A Tale of Three Cities

A TALE OF THREE CITIES

The 1962 Baseball Season
in New York, Los Angeles, and San Francisco

STEVEN TRAVERS

Potomac Books, Inc.
Washington, D.C.

Library of Congress Cataloging-in-Publication Data
Travers, Steven.
  A tale of three cities : the 1962 baseball season in New York, Los Angeles, and San Francisco / Steven Travers. — 1st ed.
     p. cm.
  Includes bibliographical references and index.
  ISBN 978-1-59797-431-8 (hardcover : alk. paper)
  1. Baseball—United States—History—20th century. 2. Los Angeles Dodgers (Baseball team)—History—20th century. 3. San Francisco Giants (Baseball team)—History—20th century. 4. New York Yankees (Baseball team)—History—20th century. I. Title. II. Title: 1962 baseball season in New York, Los Angeles, and San Francisco.
  GV863.A1T725 2009
  796.357'640973—4dc22

                                    2008047622

Printed in the United States of America on acid-free paper that meets the American National Standards Institute Z39-48 Standard.

Potomac Books, Inc.
22841 Quicksilver Drive
Dulles, Virginia 20166

First Edition

10 9 8 7 6 5 4 3 2 1

To my brother Don

Contents

Preface

It was a dark and snowy night, some time in the early to mid-1960s. The place was my parent's ski cabin in Squaw Valley, California, home of the 1960 Winter Olympics. It was a small alpine-style lodging. The perilous, icy pathway leading from a narrow, pine tree–shrouded street to the door had to be negotiated using small, mincing steps so as to avoid falling on one's face, or worse, fracturing a hip.

Located on the side of the mountain, we overlooked the valley. Below us was a cabin owned by Walt Disney. In the distance, the Olympic Village, which had since been turned into a ski mecca by the visionary Alex Cushing; an ice rink, where the United States had defeated the mighty Soviets in hockey a few years before, a precursor to the 1980 "miracle on ice"; the daunting KT-22, for only the most advanced of ski experts; and east of that, the ski jump ramp. With good binoculars one could see the competition from our balcony without paying for a ticket.

But all of that was over with, and on this night my folks were out to dinner. I was left in the cabin with my babysitter, a neighbor girl whose family lived there year-round. We had no television and boredom set in quickly. I looked around for something to occupy my attention. A board game, some toys perhaps. I opened a drawer, and there it was, in paperback, black and white, 225 pages: the *1963 Official Baseball Almanac*. On the cover, Yankees shortstop Tony Kubek completed a double play at the Stadium despite the best efforts of the Chicago White Sox's "Jumbo Jim" Landis barreling into second.

Edited by Bill Wise, published by Fawcett Publications of Greenwich, Connecticut, it was the "most authoritative . . . most complete baseball book on the market! A great buy for any fan at 50 cents!"

In the remake of *Planet of the Apes*, the apes discover an astronaut's manual along with a chimpanzee. They determine that the manual is their "Bible," the chimp their "savior," and his "return" foretold as Holy Scripture. The *1963 Official Baseball Almanac* had a strangely similar effect on me. It was, for me then and in succeeding years, my Bible, a holy book to be revered, memorized, and worshipped.

Now, what this says about me at four or five years old, when I discovered this document, is questionable. I was definitely not normal. Discovering rock music, singing, guitar-playing, a hidden copy of *Playboy*, or the actual *playing* of baseball; those are all typical events that might stir like passions. Reading books in and of itself was certainly not an unusual thing for a little boy to learn and love; Jules Verne, *Alice in Wonderland*, the Brothers Grimm—something like that, yes. But the *1963 Official Baseball Almanac*? Are you kidding?

Half that book was *statistics* that looked thus:

PLAYER AND CLUB	G	AB	R	H	TB	2B	3B	HR	SB	RBI	PCT
Pena, Orlando, KC	13	31	2	5	5	0	0	0	0	4	.161

Okay, it had pictures, too. Not pictures, as in illustrations, but photographs, and truth be told, that was what attracted me at first. I still have that dog-eared little paperback, and leafing through it reveals its true, original purpose: I turned it into a coloring book. I used crayons and a pen, outlining the features of players apparently onto a piece of paper pressed against the back in order to create images, but I also colored in the uniforms. I favored black-and-orange, particularly the San Francisco Giants' color scheme. I somehow sensed certain things, too, such as a photo of Los Angeles Angels manager Bill Rigney with pitcher Bo Belinsky. I was too young to know that Bo was a major playboy and denizen of the night, but I drew a "five o'clock shadow" on his face, apparently out of reference to the fact that he was haggard from his nocturnal activities.

But over the course of years, I started *reading* that book, and I really mean *reading* it. I poured over it, memorizing every single piece of data: every stat, every player, the fortunes of every team, the All-Star Game (there were two played in those days), the Cubs' "revolving managers," the pennant chase and playoff between the Giants and Dodgers, and of course the Fall Classic—a rain-delayed thriller won by the slimmest of margins by the Yankees over San Francisco.

I became a "62'er" of the first order. Over the years, as my knowledge base increased, other things became apparent to me. I learned about John Glenn, the astronaut who became a hero in 1962. I learned that my favorite football team, the Southern California Trojans, had won the National Championship that year. *American Graffiti* came out and asked, "Where were you in '62?" The sense of nostalgia for that year became palpable.

I learned that John Kennedy had been president in 1962. He seemed to be something out of the past, and that year was part of the past in ways that increasingly seemed to be impossible to recapture: in style, in politics, in music, and in culture. Then there were the teams: the Yankees, Giants, and Dodgers. As I developed into a baseball fan, the championship teams seemed to be the Minnesota Twins, the Boston Red Sox, the Detroit Tigers, the Baltimore Orioles, the St. Louis Cardinals, and the Cincinnati Reds. The Yankee dynasty was a myth to me; in my formative years they were "New York's other baseball team," as the Big Apple's passions were stirred by a team that was comically bad in 1962, the Mets. The Dodgers of Sandy Koufax and Don Drysdale seemed to be an old B movie, like one of those CinemaScope features in which the screen narrows in the artistic stylings of the late 1950s and early 1960s. The Giants were a shell of whatever I knew them to have been in 1962; fans stayed away from Candlestick—which within a decade was old, resembling a prison—their stars over the hill. Bay Area sports excitement resided in the East Bay: the three-time champion A's, Al Davis's marvelous Oakland Raiders, and Rick Barry's shoot 'em up Golden State Warriors.

I developed an incredible baseball library: *The Glory of Their Times* by Lawrence Ritter, *Ball Four* by Jim Bouton, Pat Jordan's wry reminiscences of a failed minor league career, anything and everything else. I still have all those books, wonderful works inscribed with love by my mom and dad: "To our darling boy from Mommie, X-mas 1969," or "To Champ, this brings back memories, Love, Dad, 1970."

Above all others, however, stood Roger Angell's *The Summer Game* (1972). Angell did not even think of himself as a professional sportswriter. He wrote from a fan's perspective, choosing to mingle with fans in the stands instead of a press box. Every year he took a baseball journey and wrote about it in the *New Yorker*. He devoted a particularly large amount of attention to the 1962 season; first, the nascent Mets; then, the unfolding pennant chase played in the glorious California sunshine between the Giants and Dodgers; and finally, a World Series that combined all the old "subway series" elements of John McGraw versus Babe Ruth updated to Mickey Mantle versus Willie Mays, complete with jet air travel. Angell stirred all my old pangs, shedding new light on the summer of '62.

In a high school history class they showed *The Missiles of October*, a docudrama starring William DeVane as JFK and Martin Sheen as Bobby Kennedy. It was a hard-hitting, sober look at the Cuban Missile Crisis, but what struck me was that it all happened in 1962, the year of my great fascination. To think, all I cared about was Pete Runnel's batting average and the fact that Sandy Koufax hurt his finger at midseason, and now I learned that much had occurred beyond the bounds of Fenway Park or Chavez Ravine.

Through baseball, I developed a focal point for history. If something happened in 1914, I knew that Chief Bender had jumped to the Federal League that year. Pearl Harbor occurred the same year Joe DiMaggio hit in 56 straight games and Ted Williams was the last of the .400 hitters. I had remembered Bobby Kennedy running for president in 1968, but all I recalled of the campaign was that he was always surrounded by Mexican farmworkers, which seemed incongruous. *The Missiles of October* showed him to be a man of power, a hawk and war architect suddenly questioning the use of force, and therefore it helped me to understand the RFK I knew from 1968—a man tempered by his experiences.

Three things occurred to me since I came to worship the *1963 Official Baseball Almanac*. First, I went beyond just reading about baseball to actually playing it—pretty well. Well enough to help Redwood High School, located in the San Francisco suburb of Marin County, win the mythical national championship in my senior year of 1977. Well enough to earn a full-ride scholarship to college and make all-conference as a pitcher. Well enough to play a few years of professional ball, in the St. Louis Cardinals and Oakland A's organizations, and to strike out 1989 National League MVP Kevin Mitchell three times in one game and K 14 Kingsport Mets on a hot July night in 1981. As Casey Stengel once said, "You could look it up."

The next thing that happened to me was that while I never lost my passion for baseball, as a fan and a player, I developed just as much passion for history, politics, and as a direct result, for writing. Being a millionaire baseball star was not my destiny. Being a writer and historian was.

Most important, I stopped worshipping the *1963 Official Baseball Almanac*, or *The Sporting News Official Baseball Guide*, or the works of Pat Jordan and Roger Angell. I started worshipping the *Holy Bible* instead, directing my admiration not for Mickey Mantle or Willie Mays or Don Drysdale, but for the Lord Jesus Christ.

So it is that I temper my writings with an understanding of the things that are truly important. But somehow baseball has never slipped too far away, even as I endeavor to find Truth. My love for baseball is in fact spiritual, as is my love for America. This is a book not merely about baseball, but about America.

Acknowledgments

Thanks to Kevin Cuddihy, Jennifer Waldrop, and Sam Dorrance of Potomac Books. Also thanks to John Horne and Pat Kelly of the Baseball Hall of Fame and Mary at George Brace Photos in Chicago. Thank you to the New York Yankees, the Los Angeles Dodgers, the San Francisco Giants, the New York Mets, and the Los Angeles Angels. Thank you, Bruce Macgowan, Lon Simmons, Blake Rhodes, Vin Scully, Donna Carter, Willie Mays, Willie McCovey, John Shea, Glenn Schwarz, Dale Tafoya, the late Bo Belinsky, and the late Bill Rigney. Thanks to my wonderful daughter, Elizabeth Travers, and my supportive parents. Above all others, my greatest thanks go to my Lord and Savior Jesus Christ, the source of all that is decent and true.

Introduction

In some respects, 1962 was the last year of American innocence. It preceded the assassination of John F. Kennedy; Vietnam and the antiwar protests; the explosion of drug use and the advent of the sexual revolution; and Watergate. All of these events led to a great division of American culture. But 1962 also represents one of those years that stand out in history, like 1776, 1865, 1927, 1945, 1989, and 2001. It was a year of enormous cultural change, in which the tides of modern politics were formed, thus shaping the world we have lived in since.

It was also one of the greatest years in the history of sports, marked by a particularly great California sports season in which the Southern California Trojans won the National Championship in football, the recently arrived Los Angeles Lakers started their famed rivalry with the Boston Celtics, and the transplanted New York teams—the San Francisco Giants and Los Angeles Dodgers—intensified their rivalry in ways never even seen back east.

In one of the greatest pennant races of all time, the Giants survived to overtake the favored Dodgers, only to face the fabled New York Yankees— the winner of New York's war of baseball attrition—in a classic World Series for the ages.

The year's heroes included the Yankees' Mickey Mantle and Whitey Ford, the Giants' Willie Mays and Willie McCovey, and the Dodgers' Sandy Koufax and Don Drysdale. It was a year that included Hollywood's adoration of the Dodgers; San Francisco's battle between inferiority and superiority; and the ascendancy of New York, the New Rome, as the ruler of sport and society. We also see the Los Angeles Angels in the Sunset Strip summer of '62, and across the continent the comical New York Mets as a sideshow. Five teams, one great year.

ONE

A Palace in the Hills

"GET YOUR WHEELBARROW AND SHOVEL. STOP.
I'LL MEET YOU IN CHAVEZ RAVINE."
—*Walter O'Malley's telegraph to L.A. Mayor Norris Paulsen, 1957*

The Los Angeles Dodgers and San Francisco Giants moved to California in 1958. Roy Campanella's special night in 1959 was seen as the "debutante ball" of the Dodgers. Five months later Los Angeles won the World Series. For decades, the University of Southern California Trojans and UCLA Bruins were America's dominant collegiate sports powerhouses. Crowds of over 100,000 came out to watch USC, UCLA, and Rams football games at the Coliseum. The 1932 L.A. Olympics had been the most successful to date. In 1962 Hollywood was the world's cultural touchstone, and politically the Golden State was the most important in the nation.

Despite this, Los Angeles and California were seen as "minor league," far removed from the long-held eastern salons of sports influence. It was not until April 10, 1962, that they entered the "Major Leagues." That was the day that the Dodgers hosted the Cincinnati Reds in the first game ever played at Dodger Stadium.

When the world got a look at Dodger Stadium in all its glory, the true greatness of the Golden State could not be denied. Here was the finest sports palace ever conceived, Manifest Destiny for the twentieth century, something greater than the sum of merely human parts. Baseball, America, and Los Angeles, California, would never be the same.

Until Dodger Stadium was built, the Dodgers and Giants were roughly equal rivals. The Giants had won five World Championships (1905, 1921, 1922, 1933, 1954); the Dodgers two (1955, 1959), but the Dodgers seemed to have achieved an edge in the final New York years and the early California seasons .

That edge had demonstrated itself in the 1955 World Series victory followed by the National League championship in 1956. Manager Walt Alston presided over the "Dodger way," a victorious formula of sorts that had been the product of such baseball minds as Lee MacPhail, Branch Rickey, Buzzie Bavasi, Fresco Thompson, and Al Campanis.

The Giants, on the other hand, had fired Leo Durocher and gone through a succession of managers. They had opened their new stadium, Candlestick Park, two years earlier, but it was a dud; immediately old, dirty, and uninviting. Dodger Stadium was a shot across the bow at the Giants, but it was also a signal moment in a long-held rivalry that existed before Californians ever thought about Major League baseball.

San Francisco despised Los Angeles. San Franciscans despised Los Angelinos. Los Angeles and Los Angelinos did not particularly care. San Franciscans hated them even more for caring so little. San Francisco was a schizophrenic town with equal parts inferiority complex and superiority complex. They thought of themselves as the Paris of the West, the New York of the Pacific; L.A. was a land of rubes. There was no city there, no base, no monument to greatness . . . until now.

San Francisco started out as the important California city, but the building of the Owens River Valley aqueduct and two world wars had changed that. The University of California and Stanford University built impressive stadiums in the early 1920s. Stanford lobbied for the Rose Bowl game to be moved up north. Southern California responded by building two stadiums—the Rose Bowl in Pasadena and the Coliseum near downtown L.A. Both dwarfed the northern stadiums. Instead of being compared to Cal and Stanford, they were compared to the "House That Ruth Built" (Yankee Stadium) and the Roman Colosseum.

California's "Wonder Teams" and Stanford under coach Pop Warner were the two great college football dynasties of the early 1920s, but they quickly became overshadowed by Knute Rockne and Notre Dame. When Southern California started their great rivalry with the Fighting Irish, it established the Trojans as the other major grid power, further pushing Cal and Stanford into the shadows. A sense of jealousy pervaded the northern schools, infusing the region in ways that became sociopolitical. Then UCLA came into their own. The Bruins, not the Golden Bears or Indians, were USC's main conference rival, winning the 1954 National Championship in football and later establishing themselves as the greatest basketball dynasty of all time.

In the 1950s and early 1960s, California, reeling from a recruiting scandal in which Stanford "turned them in," scaled back sports. A program that had produced four National Champions in football, two in baseball, one in basketball, plus numerous Olympians, became a joke and has never truly recovered.

Political power shifted from the north to the south. Earl Warren was from the Bay Area and attended the University of California. He became governor and was tapped by Thomas Dewey as his vice presidential running mate in the losing 1948 election. Richard Nixon was from the Los Angeles area. He represented a growing, more powerful electorate than Warren, and rose to greater heights. Ronald Reagan would also tap into the same Orange County conservatism that propelled Barry Goldwater to the 1964 Republican nomination, and eventually would represent the dominant political ethos in America.

All of these factors—the Rose Bowl and Coliseum being better recognized than Cal's and Stanford's stadiums; the Trojans and Bruins dominating the Golden Bears and Indians; political power shifting to the Southland, leaving Northern California marginalized towards the Left—combined to frustrate denizens of the San Francisco Bay Area. On top of that, they saw that the center of business in the Pacific Rim was no longer San Francisco, but Los Angeles. Then there was Hollywood. The imprimatur of glamour, of beautiful women, hot nightlife, golden beaches, and Tinseltown fame overshadowed foggy San Francisco, which seemed to fall short in every way a city can be measured against another one. San Franciscans looked at their beautiful scenery, their identifiable, skyscraper city center, their supposedly more literate, cultured population, and tried to look down their noses at the churchgoing Midwestern transplants who made up the L.A. Basin. They seemed to be desperately attempting to convince themselves of their elitism. The harder they tried, the more they failed.

When Dodger Stadium was built, it was the final insult. San Francisco had gotten a stadium done faster, in 1960, but there was little hiding the reality of

Candlestick Park: a dismal failure in every way. Now Los Angeles had created pure excellence. It was self-evident truth. It needed no commentary. Los Angeles was superior to San Francisco.

During the 1956 World Series between the Brooklyn Dodgers and New York Yankees, Dodgers owner Walter O'Malley observed something that more than piqued his interest. He saw Kenneth Hahn, a rising and influential Los Angeles city councilman, in the company of Washington Senators owner Calvin Griffith. Everybody knew what they were speaking about: Hahn was trying to talk Griffith into moving the moribund Senators franchise to Los Angeles.

Los Angeles had been discussed as a potential destination for Major League Baseball since 1941. The weather was perfect and the population grew and grew and grew. Capacity crowds filled the Rose Bowl and the Coliseum. Fans were rabid for athletics in California. On top of that, an enormous number of superstar athletes in all sports were from the Golden State. The success of the 1932 Los Angeles Olympics seemed to demonstrate that Los Angeles had the ability to choose not to participate in the Great Depression. Out west, there was a different mindset, a new way of thinking, an enlightened approach to race, to culture, to society, that was more forward looking. It was the future.

On December 7, 1941, the St. Louis Browns were expected to announce at the winter meetings that they were moving to Los Angeles. When the Japanese attacked Pearl Harbor and the West Coast was threatened in the early days of World War II, those plans fell by the wayside.

When the war was finally won in 1945, the country began to turn its attention to other endeavors. In 1946, Branch Rickey signed the first black player, a young infielder from UCLA named Jackie Robinson. In 1947, in the skies over the high California desert, Chuck Yeager broke the "sound barrier." This made jet travel feasible, and more importantly, commercial.

In the early and mid-1950s, a flurry of franchise shifts took place, with varying degrees of success. The Browns did move, but not to Los Angeles. Chicago Cubs owner Philip K. Wrigley owned the L.A. market. His team trained at Catalina Island, off the Southern California coast, during Spring Training. The Los Angeles Angels' franchise played in the West Coast version of Wrigley Field, a quaint little ballpark located on a street called Avalon, in south L.A. The Pacific

Coast League was competitive, successful, and had loyal fan support. Numerous well-known big leaguers competed in the PCL. Many of the league's greatest stars were local products who moved from nearby high schools to the Angels, Hollywood Stars, San Diego Padres, San Francisco Seals, Mission Reds, Oakland Oaks, Sacramento Solons, Seattle Rainiers. and Portland Beavers. But it was still the minor leagues.

With L.A. apparently controlled by Wrigley, who would never consider moving the Cubs out to the coast, the Browns—long in the shadow of the Cardinals—moved to Baltimore. The Boston Braves, who despite having played in the World Series as recently as 1948 were a distant second in popularity to the Red Sox, moved to Milwaukee. The Philadelphia A's, a one-time American League powerhouse, had lost a war of attrition to the Phillies. They packed up their bags and made their way to Kansas City.

The most successful of these franchise shifts were the Braves. County Stadium in Milwaukee was a wide-open facility with a large parking lot and easy road access. The car culture was in full swing. It was the Baby Boomer generation, a period of post-war prosperity of unprecedented proportions. The Great Depression, the Dust Bowl, the New Deal, the failed America of John Steinbeck's novels, was completely overshadowed by the success of free market capitalism. In Oklahoma, Bud Wilkinson's Sooners were the dominant college football power; their games sold out, eclipsing old stereotypes of Okie poverty. In Milwaukee, attendance topped two million. Families of four came out to the park. They bought expensive new cars, paid for gas and parking. They paid for souvenirs and ballpark food. After the game they frequented local restaurants and businesses. Baseball in Milwaukee was integrated into the economy of an entire community.

Post-war success seemed to have resonated everywhere except in Brooklyn. During World War II, blacks from the South moved to big cities to work in the shipyards. It was a new, mobile population, and the demographics of Brooklyn changed. Blacks and Puerto Ricans began to replace the traditional Irish Catholic and Jewish citizenry of Brooklyn. Levittown was built; a planned, suburban community on Long Island. "White flight" took place. Whites moved out of the city to Westchester, to Long Island and Queens, to New Jersey and Connecticut. Retirees found new lives in Miami.

Walter O'Malley and Branch Rickey had courted the black and Puerto Rican fan base. When Robinson was signed and brought to Brooklyn in 1947, they were an integral part of the team's support, financially and otherwise. But a fissure occurred between O'Malley and Robinson. O'Malley, who had been born into wealth and graduated from Fordham Law School, hated Rickey and bought him out after annexing shares over a period of years. He had total control of the Brooklyn franchise. O'Malley fired employees who so much as mentioned Rickey's name. Only those considered indispensable to the club's operation were retained from the Rickey era. Robinson admired the "savior" Rickey and openly supported him, which infuriated O'Malley.

The Dodgers of the late 1940s and 1950s were some of the most successful in the club's long history, but attendance dipped. It perplexed O'Malley. Here he was, a smart, successful attorney and businessman, living in America at a time of huge economic growth, but he was not benefiting from it. Other cities were. The new franchises out west, particularly Milwaukee, were breaking new ground, creating paradigm shifts in what a sports business could be. Just over the Brooklyn Bridge, Manhattan was prosperous, a glamorous, Frank Sinatra town of Broadway shows, hot nightspots, business tycoons and their trophy women. Wall Street executives lived posh country lifestyles in Greenwich and New Canaan, Connecticut, or Westchester County; easy train access whisking them back and forth from the city where they seemingly ruled this brave new world; masters of the business universe, patricians of the New Rome.

With all of this going on, O'Malley sat in his office with Buzzie Bavasi and looked out his window. What he saw filled him with despair. A long line of blacks and Puerto Ricans were standing outside the welfare office, waiting for relief checks. These were not people with discretionary income who were going to spend what they did have on Dodger tickets.

"Why are we catering to these people?" O'Malley asked Bavasi. There was no good answer to that question.

A conundrum developed. O'Malley wanted a new stadium and new fans. There was little available land in Brooklyn, but worse, there was no freeway access. The "new fans" were really the old ones who had moved away. They would have to come from the suburban enclaves of Jersey, Long Island, and Connecticut. They would need to come in cars. Without freeways, getting in and out of antiquated Brooklyn was problematic. Little Ebbets Field only held only 32,000 fans. O'Malley commissioned famed architect Buckminster Fuller to draw plans for a domed stadium at Atlantic and Flatbush, above the Long Island Railroad depot.

To New York City building czar Robert Moses, the answer seemed obvious. He wanted a modern park built in Flushing Meadows, adjacent to La Guardia Airport and across from the future site of the World's Fair. He formulated plans to erect a new stadium in Queens. But the Dodgers were psychologically tied to their Brooklyn identity. A move to any other borough was seen as betrayal. Already struggling in a three-way battle for the New York fan base with the Giants and Yankees, O'Malley was concerned that if he lost the Brooklyn identity the team would suffer at the gate.

In Moses, O'Malley had met a man he could not defeat in a political power struggle. As in Sun Tzu's The Art of War, O'Malley understood that withdrawal might be his best option. There were rumblings that the Dodgers might move, but nobody took it seriously. It was out of the question, unthinkable, heresy. But there were signs of impending doom. O'Malley played a series of games in Jersey City, New Jersey, ostensibly testing the waters.

Brooklyn's great rivals, the Giants, also suffered attendance downturns. Their stadium, the Polo Grounds, was located in an even worse neighborhood. Coogan's Bluff in Harlem was now crime ridden. Their Bronx neighbors, the Yankees, faced similar problems, but the pinstripers were a dominant team that won the battle for the Manhattan, New Jersey, and Connecticut fan base needed for success. Yankee Stadium also had the advantage of easy freeway access, meaning suburban fans could pop in and out without risking the mean streets as they did in Brooklyn.

A bitter novel, Last Exit to Brooklyn, embodied the desultory situation of the borough in the 1950s. O'Malley's plans for a new stadium, for a "geodesic dome" and other alternatives, were put down at every turn. But he showed his hand when he turned down a deal with a firm that planned to build a Brooklyn stadium. However, the Queens stadium project did not appeal to O'Malley. He felt that if he acquiesced to such a venture, not only would the club lose its Brooklyn identity, but a palpable shift in power and even club control might be lost to Moses, who ruled over all he surveyed in New York like a modern Caesar.

When Jackie Robinson was traded to the Giants and Sal Maglie, a longtime hated Giants pitcher, became a Dodger, all seemed to have been turned around. It was a foretaste of cataclysmic change. So it was during the 1956 World Series when O'Malley saw Kenneth Hahn talking shop with Cal Griffith. He knew the future was in Los Angeles. Whoever harnessed it would ride the whirlwind. O'Malley could not stomach the prospect of Cal Griffith being such a pioneering figure. New York literally was not big enough for O'Malley and Robert Moses to coexist. A three-team big league city was apparently a failure, especially in the car culture. O'Malley wrote a note to Hahn and had an usher deliver it. It asked Hahn not to accept any deal with Griffith or anybody else until he had a chance to speak with O'Malley.

"Being two miles away was the same as being 3,000 miles away," Buzzie Bavasi said. "Walter wanted to own his own stadium, even in New York. And Los Angeles was prepared to help him get it."

After losing a seven-game Series to the dominant Yankees, the Dodgers immediately departed for an exhibition tour of Japan. Disappointed over the World Series loss, nobody had the heart for it. Jackie Robinson refused, and it was the last straw. He was traded to the Giants, but chose to retire instead of becoming a teammate of Willie Mays, possibly returning to his home state to finish out a Hall of Fame career.

The team's plane stopped in Los Angeles on the way to Japan. O'Malley met with Hahn, who held some major cards. Aside from Griffith, he was entertaining inquiries from Giants owner Horace Stoneham, who was rumored to be ready to move his team somewhere out west. O'Malley knew he needed a rival in California, and that would naturally be Stoneham's Giants. O'Malley also knew that the jewel in the Golden State would be Los Angeles; not San Diego, not San Francisco. He immediately set about securing L.A. and steering Stoneham to San Francisco. San Diego, located 100 miles south of Los Angeles, would be "Dodgers country." Its minor league operation would fall by the wayside, replaced by media and radio attention devoted to the new team in L.A.

O'Malley tried to keep his cards close to the vest, but Hahn put on a full court press. Hahn played the Senators and Giants against O'Malley, as if any big league operation would be of equal value. In truth, he salivated over the Dodgers. They were by far the most attractive prospect for a number of reasons.

O'Malley understood what he had and acted on it, secretly committing to the City of Angels.

What clinched the deal was O'Malley's declaration that the city would not be required to build him a stadium. In bureaucratic New York, old school corruption going back to the days of Democrat-controlled Tammany Hall was still in place, embodied by Moses. The concept that a private corporation could secure a plot of land large enough for a ballpark, build it on its own, and operate such a venture in an act of unfettered capitalism, was unheard of. It would certainly take Moses out of the picture, and that was not to be.

But Los Angeles was still a Republican city; a wide-open, business-friendly atmosphere in which entrepreneurial capitalism was the driving force of a growing, unbounded, we-can-achieve-anything culture. It was O'Malley's kind of place. Hahn and the L.A. politicians knew their biggest hurdle would be the stadium issue, resulting in the inevitable, age-old complaints about such an expense when schools, hospitals, and the poor needed the money instead. Then O'Malley delivered a bombshell: Manna from Heaven. He would build the ballpark. He would also reap the benefits. The city of course would be spared the initial costs, but the value—public relations and monetary—would be incalculable.

All O'Malley wanted was land. The city and county of L.A. had plenty of that. It was a huge, wide-open swath of mountains, hills, valleys, and basins, all crisscrossed by new modern freeways, courtesy of a visionary highway act signed by President Dwight Eisenhower. O'Malley seemingly had his choice, but that choice was not a hard one to make. A couple of miles from downtown Los Angeles was a pleasant hill and wide plateau overlooking the city. It was perfect. He originally found it on a map at a gas station. It was called Chavez Ravine. The city had tried to make it a recreation site, but squatters' shacks and scattered herds of goats still roamed amid the refuse. O'Malley swapped the Watts property where Wrigley Field was for the 300-acre landfill. A close referendum would grant it to the Dodgers, and groundbreaking would take place in 1959.

But first O'Malley had to deal with the exodus from New York. It was an incredible high-wire act of deception, all designed to slowly, imperceptibly prepare the public for an inevitable outcome in a manner with as little shock to the system as possible. Throughout 1957, O'Malley pretended to negotiate with the powers that be, but eventually played his hand when he sold Ebbets Field to a commercial developer. When no alternative was effectuated—a Brooklyn stadium site or the Moses site in Queens, the writing, as in the Old Testament, was on the wall. O'Malley would be the modern Moses who led the Dodgers to the Promised Land of California. Robert Moses would be left to pick up the pieces in a city he ruled like a Pharaoh.

Fans observed this; one small step followed by another, instead of a single announcement. They began to accept the inevitable. Both the Dodgers and Giants had disappointing seasons in 1957, so attendance was down at both Ebbets Field and the Polo Grounds. O'Malley pointed to this as reason for the move.

When the news hit that O'Malley had purchased the Cubs' minor league franchise in Los Angeles, along with L.A.'s Wrigley Field, the cat was out of the bag. Then O'Malley got Stoneham on board. Stoneham was painted a dark scenario. If he went it alone in New York, or moved to Minnesota, he would not have his main rival to help power the transition. Stoneham was doing so poorly financially that he owed money to the stadium concessions.

The Giants' owner was completely fed up with the ancient Polo Grounds, now located in a war zone. He was prepared to move to Minneapolis anyway, regardless of O'Malley's departure. O'Malley simply made him change his plans for the better—San Francisco, California, a New York-style town steeped in the traditions of Joe DiMaggio and the PCL Seals, the most legendary of all minor league teams. The rivalry would flourish on the West Coast.

The Boston Red Sox owned the San Francisco Seals. Red Sox owner Tom Yawkey sold his territorial rights to Stoneham in exchange for Minneapolis, at a price of $25,000. On May 29, 1957, the Dodgers announced the move. In August, the Giants followed suit.

"I feel sorry for the kids, but I haven't seen much of their fathers lately," Stoneham said.

For Brooklyn fans, the retelling of this story resembles the Zapruder film, as if in watching it somehow it will turn out differently, but it never does. Their team was a beloved institution. There was a sense of family in Brooklyn that had not existed with the Giants (at least not recently), and certainly not with the corporate Yankees, who like the Americans in Iraq simply prevailed in a war of attrition and strength because they were too big, powerful, and rich to be toppled.

The relationship of the players and owners, however, was the polar opposite. Stoneham was a "real baseball fan as an owner," his close aide, Chub Feeney said. "Winning meant a lot to him and the team meant a lot to him. He was a rooter." Stoneham was known for his generosity with Giants players, whom he viewed as part of a larger family. O'Malley, with slick hair, three-piece suits, and a large paunch, looked the part of a big city bank president. Stoneham, with his rosy cheeks, thinning hair, and thick, dark glasses, was a round-faced man who resembled the comic Drew Carey. His persona was more like a regional branch manager.

Stoneham loved to drink, an occupation that coincided with watching his team. According to rumor he killed a man in a drunk-driving incident in Scottsdale, Arizona. He had been duped into accepting San Francisco, as if it was equal in value to Los

Angeles. There was a sense that California was one big tropical paradise and little regard for the enormous physical disparities within its 900-mile north-south borders. Even within the Bay Area itself, temperatures varied greatly. Walnut Creek, for example, a bedroom community located over the hill past Oakland in the East Bay, could be steaming hot at 90 degrees on the same day that San Francisco was foggy and windswept at 55 degrees.

Stoneham emphasized one thing above all other criteria: He wanted parking at his new stadium. Parking, parking, parking. Neither L.A. nor San Francisco had much in the way of public transportation. San Francisco's bus service was better than L.A.'s, and a commuter train connected people between The City (its denizens used caps) and the peninsula towns of Burlingame, San Mateo, Palo Alto, and Mountain View. For the most part, however, its citizenry traversed the freeways and numerous bridges (the Golden Gate, Bay, and eventually the Richmond–San Rafael, San Mateo, Dumbarton, Carquinez, and Benicia) by car.

There was available downtown land near Powell and Market streets, which would have been an excellent spot. Located not far from where the current AT&T Park stands, it would have offered reasonable weather. Certainly there would have been wind and fog, but it would have been acceptable. Financial district foot traffic, cable cars, ferry service, municipal bus lines, the Southern Pacific train, and eventually the Bay Area Rapid Transit (BART) would have provided easy access. Stores, bars, and restaurants would have benefited from the nightlife and "this is the place to be" vibe that AT&T Park now provides. It was not chosen because local businesses did not want increased traffic congestion. Stoneham lacked the vision to fight for the downtown stadium; all he saw was a big parking lot. In addition, eminent domain laws would have cost The City $33 million to pay off citizens forced to leave properties.

San Francisco Mayor George Christopher saw how O'Malley had manipulated the gullible Stoneham. He set out to do the same thing. Christopher had a sweetheart deal with a construction magnate named Charlie Harney. Harney owned tons of regular old dirt. He needed a place to put it that would pay him for it. Within the jurisdiction of the city there were only so many places that could accommodate Harney's dirt.

They decided on nondescript Candlestick Point, sitting on a section next to San Francisco Bay that was not officially in The City. It was an unincorporated area owned by Harney. Candlestick Point was located next to the Bayshore Freeway, which connected The City with the airport, which was almost as much of a boondoggle and likewise not in The City. Stoneham was told of the Bayshore location. He had visions of a baseball version of Fisherman's Wharf, a marina-style stadium perhaps, accompanied by waterfront vistas. In fact, the section of bay that Candlestick Point is located on is one of the farthest from the East Bay on the other side. Furthermore, the East Bay area across from Candlestick is much flatter than the scenic Oakland and Berkeley hills to the north, with the lights of Oakland and the Bay Bridge providing spectacular visuals. Trying to locate the East Bay from Candlestick Point is almost as difficult as trying to spot England on the horizon across the channel from France.

A bluff overlooked the site, which was curved away from the downtown Embarcadero area in such a way that there was absolutely no evidence of the beautiful downtown San Francisco skyline to the north, or even the mountainous peninsula to the south. It just sat there. The neighborhoods adjacent to Candlestick Point—Bayside, Hunter's Point, and Potrero Hill—were headed in the same direction as the Harlem slums where the Polo Grounds had been. Stoneham was painted a portrait of racial harmony, of new thinking in California, but, in truth, the black community of San Francisco lived in sullen isolation, well away from The City's frolicking financial district or the tony neighborhoods of St. Francis Woods, Mt. Davidson, Twin Peaks, and the Sunset.

There was no fan-friendly business within miles and miles and miles of Candlestick—just slaughterhouses, packing plants, and a few liquor stores. An eyesore for the ages, a huge crane dominating a nearby naval shipbuilding facility, blocked whatever views of the bay that there might have been. Fans exiting Highway 101 found themselves on narrow streets that quickly became traffic heavy before and after games with any kind of large attendance. Local kids threatened to vandalize cars unless money was extorted from frightened drivers. But all of this was nothing compared to the elements.

Christopher and Harney knew that Stoneham was a man who wanted to get to his drinking early. They arranged for a tour of Candlestick Point around 10:30 AM. Mark Twain once said, "The coldest winter I ever spent was a summer in San Francisco." The best time of year there is the fall, the Indian summer months of September, October, and early November. Instead of directing Stoneham to Candlestick on one of those Mark Twain days—cold, drizzly, windy—they drove the owner out on a sunny, clear morning. All Stoneham seemed to see was room for parking. Of course, that room was still part of the bay. This was where Harney's dirt would be dumped, creating landfill and a toxicological disaster. On top of that, nobody understood much about earthquakes back then, other than that the Big One had virtually destroyed the entire city only 50-some years before that. Sure, go ahead, build a stadium on the shifting sands of loose dirt dumped into the water!

Stoneham enthusiastically endorsed the whole plan, hook, line, and sinker. Christopher and Harney just looked at each other. This was a savvy New York businessman? The West Coast rubes had pulled the dirt right over his head. Stoneham was spirited away and by 3:00 PM was in his cups. Around that time, a violent windstorm descended on Candlestick Point. It was like something out of *Lawrence of Arabia*, like a Biblical fog that could have killed every first-born child on the point if it had been fit for human habitation in the first place. Dust from the nearby bluffs swirled in a sea of drifting garbage wrappings. Fetid smells filled the air, but Stoneham did not see, feel, or smell it. It was cocktail hour.

Walter O'Malley toured Wrigley Field, a quaint little park located in an industrial area that was becoming more and more crime ridden. It held about 22,000 fans. The Hollywood Stars had a stadium located where the CBS Television studios are currently located. That neighborhood was better, but the capacity was not. There were no alternatives. Everyone assumed O'Malley's team would play at Wrigley Field until Dodger Stadium was built, just as the Giants would play at little Seals Stadium until Candlestick Park was erected.

"What about the Coliseum?" O'Malley asked.

His tour guide scoffed at the notion. The Coliseum was strictly a football stadium with a track. But O'Malley knew it held 100,000 fans. "Walter was a business man—first and only," said Bavasi. "He was not a baseball man and admitted as much. He left that part to others. Contractual work with television and radio was about all he was interested in. He was not an emotional man and he never got close to any of the players."

O'Malley saw dollar signs in each of those 100,000 seats. He decided the Coliseum, not Wrigley Field, would be the home of the Dodgers. He appeared before the Los Angeles City Council in 1957, asking for permission to play four seasons at the Los Angeles Memorial Coliseum. There was one dissenter, John Holland, who turned out to be in league with C. Arnholt Smith, who was lobbying for the prized first big league franchise in San Diego, not Los Angeles. Smith later did time for fraud, and Major League Baseball did not arrive in San Diego until expansion in 1969.

Between 1958 and 1961, the Dodgers played in the venerable stadium, which, all things considered, must be the most famous all-around sports facility in the world. If there was any competition for such a moniker, the Dodgers' four years there ended the discussion.

It was built in 1923 to serve a number of purposes. First and foremost, it was erected to house the University of Southern California Trojans. USC had emerged as a major university in the years immediately after World War I. Long overshadowed by the respected University of California–Berkeley and Stanford University, USC now accommodated a large urban population and grew in prestige because of it. In 1919 the university hired Elmer "Gloomy Gus" Henderson to coach the football team, which until then had been a second-rate outfit, not considered a big-time collegiate program like those at Pacific Coast rivals Cal, Stanford, Washington, Washington State, and Oregon.

Henderson quickly turned the team into champions. In 1922 the Trojans entered the Pacific Coast Conference. Stanford lobbied to get the Rose Bowl game, previously played at Tournament Park, where Cal Tech is now located in Pasadena. The city of Pasadena responded to Stanford's challenge by building the Rose Bowl in the Arroyo Seco in 1922. USC christened it by winning the first Rose Bowl game played there, beating Penn State, 14-3, on January 1, 1923.

In 1923 the Coliseum was built, seemingly one-upping Pasadena. The stadium was located across the street from the university and eventually lured the 1932 Olympics and the growing football aspirations of nascent UCLA. Started as the Southern Branch of the University of California system, UCLA was located on Vermont, near Griffith Park, but quickly outgrew its humble beginnings. The school moved to a location in Westwood that seemed preposterous at first.

"Nobody will go all the way out there," people said of Westwood. Everything west of Western Avenue was rural until one got to Santa Monica, where the West Coast version of the Gatsby crowd frolicked in their exclusive beach cottages. Ironically, UCLA had enough open space to build a stadium larger than the mightiest South American soccer colossus, but chose instead to rent the Coliseum, meaning their fans had to drive to USC and walk across their rivals' campus shrines in order to watch the games.

When the USC–Notre Dame football rivalry began in 1926, it ensured huge crowds at the Coliseum. When Coach Howard Jones turned Troy into a collegiate dynasty with four National Championships between 1928 and 1939, the Coliseum was packed, the Trojans the cause célèbre of Hollywood. UCLA moved in, and when Jackie Robinson starred for the Bruins, they too filled the stadium. Games played between the integrated Trojans and Bruins in the 1930s were nothing short of social statements a decade before baseball broke the color barrier.

The 1932 Olympics were a huge success. USC athletes dominated for the American team, giving the school and the city the imprimatur of "Sports Capital of the World" when Troy won their second straight national title in 1932.

The Coliseum was the home of the mighty Trojans and the mighty Bruins, who by the 1950s were challenging and beating USC. The Los Angeles Rams moved in and won the 1952 National Football League crown. Crowds of well over 100,000 fans came to watch USC–UCLA, USC–Notre Dame, and Rams-49ers spectacles.

In addition to pro and college football and the Olympics, the Coliseum was the site of the popular East-West Shrine football game, a prep extravaganza. It hosted the Los Angeles City Section and California Interscholastic Federation–Southern Section championship games. Many stars played high school, college, and pro football in the Coliseum. The USC track team, probably the single most dominant collegiate sports dynasty in history with 26 NCAA championships, ran their major meets in the Coliseum. In its heyday, close to 100,000 people came out to watch the USC-UCLA meet.

For many years, the Pro Bowl game was played at the Coliseum. In 1984 a second Olympics was held there. Every major rock band—the Who, the Rolling Stones, Led Zeppelin, and many more—played to sold-out Coliseum crowds. In 1945 war hero George S. Patton addressed a capacity nighttime crowd when he returned to his hometown after defeating Nazi Germany. Billy Graham held Christian revivals in the Coliseum, filling every seat.

The adjacent Sports Arena, built in 1959, was—and this is not a misprint—the finest basketball arena in the nation in its early days. The home of USC until 2006, it was also UCLA's arena when it won its first two NCAA titles; the Lakers' arena until the Forum was completed in 1967; and the home court of the ABA's Los Angeles Stars. John F. Kennedy accepted the Democratic presidential nomination there in 1960.

In 1958 the Dodgers struggled in their first year, finishing seventh, but were successful at the gate. More than 78,000 attended the first game played at the Coliseum, and a total of 1.8 million passed the turnstiles that season. The Dodgers won the 1959 National League pennant playing at the Coliseum. They set the all-time attendance records, drawing crowds of more than 90,000 fans for each of three World Series games against the Chicago White Sox en route to the World Championship. Home plate was set next to the entrance where football teams emerge, with left field a scant 290 feet away. A high screen was erected so that balls would not fly out of the stadium. The result was that legitimate line drive homers would hit the screen and, if played correctly by the left fielder, could be held to singles. Conversely, lazy, arcing pop-ups would drift over the screen for home runs. A journeyman outfielder, Wally Moon, seemed to specialize in these "Moon shots."

The farther the stands and the screen extended toward center field, the farther away they were from home plate. Deep center field was a considerable distance, and in order to make up for the ridiculous left field dimensions, right-center field was so deep that Babe Ruth or Barry Bonds would have had little chance of homering there. Duke Snider, a left-handed slugger in the bandbox Ebbets Field, was completely destroyed by the Coliseum. When Willie Mays first saw the place, he approached Snider during batting practice.

"Duke, they just killed you, man," he exclaimed in his high-pitched whine.

Right-handed pitcher Don Drysdale emerged as a star. In 1961 young Sandy Koufax came into his own. Slowly, manager Walter Alston transitioned from the aging, veteran stars of Brooklyn—Snider, Pee Wee Reese, Gil Hodges—to a team with a Los Angeles identity: Frank Howard, Maury Wills, Tommy Davis. The Dodgers were generally contenders after their first season, as were the Giants in their first four years in San Francisco.

On April 15, 1958, 23,449 San Franciscans arrived at Seals Stadium to watch their new heroes defeat their old rivals, Don Drysdale and the Dodgers, 8-0. The Giants drew 90 percent capacity of the stadium located at the corner of Seventh and Bryant streets in their first year. The club quickly built itself up on the strength of new, young San Francisco stars like Orlando Cepeda, Willie McCovey, and Juan Marichal. But they never reached the World Series, as L.A. had in 1959. The Giants lost seven of their last eight games to blow the pennant after being in first place all season that year.

San Francisco did pass a $5 million bond issue to build a modern stadium. Charlie Harney sold his land to The City for $2.7 million on the proviso that he be put in charge of the construction project. He pledged to complete the park "in eight months." The graft and corruption in San Francisco was rampant, with Mayor Christopher and Harney smiling all the way to the bank. The stadium project became a model for bad planning, bad government, and bad bureaucracy.

Dirt from Harney's nearby hill was used as landfill, but it sheared off the windbreakers. Chub Feeney came out to observe progress and saw cardboard boxes blowing around. "Does the wind always blow like this?" he asked with desperation in his voice and visions of a bleak future in his eyes.

"Only between the hours of one and five," answered a crewmember. The workers just laughed. They had theirs, the union had theirs; the suckers from the Big Apple were committed to their incompetence with no recourse. Certainly they lacked the will to insist on excellence.

The smell of clams and polluted water "thicker than Los Angeles smog and fouler than Canarsie garbage" permeated the environment, wrote Southern California writer Arnold Hano, who was familiar with the air quality down there.

Harney thought the stadium would be named after him. The winning contest name, however, was the uninspiring, unoriginal Candlestick Park. Nobody ever really figured out why the park was called Candlestick Point in the first place. It meant nothing and stood for less. After Harney heard it was not to be named after him, work slacked off and the completion date was pushed back. Eventually a grand jury probed the payment of Harney's parking contracts, a notoriously crime-addled business run largely by organized crime in San Francisco to this day. The Teamsters' strike delayed installation of key stadium components. Then Harney refused to allow the Giants to observe their future home. The city fire marshal inspected the place and called it a "fire trap." Eventually, Candlestick was reinforced with concrete, the first stadium ever constructed in that manner.

When Candlestick Park went up in 1960, Vice President Richard Nixon inaugurated it by calling it the "finest baseball stadium in the world." That review resonated for about a game or two. Fans were literally blown away. On the very first batting practice swing Willie Mays took, he connected and the wind sheared his bat in half.

The opener drew 42,269 fans. Distinguished guests included Nixon, California Governor Edmund "Pat" Brown, Commissioner Ford Frick, and ex-manager John McGraw's widow. The Giants beat St. Louis, and superstar center fielder Willie Mays drove in all their runs.

Both the Dodgers and Giants were close in 1961, but Cincinnati captured the championship. Mays somehow had not excited the populace. He seemed to always pop up in the clutch with the bases loaded. He was a New York creation, Leo Durocher's prodigy, not a homegrown product like the more popular Cepeda.

Candlestick was a liability from the very first season and never improved. Dodger fans who traveled north made fun of it. "The Candlestick weather leaves you depressed," said shortstop Eddie Bressoud. Opponents were just happy to leave. Pittsburgh pitcher Vernon Law said he would not report to San Francisco if he were ever traded there.

"Never mind the hot coffee, get me a priest!" Cardinals' announcer Joe Garagiola joked while enduring a game in its cold, breezy broadcast booth.

"No one liked playing there," pitching coach Larry Jansen recalled. "Every team that came in hated it, but I told the pitchers this was our home and we'd have the edge if we just prepared ourselves mentally and physically. Wear longjohns, wear a choker around your neck and warm up an extra five minutes."

Willie McCovey hit an infield pop-up that carried for a homer. Diminutive relief pitcher Stu Miller's glove stuck to the fence, and he was "blown off" the mound during the 1961 All-Star Game, causing a balk. On that July day, 100 fans were treated for heat prostration. Then swirling winds caused a huge temperature drop and the infamous gustblown Miller incident. The wind caused seven errors by both teams, an All-Star Game record. Roger Maris, the superstar right fielder of the New York Yankees, was in shock, saying Candlestick should have been built "under the bay."

"Chewing tobacco and sand isn't a tasty combination," remarked Baltimore relief pitcher Hoyt Wilhelm. To spit in the wind at Candlestick Park was hazardous.

"Whatever this is, it isn't a Major League ballpark," wrote Arthur Daley of the *New York Times*.

On one occasion, a pop fly off the bat of Pittsburgh's Don Hoak was actually lost. It was called foul and the game was held up for 15 minutes. A coiled heating system may have been the most famous example of San Francisco incompetence. Built under the seats to warm the behinds of frigid fans, it never did work. Famed attorney Melvin Belli froze his toes and sued, winning full damages: the price of his season ticket, which he paid to San Francisco for the planting of trees, but "not at Candlestick," he said. "They would freeze out there."

Stoneham had a legal waiver printed in the program disavowing future responsibility for malfunctions. Women complained about their nylons torn by the seats. Heart attacks occurred when people walked the steep hills to get to the park in the brutal bayside conditions. "Cardiac Hill" got its name when 16 people died traversing it. In 1962 the elevators failed. Also, $55,000 was paid to a Palo Alto firm to study the wind, but no answers were forthcoming.

"It's an act of God!"

It was a waste of dough, just like the money paid to Harney.

It had open-ended bleachers, and the monstrous shipbuilding crane loomed beyond like the alien space ship in Independence Day. Anything hit in the air was an adventure. Dust swirled amid hot dog wrappers. The players despised everything about the place. It had no redeeming qualities whatsoever, except that people who wanted to leave were allowed to. At night, a fog rolled in like the darkness over Old Testament Egypt on Passover.

Fans from warm surrounding communities showed up for midsummer games in shorts and T-shirts, then froze to the bone. There was no relief under the stands, which became wind tunnels, even worse than the open spaces. After games, fans were met head-on by the howling elements. Whitecaps roiled the bay. Cracks immediately appeared in the parking lot cement, since it had been laid over landfill. The city-employed stadium operations crew did not pick up broken glass; they were all bored, lifeless, and made fans feel unwelcome.

The concessions were blasé, hot dogs were cold, and the buns were soggy. Beer was warm. Concessionaires were rude. The bathrooms stunk of vomit and urine. Candlestick Park was dirty the day it opened and never got better. The city-built, owned and controlled park was a symbol of government inefficiency. San Francisco, once considered a can-do city that, after the 1906 Great Earthquake, had rebuilt itself in time for the Pan-Pacific Exhibition of 1915, lost enormous prestige.

When fans left Candlestick, they had no restaurants, bars, or any other places to go. Whatever was there was dangerous and uninviting, anyway. South San Francisco, the nearest civilization to the south, had no nightlife of any kind. It was, literally, an "Industrial City," which advertised itself as on a nearby bluff much the way high schools put up a giant "D" or "R" on hills overlooking campuses. Someplace that nobody even knew how to get to, called Brisbane, existed somewhere west of the stadium. It was of no use beyond a postal annex.

The downtown fun spots of Union Square, the marina, and Fisherman's Wharf required a car ride on the freeway, or through the ghetto, then exiting and negotiating major parking hassles. There was little ancillary benefit to The City. Most fans just wanted to get home. If they lived on the peninsula, they never came close to San Francisco proper coming or going from Candlestick.

Then there was the park's effect on Mays. The winds just pushed his powerful shots back onto the field of play. He was forced to alter his swing and become an off-field line drive hitter. Candlestick Park eliminated any chance he had at break-ing Babe Ruth's career home run record of 714. The place was a disaster with a capital "D."

By 1962 fans were frustrated with the club. "San Franciscans [who expect a pennant] are advised to stay away from coarse foods . . . avoid stimulants that irritate the stomach walls . . . if seized by a choking feeling, lay quietly and well-covered until your physician arrives," wrote Mel Durslag of the *Los Angeles Herald Examiner*. The well-aimed barbs from Los Angelinos toward San Franciscans came early and often.

Candlestick was a model of how *not* to build a stadium, first learned by the Dodgers. Candlestick Park was—and still is—the laughing stock symbol of San Francisco ineptitude in the face of Los Angeles excellence. L.A.'s efforts at building Dodger Stadium went smoothly. A New Yorker, Captain Emil Praeger, was the chief architect. Vanell Construction built it to perfection: every seat unobstructed, spacious parking for 16,000 cars, and all landscaped with exotic tropical shrubs and palm trees.

Despite all of this public evidence of San Francisco's inferiority, San Francisco and San Franciscans insisted on the myth that they were instead superior! The leading lights of this subject were two local gossip columnists, Herb Caen and Charles McCabe, and a politico named Art Hoppe. Hoppe was paid good money every first and 15th of the month to dispense lies about America. Truth was not his ally, so he found other means of earning his pay. Caen and McCabe wrote provincial articles extolling the virtue of all things in The City Caen called, in those pre-Saddam Hussein days, "Baghdad by the bay." Caen was a talentless hack whose stock in trade was identifying people more impressive than he was, finding out some secret about them, then printing it in the paper. McCabe at least had some style. They wrote for a rag called the San Francisco Chronicle, which was thin and unimpressive. The Chronicle had little if any reportorial presence in places where the news was being moved and shook; Washington, New York,

Southeast Asia (where American involvement in Vietnam was escalating), or in Europe. Most of the important stuff just came in from the wire services.

Its sports section was printed on green paper and called the "Sporting Green." They did employ a couple of good baseball writers, but the whole emphasis was on the Giants with a "homer" point of view. It was skimpy and scant. High school sports got no love whatsoever. Reading the Chronicle took a couple of minutes. There was no there there.

The afternoon paper, the Examiner, was better, but no great prize. Again, the contrast with Los Angeles excellence manifested itself, this time in the form of the Los Angeles Times. The Times was a conservative paper owned by the Chandler family. They had a large circulation and catered to a mostly white, Christian readership populating suburban enclaves such as Pasadena, Palos Verdes Estates, and Orange County. It was written for people embodied by the parents of Benjamin Braddock (Dustin Hoffman) in The Graduate. The Times put its weight behind Richard Nixon, a local congressman fighting communism who served on the House Un-American Activities Committee during the contentious Alger Hiss affair. The paper backed Nixon through his Senate election, his vice presidency under Dwight Eisenhower, and a 1960 campaign he won but for stolen votes in Illinois, and "tombstone votes" in Texas.

But the Stanford-educated Otis Chandler eventually took over the family business. He was conservative, but bound to remake the paper not as a mouthpiece for the Republican Party, but to turn it into a world class journalistic organization on par with the New York Times, Washington Post and the Times of London. Chandler succeeded by opening bureaus in every major news center; not just New York and D.C., but the Deep South where the civil rights struggle was underway; in Asia where the Cold War was getting hot; in Moscow, London, Paris and everywhere else opinions, politics, and policy were being made, formed, and expressed.

The Times also covered local and state issues with a fine-tooth comb. Its editorial page was diverse, thought provoking, and worthy. Its coverage of the film business was equal to trade magazines like the Hollywood Reporter and Daily Variety. But what separated the Los Angeles Times from all competition, making it the best newspaper in the world, was an unbelievable sports section. It was like picking up a copy of the Sporting News seven days a week. It covered high school sports and blanketed the Angels, Lakers, USC, UCLA, and all other athletic endeavors. A talented staff of columnists, reporters, and beat writers covered the colorful commentary of USC coach John McKay, the Southern homilies of UCLA coach Red Saunders, the dry wisdom of Bruins basketball coach John Wooden, and the odd Kabuki dance between the Dodgers' front office and manager Walter Alston.

The heart of the Times was a brilliant wordsmith named Jim Murray. Murray, like so many on the West Coast, was an East Coast transplant who came to the paper from Time magazine, where he covered Hollywood during an era of true decadence; the last of the studio system, Mob influence and Frank Sinatra's Rat Pack. Murray once went on a date/interview with Marilyn Monroe, which was broken up when the sex symbol excused herself to leave with another guy. Joe DiMaggio had been lurking in a nearby booth at the Brown Derby.

Murray came to the Los Angeles Times in 1961. He wrote with a social pathos, imbuing his sports reportage with observations that the University of Alabama, for instance, was not deserving of the term National Champion so long as they neither played integrated opponents, traveled to the North, nor had black players on their roster themselves. It also did not make sense to call the Crimson Tide the number one team when they lost their bowl game after the final Associated Press poll. Murray was, quite simply, the best sportswriter who ever lived.

The difference between Murray and the San Franciscans' Hoppe, Caen, and McCabe was a chasm wider than the Grand Canyon. The elitist view of themselves was embodied by a 1960s column McCabe wrote in which he claimed to have been spared a parking ticket in Paris when the gendarme learned of his San Francisco pedigree.

"You mention that you are from San Francisco and you are immediately a gent, as distinct from the yahoos who bully blacks and throw tear gas at kids . . . and live in ticky-tack houses and go to ticky-tack supermarkets," McCabe wrote. He somehow determined that the reception given to black jazz artists (who achieved superstar status in New Orleans, for the most part) in Paris nightclubs equaled the "grace" that would have been accorded the descendants of a million slaves had they lived amongst the French populace.

A San Franciscan, "in the eyes of most Europeans," is really "a civilized European," and The City was an "Arcadian enclave" separated from the backwards burgs of America's "fly over country."

"San Francisco, like John Kennedy, has been formally canonized in Europe," McCabe wrote. "It comes as no news to anyone that Europeans hate our guts," he continued, apparently quite distressed that a continent that in the twentieth century started two world wars killing 150 million people, as well as a political ideology—communism—that by the 1960s was well on its way to "achieving" its eventual total of 100 million murdered human beings, somehow "hated" the very people who were responsible for ending both world wars and thus the 150 million dead; and would eventually end communism and its 100 million murders. This was like the convicted mass killer who hates the prosecuting attorney who puts him behind bars, then has the temerity to possess knowledge of his crimes!

McCabe also seemed resilient to the rather obvious fact that the Vietnam War we were fighting at that very time was one we were engaging in because the French themselves had mucked it up so badly in the first place. He no doubt remained clueless to the fact that the Middle East was a mess not because of America, but because the French, after the Sykes-Picot Agreement (1916) had tried to colonize Syria, Lebanon, Algeria, and other Arab populations, used the Foreign Legion to brutally suppress inevitable rebellions, then again left it up to the United States to pick the pieces.

McCabe in his column wailed against our nation's tendency towards wealth and power thrust upon the whole world. The elite columnist again seemed unable to see that which was placed before his eyes. Here were a few tiny agrarian colonies, separated by an ocean from the salons of political, economic, and military influence, yet in a scant 200 years we had become the most powerful empire in the annals of mankind. McCabe and his kind were the last people on God's Earth to embrace knowledge of the fact that such a thing could happen only by a divine, guiding hand.

The "traveling American . . . tends to be a quite awful advertisement for his country," he wrote, apparently in all cases with the exception of those times when the "traveling American" is feeding starving Berliners; liberating Nazi-occupied France; providing an alternative to the gulags and concentration camps for millions . . . all at great cost in treasure and life, and apparently out of pure benevolence!

"He does not care about people in Paris," McCabe wrote, which is like saying the policeman who saves the life of a man does not care that the man hates him for saving his life. Apparently, Jack and Jacqueline Kennedy were the sole antidotes to American rudeness. Cheating on a man's wife was a virtue the French could admire, in McCabe's view.

While the Dodgers toiled with a considerable degree of success in the Los Angeles Memorial Coliseum, Walter O'Malley set out to build a baseball palace that would stamp greatness upon his legacy. Brooklynites called him the "most hated man since Adolf Hitler." If O'Malley were going to be given credit as a visionary and important figure in the game's history, his Dodger Stadium would have to be his monument.

He had found Chavez Ravine, a plot of undeveloped city-owned ground, given to him to do with as he pleased. Illegal Mexican immigrants, "squatters" in O'Malley's view, inhabited the area. They camped out rent- and tax-free. The Arechiga family lived there and put up a big stink over the proposed stadium, even though they did not own the land. Many do-gooders and bleeding hearts found solitude in their plight. The city then paid Arechiga and others for the land they did not own, and the construction crews moved in.

By 1962 the project was completed, ready to be unveiled in all its glory. It was immediately unique in its design, architecture, and location—a place of wonder. Sitting on a rise about two miles from downtown, it was totally surrounded by urbanity—freeways, a teeming population, skyscrapers, sprawl—yet in traveling up a slight but steady palm tree–lined grade, fans had the immediate illusion, in true movie style, of a park—in a park, amid foothills and foliage. The view at night was spectacular: a lit-up downtown, and beyond that the vast basin of countless film and photo images. Its parking lot was spacious, with ticket holders directed to convenient spots near their seats. Freeway access from every area of Los Angeles seemingly directed all roads to Dodger Stadium.

Next to the Dodger offices fans traversed a steep stairwell under a cluster of greenery designed to resemble the Hanging Gardens of Babylon. Fans felt as if they were on tour of a John Huston or Cecil B. DeMille movie.

In contrast to the filthy, stinking Candlestick, Dodger Stadium was so clean fans felt they could eat dinner off its polished floors. The bathrooms were pristine. The concessions offered many choices—fresh, tasty foods, and grilled Dodger Dogs on crisp buns. Cheerful concessionaires sold bright souvenirs. Ushers directed fans to their seats with service and a smile.

The stadium was built for maximum fan comfort, a baseball-only facility in which all seats were angled toward home plate instead of toward a 50-yard line location hidden behind a pillar in right field. Seats were built wide with plenty of legroom. No more hard, wooden benches. Its luxury boxes were an innovation that O'Malley came up with after seeing similar seating arrangements during the exhibition tour of Japan.

The Diamond Room catered to stars and celebrities, who enjoyed posh accommodations, gourmet food, and cocktails while watching the game. Despite this, part of the fan experience at Dodger Stadium immediately included hobnobbing with movie stars, as the park was located 15 minutes from Hollywood Boulevard. The comingling of average fans was immediately an easy going affair, with a sense of democracy among Dodger Stadium fans. A wide diversity of people came to share their love of baseball and the team. There had been a long-simmering feud between the Latino and white populations of Los Angeles. Dodger Stadium went a long way toward healing much of that divide.

The warm weather gave the palm tree–studded stadium a sense of tropical paradise—shirtsleeve crowds and plenty of girl watching. The team immediately chose to play Saturday night games, a first that gave fans a chance to enjoy a weekend at the beach and still make it to the ballgame. With Vin Scully announcing into fan-held transistor radios, Dodger Stadium somehow seemed wholesome, "something good," as James Earl Jones said in Field of Dreams. It was a family oasis in the middle of a city rife with smog, traffic, crime, prostitution, X-rated movies, gangs, corruption, and greed. Fans arrived at Dodger Stadium and it was like "dipping themselves in magic waters." It was immediately modern and at the same time nostalgic.

When the first game was played on April 8, 1962, the hoopla was extra-ordinary. Baseball Commissioner Ford Frick, National League President Warren Giles, and Roman Catholic ecclesiastic James McIntyre were among the honored guests. An army of blue-shirted usherettes met a crowd of 52,564. Every review was A-plus. The place was fantastic in every way; the greatest stadium in all of sports.

A video of O'Malley shows him sitting in his luxury suite, overlooking the field like a potentate. He smiles and puffs on his big cigar, secure in the knowledge that after all the lawsuits, bad press, and angst, he had pulled it off; he was one of the "lords of baseball." Not even a 6–3 loss to Cincinnati could dampen spirits.

San Franciscans grudgingly acknowledged the greatness of Dodger Stadium. Some things were just too spectacular to deny. They would find fault with the Dodgers and their fans, who tended to leave in the seventh inning to beat the traffic, but the stadium itself was a monument.

It certainly did not look good for "Frisco," the nickname San Franciscans hated in April 1962. The two teams had been in California for four seasons. The only team to make it to, and win, a World Series was Los Angeles. Candlestick was a joke. NoCal was getting fed up with SoCal hegemony. USC went unbeaten, shut out Notre Dame, 25-0 and defeated Wisconsin in the Rose Bowl, 42-37, to capture the National Championship. The Lakers extended Boston to seven games in the NBA Finals.

The Trojans and Bruins regularly dominated Cal and Stanford in all sports. The dynamic of the schools was beginning to take on a political edge, with Cal and Stanford playing the role of jealous losers forced to lie about their opponents.

While L.A. had the Lakers, the Warriors did not move to San Francisco from Philadelphia until the 1962-63 season. The expansion Angels looked to be a mini-success. The A's were still in Kansas City, six years away from their move to Oakland. The Rams consistently had the upper hand over the 49ers. The Raiders were nobodies playing on a high school field. Now this fabulous new Dodger Stadium threatened to catapult the already-favored Dodgers to a big championship season. Willie Mays and the Giants were The City's last, best hope to prevent more indignity.

TWO

Empire

"I am not superstitious, but I do think it is bad luck
to bet against the Yankees."
—*Ring Lardner*

The history of the New York Yankees up until 1962 was of course magnificent; the team was over and above any sports franchise at any level, anywhere. There had been many times in the past when the Bronx Bombers were deemed unbeatable, at the top of their game, a surefire favorite to win the pennant and capture the Series. There may never have been any season, however, in which Yankee confidence was greater than it was entering the 1962 campaign.

This was the baseball version of America at the very peak of its glory. They were Rome after Caesar's triumphs; MacArthur on the deck of the "mighty Mizzou." First, they won the battle for New York that had long been fought between the Giants, Dodgers, and themselves. In the beginning, the Giants owned the town. The Yankees were "Johnny-come-latelies," a low rent team of . . . renters in a new league. It took years before they even settled on the name Yankees. Somehow this had to happen, because it would have been hard to imagine such a force of nature going by the name Highlanders.

The Dodgers never matched the Yankees on the field, but they engendered a love that the pinstripers could never seem to get. They were like Marcus Licinius Crassus, the Roman general played by Sir Laurence Olivier in *Spartacus*, who steals the slave girl Varinia from Kirk Douglas. He lavishes her with the good life but cannot buy her love. Olivier's response was to crucify Douglas and the rest of the slave rebellion in a gruesome spectacle along the Appian Way.

The New York City baseball version was less horrible but served the Yankees' purposes just the same anyway. The Dodgers and Giants were run out of town, leaving the Big Apple uncontested. The New York Yankees owned the city, every single borough. Whether they liked it or not, the residents of Brooklyn, Queens, Staten Island, Harlem, and the rest of the city had been colonized by the New York Yankees, Inc.

With the Dodgers and Giants gone, New York immediately consolidated its power, like a politician who runs unopposed in the primaries and spends all his money to easily win the general election. They captured the 1958 World Championship. In 1961 the Yankees did not merely win; they rolled through opposition like George Patton's tanks in the late winter and early spring of 1945.

Many people still refer to the 1927 Yankees as the greatest team of all time, but the 1961 version may well have been better. New manager Ralph Houk's team got off to a relatively slow start and faced competition from a strong Detroit Tigers ball club (101-61) that featured Norm Cash (.361 with 41 homers and 132 RBIs allegedly using a corked bat), Rocky Colavito (45 homers, 140 RBIs), the great Al Kaline (.324), and pitchers Jim Bunning (17-11) and the "Yankee killer" Frank Lary (23-9).

But once the "M & M boys"—Mickey Mantle and Roger Maris—got going, New York could not be stopped. Maris led the way, earning his second straight Most Valuable Player award while breaking Babe Ruth's all-time home run record with 61 along with 141 runs batted in. Mantle, burdened by a late-season injury that prevented his breaking Ruth's mark, still finished with 54 home runs, 117 runs batted in, and a .317 average. First baseman Bill "Moose" Skowron added 28 homers and 89 RBIs. Second baseman Bobby Richardson played great defense and teamed with shortstop Tony Kubek to form one of the best middle infields in baseball. Clete Boyer was a fine-fielding third baseman.

Yogi Berra mainly played left field, having ceded catching duties to Elston Howard. In 1961 Berra hit 22 homers and batted .271. Mantle (center field) and Maris (right field) were exceeded defensively by only two National Leaguers, Willie Mays and Roberto Clemente. It was as complete a lineup as can be imagined. Houk had kept it set throughout the year, instead of platooning right-handers and left-handers as Casey Stengel (1949–60) had done. Utilityman extraordinaire Johnny Blanchard contributed 21 home runs and a .305 average.

The pitching staff was airtight, led by Cy Young award-winner Whitey Ford in his best year ever (25-4, 3.21 ERA). Bill Stafford (14-9, 2.68), Ralph Terry (16-3, 3.15), Rollie Sheldon (11-5), Jim Coates (11-5), Bob Daley (8-9), and ace relief pitcher Luis Arroyo (15-5, 29 saves and a 2.19 earned run average) gave New York mound dominance.

New York had powered their way to a 109-53 record, eight games better than Detroit, then obliterated the Cincinnati Reds in an anticlimactic five World Series games. Ford shut out the Reds, 2-0, in the Series opener. In game four at Crosley Field, Ford had to retire in the sixth inning after suffering an ankle injury but was the winning pitcher in a 7-0 victory. That extended his streak of consecutive scoreless innings in World Series play to 32, eclipsing the old record by Boston's Babe Ruth set in 1918.

Cincinnati's Frank Robinson was held to a .200 Series average. Maris contributed only one homer and Mantle was still wobbly from late-season health issues, but there was, aside from Joey Jay's 6-2 win in game two, no stopping the Yankees.

As the team gathered in St. Petersburg, Florida, for Spring Training in 1962, they were the kings of baseball, of all sports, and perhaps most important, of New York, which some people considered to be more important than all of America or even the world. There was a mosquito in their midst, but they hardly noticed it. The expansion New York Mets were congregating for their first season.

Commissioner Ford Frick, who always adhered to the Yankees' interests as if he were on their payroll, had opposed the Mets, but inexorable forces within the media and political circles had made their creation a fait accompli. They would play at the Polo Grounds (Ebbets Field had been torn down to build apartments immediately after the Dodgers' departure), which seemed to be a joke. But the Mets had one little, tiny card in their deck. Casey Stengel was their manager. They also featured several old Dodgers who were expected to draw fan support.

The Yankees, for all their bluster, had not really increased their attendance in the four years between the Dodgers and Giants leaving and the arrival of the Mets. It was the old "love me . . . how much can I pay you to love me?" theme. But on the field, and in the general psyche of baseball, they were all-powerful and gave scant thought to anything the Mets were doing.

The club assembled in sleepy St. Pete was now Ralph Houk's team through and through. In 1961 Houk had replaced a legend. He immediately established his own identity by deviating from Stengel's old stratagems. After some early ups and downs, his methods proved to be at least as effective, if not superior.

Houk described himself "as corny as Kansas in August." He was born near Lawrence in 1919 and grew up on a farm. A high school football hero, he turned down scholarships to Kansas and Oklahoma in the pursuit of professional baseball. Two Yankees scouts teamed up to get his name on the dotted line for $200. One "negotiated" while the other regaled scouts of other teams with old Babe Ruth stories to derail them from signing Houk. By the time they caught on, the young catcher was a Yankee.

The 1962 Yankees were a team in semi-transition, but it was a good thing. For years, they had produced young players through their great farm system but also brought in numerous key players in trades with the Kansas City A's. Charlie O. Finley was a cantankerous midwestern insurance magnate by way of Alabama. He owned the A's after the death of Arnold Johnson and vowed to cut off that spigot. In the spring of 1962, the club had numerous young stars threatening to break into the big leagues. It appeared that the Yankee dynasty would never end; it had an endless supply of talent to keep the train rolling.

At first base, veteran Moose Skowron was trying to fend off the advances of a hotshot rookie named Joe Pepitone. Skowron, born in Chicago in 1930, had been a Yankee mainstay since breaking in, in 1954, hitting .340 in 87 games. He hit .319 his first full year (1955) and bested the .300 mark three times after that. Skowron hit for solid power, slamming 28 homers in 1961.

Skowron, 31 in 1962, was in many ways the typical Yankee. He was big, powerful, self-assured, and proud to wear the pinstripes. Players who showed any lack of respect for Yankees tradition had to deal with Moose. He was a man's man and enjoyed life on a team of life-enjoyers.

The player creeping up on him, ready to take his place as the Yankee first baseman, was one of those youngsters who lacked what Moose and others saw as the proper respect for Yankees tradition. Twenty-one-year-old Joe Pepitone was a 6'2", 185-pound left-handed gloveman straight out of a Martin Scorsese movie; a swarthy, bushy-browed Italian American, a young Al Pacino–type. Pepitone loved to party, loved the ladies, found baseball to be a means to an end, and despite his Bronx upbringing did not bow at the altar of Yankee glory.

In the minor leagues, Pepitone found a kindred spirit, an Orioles farmhand named Bo Belinsky. In Aberdeen, South Dakota, Pepitone and Belinsky hooked up, chasing local girls. Belinsky's manager was Earl Weaver, who later skippered the big club to the 1970 World Championship.

"Pepitone shows up in a convertible," recalled Weaver. "I see Bo get in the passenger's seat, and I call out to him to be careful, not to get in trouble. He never paid any attention as the car fishtailed out of there, kicking up dust all over the place, tires screeching. I thought, 'Where the hell are they going, there's nothin' to do in Aberdeen?' but those two, they'd find it. Oh my, they were pistols."

Houk had little idea how to deal with this "new breed" of player, but Pepitone was a slick fielder who would eventually have his day. Skowron was determined to hold him off at least one more season.

The team was divided between the partiers—Mantle, Ford, Blanchard—and the family men. Richardson and Maris were the leading family guys. It was this quality of his personality that had given Richardson the edge in the first place.

Born in Sumter, South Carolina, the 5'9", 170-pounder was a devout Christian who did youth work in the off-season. He came up in 1955, but the job belonged to fan favorite Billy Martin. George Weiss and the Yankee brass, however, were not enamored with Martin, who not only drank too much but also did not hold his liquor well. Martin, according to the company line, led Mantle astray. There was hypocrisy in this, of course, since Whitey Ford was in on the fun, too. But Ford was the "Chairman of the Board." Casey Stengel loved Martin, a scrappy Berkeley, California, native who had played for him with the Oakland Oaks when Casey's team won the PCL pennant. Martin, however, did not fit the Yankee image of the 1950s.

He was part Portuguese, and despite being a believing Catholic himself, constantly gave in to the temptations of the road and the allures of groupies. When Martin got into a celebrated brawl at the Copacabana in 1957, it was the excuse Weiss needed to get rid him. He was shipped to Kansas City, and Richardson was made the starter.

In 1958 Richardson seriously thought about quitting baseball to pursue the Christian ministry. "I didn't feel as though my future was too solid as I had played only on a part-time basis in 1956 and 1957," he said. "I was thinking of going to school to get prepared for youth work."

In 1959 Richardson hit .307, and in the 1960 World Series set a record with 12 RBIs, earning the MVP award; he was the only player from a losing team to win the award. He slammed two doubles, two triples, a grand slam, and batted .367.

"I always thought records like this belonged to men such as Babe Ruth, Lou Gehrig, and Joe DiMaggio," said Richardson. "I certainly shouldn't be classified in their category."

"He has wonderful hands, so quick and sure," remarked Houk. "He can make the double play on the pivot and he can make it on the starting end."

Clete Boyer had no competition at third base. His brother Ken was a star with the St. Louis Cardinals who, two years later, would lead the Redbirds to t he 1964 World Series victory over the Yankees. The Boyers hailed from Missouri. Both came to the Major Leagues in 1955. Ken was the better hitter, but other than Baltimore's Brooks Robinson, Clete was as good a defensive third sacker as there was in baseball. He was a quiet, unassuming midwesterner, the consummate professional overshadowed by Robinson, who captured all the Gold Gloves he otherwise would have won. Clete came to the Yankees as part of the Kansas City pipeline in 1959. He hit only .224 in 1961, but that was what was expected of him.

At shortstop, 25-year-old Tony Kubek was a 6'3" Milwaukee native whose size foreshadowed the big shortstops of later years—Cal Ripken, Alex Rodriguez, and others. Kubek replaced Phil Rizzuto and provided solid play offensively and in the field. However, his career was marked by one unfortunate incident. In game seven of the 1960 World Series a seemingly routine groundball took a bad hop and hit Kubek in the Adam's apple, giving Pittsburgh the life needed to win an improbable 10-9 clincher. Pictures of Kubek, sitting on the infield dirt, his hand to his throat while surrounded by concerned teammates, still frustrates Yankee fans to this day.

Behind the plate was Elston Howard. Few teams in Major League history had so much talent behind the plate as the early 1960s Yankees. Aside from Howard was the Hall of Famer Berra, the steady John Blanchard, and in the minors a future big leaguer named Curt Blefary.

Among social sports pioneers, Howard was an unsung hero. Jackie Robinson broke the color barrier in 1947, and the National League set the pace. Between 1949 and 1961, 10 National League MVPs were black. All the American League MVPs had been white. Bill Veeck, owner of the Cleveland Indians, had followed up on the Robinson signing by bringing in Larry Doby and Satchel Paige in 1948, the year the Indians won their last World Series. However, Veeck went to the St. Louis Browns before taking over ownership of the Chicago White Sox. His travels derailed some of his efforts at further breaking social barriers. The junior circuit tended to follow the lead of the Yankees and Boston Red Sox.

Boston was alleged by the likes of Bill Russell and Reggie Smith, among others, to be the most racist city in sports. Owner Tom Yawkey was a leading dissenter when Branch Rickey introduced Robinson, and a few years later the Bosox turned down Willie Mays. If the Yankees were a racist organization, they kept that under wraps. There was no evidence of official policy or directive against the signing of black players, and their ownership had not protested integration.

Certainly, New York was a liberalized town, as receptive as any other than California cities to black pro athletes. Columbia University had All-American black football players during the 1910s. After initial resistance, Brooklyn took to Robinson with open arms. Willie Mays was a folk hero at the Polo Grounds, located in a Harlem neighborhood that could be seen from Yankee Stadium. The Bronx, traditionally a Jewish, Italian, and Irish borough, was by the 1950s becoming filled more and more by blacks, so the Yankees were well situated to lead the way in the American League in this area.

But the Yankees were conservative. They were the Republican Party, country club elites, Wall Street pinstripers. Their crowds resembled the New York Stock Exchange. Women in fur stoles and vanity sunglasses accompanied the men. Fans sat in the stands like Roman senators contemplating the proceedings. The front office calculated that if the club won, they filled Yankee Stadium, and if the "wrong" black player were brought in—well, why rock the boat?

A handsome, womanizing Caribbean first baseman, Vic Power, was traded from the organization before he could make his big league debut because he liked white women too much. The Power situation served as a cautionary tale to the club. Even Robinson by the 1950s, originally perceived as the "perfect" black pioneer, was to the Yankee way of doing things a real "clubhouse lawyer." They did not want some pinstriped black player on a racial soapbox.

Elston Howard would take some heat for not speaking out, but in the context of his times, the way he handled his business did as much if not more for black athletes in his way as he would have as an agitator; probably he was more effective. Born in St. Louis in 1929, Howard broke in as the first black Yankee in 1955. It was not easy, not because he was black but because he threatened three-time Most Valuable Player Yogi Berra, the regular catcher. A strong, line drive–hitter from the right side, Howard was an important utilityman who played in the outfield and, year by year, caught more and more games.

The staff liked him. Berra, for all his talents, did not look the part. He was short and squatty, getting the job done but looking funny doing it. Howard was the quintessential big, athletic catcher. His respectful manner around white people worked well with the great Yankee pitching staff, and a form of affirmative action began to take place, with many going out of their way to praise Howard. He needed no extra help. Howard was a tremendous talent, albeit one who developed steadily over a period of years.

In 1961 he finally caught more than 100 games (111) and batted a sterling .348 with 21 home runs and 77 runs batted in for the World Champions. By 1962 the catcher's position was all his. Berra was still around, but to his credit he had been helpful with Howard only when he took over his position. Howard was a quiet, dignified family man who lived with his wife in the white suburb of Teaneck, New Jersey. Many black athletes in New York, like Don Newcombe, made the rounds of black jazz clubs and were considered ladies men. Howard was a churchgoer who spoke glowingly of his love for the Yankees. He was eternally grateful to the club for the opportunity. While the inequities of society were obvious, and such talk might have seemed obsequious to some, it rang with truth. Howard meant it. And after all, he *had* been given a fabulous opportunity, the chance to be part of the Yankee legacy, which most players would do anything to do.

Backup catcher Johnny Blanchard was a throwback, a rough 'n' tumble old school guy who loved to hoist a few in the company of Mickey Mantle. Blanchard liked the ladies and the New York nightlife. He was a shot 'n' a beer guy from Minnesota, big and burly. His voice and laugh filled up the room. His visage was that of a pioneer in a covered wagon; he had a handsome, tough guy face out of the John Wayne mold. He was a hardcore American, typical of athletes in his political views, which leaned like so many toward Red-baiting during this era of Cold War tensions. He was proud to be a Yankee, knowing that he had a reputation because he wore the pinstripes. He may have started someplace else but would have done so anonymously. Like Skowron he clung tenaciously to the Yankee way, setting rookies straight if they veered from the path.

In 1962 a few of these 1960s kids started to infiltrate the system, but their efforts were not yet subversive. Blanchard did not play much, but like Ralph Houk before him never complained about his role as a bullpen catcher. He hit over .300 in 1961. Newcomers were taken aback that a player of such marginal importance in the scheme of things was such an important man in the club's social order, but on a club that included Mantle and Ford, the ability to drink and chase women was a big plus.

The hottest of the hotshot rookies was left fielder Tom Tresh. He was seemingly born to be a Yankee, and certainly not one of the so-called subversives. Expectations for him engendered talk of Joe DiMaggio and Mickey Mantle. Tresh used a Mickey Mantle model glove, wore T-shirts with portraits of Roger Maris and Yogi Berra printed on them, and grew up cutting and saving clippings of Yankee games in the newspaper.

In 1962 he was 24 years old, a blond All-American who had signed for $30,000 out of Central Michigan University. Tresh was an outfielder-shortstop, a rare combination. With Tony Kubek set to do a stint in the Army Reserves in 1962, Tresh entered Spring Training in a battle with another minor leaguer, Phil Linz, for the chance to fill Kubek's place in his absence. Tresh won the job and would play shortstop until Kubek's return.

Tresh's father, Mike, had been a catcher for the Chicago White Sox, but "Even when I went to a game when my father was catching, I always dreamed of one day being a Yankee," Tresh said during Spring Training. "I'd rather sit on the Yankee bench than play for any other team."

Right-handed pitcher Ralph Terry turned 26 prior to Spring Training in 1962. Despite having gone 16-3 in the 1961 regular season, he still had something to prove because of the pitch to Pittsburgh's Bill Mazeroski in 1960 that ended game seven of the World Series, one of the bitterest pills the club ever swallowed.

In the 1961 Fall Classic, Terry was the single mound failure in a five-game win. Cincinnati's Joey Jay beat him 6-2 in game two to even the series at one. In game five Terry was knocked out of the box in the third inning, but the Bronx Bombers overpowered Jay and the Reds, 13-5, to take the title.

After throwing the hanging curve to Mazeroski, Terry gulped down five martinis and did not taste a thing. "I was in a state of shock," he said. Terry was everything Whitey Ford was not. Whitey was a mound maestro. Terry, at 6'3", 195 pounds, was physically the ultimate pitcher. He came up out of Dust Bowl Oklahoma, which by the 1950s had seen a major image change courtesy of Mickey Mantle, Bud Wilkinson, and the OU Sooners. He made his big league debut in 1956, but over the next seasons his great potential was stifled by the fact that he was part of the revolving door that seemingly switched players in musical chairs fashion with the Kansas City A's. The Yankee pitching staff of the era was so solid and veteran that Terry could not break into it. He was 10-8 in 1960, but his great win-loss record the next year was tempered by criticism that anybody could win with that lineup behind him.

Bill Stafford was a young New Yorker, born in the Catskills. He lived in Yonkers and was only 21 when the 1962 season started. He had gone 14-9 in 1961, but his record was well deserved. His earned run average was a fabulous 2.68. Rollie Sheldon, who lived in nearby Connecticut, wanted to prove his 11-5 mark of 1961 was no fluke. Jim Coates was a tall, slim Virginia-born right-hander, a 29-year-old four-year Yankee veteran entering the season. Coates had what might be described as a dark sense of humor and often held court in the bullpen, letting the younger pitchers know what was what. He had finished 6-1 in 1959, 13-3 in 1960, and 11-5 in 1961. Bud Daley was a veteran southpaw from Southern California, where he was born in the town of Orange in 1932 and where he still resided in the off seasons. Daley broke into the Majors with Cleveland in 1955, but the Indians' staff was one of the best in baseball history so mound time was precious. His trade to Kansas City meant, in effect, he had been traded to the Yankees, for as soon as he established himself after consecutive 16-win seasons he was traded to New York. Daley went 12-17 in 1960 and 7-5 in 1961. As a lefty, he was extra valuable and could be used as a starter or out of the bullpen. Marshall Bridges was a right-hander from Mississippi who had shown promise with St. Louis and Cincinnati before coming to New York in 1962.

Then there was Jim Bouton, perhaps the unlikeliest of Yankees. He was only six feet tall and weighed 170 pounds, but possessed an impressive fastball. Born in Newark, New Jersey, in 1939, Bouton grew up hating the Yankees because they were too dominant and too white. He was like one of those people who think it better for America to occasionally lose a war and be humiliated, just to make things fair. The fact that the Yankees were all white probably escaped the attention of most suburban New Jersey kids, but not Bouton. He rooted for Willie Mays and the egalitarian New York Giants. As a kid at the Polo Grounds, he once chased a ball hit into the stands. He and a local black kid grabbed the sphere at the same time. Bouton relinquished it out of a sense of social equity.

Bouton's family moved to Michigan, where he attended high school. He played other positions and was no barnburner at any of them. With no scholarship offers, Bouton's father gathered the few clips extolling his son and mailed them to the baseball coach at Western Michigan University, along with a note reading, "Here's a kid who can really help our Broncos. Signed, a Western Michigan baseball fan." The ruse worked and Bouton was invited to Western Michigan, which was not then (and it is not now) a college baseball powerhouse. He turned few heads in Kalamazoo, but during the summer pitched for a semipro outfit that played in the American Baseball Congress (ABC), a prestigious amateur event. Bouton beat a strong team from Cincinnati, and for the first time gained some attention. In those days, before computers, the Internet, and blanket area scouting, players could slip under the radar. Word of mouth was a big factor. Scouts started to take notice of the kid who beat the Cincinnati team.

Initially, offers and opportunities to play professionally were discussed, but nothing came of it. The tournament ended, and Bouton returned to Michigan, where he waited in vain for the phone call that never came. The signing period was quickly coming to a close, so Bouton's father went back into action. He sent letters to the clubs that had scouts who saw Jim pitch in the ABC. The letter intimated that bids were streaming in. In order to be fair, the Bouton family would entertain all offers for a specified period of time before deciding what to do.

Bouton himself said the Yankees were the only club he fooled into making an offer, but considering that he would develop into an effective Major League hurler, it appears the Yankees knew precisely what they were doing. Bouton was signed and sent to the low minors, where he toiled in places like Amarillo, Texas, and Kearney, Nebraska. He loved every minute of it, mainly because he was at heart a fan who could not move past the concept that he had fooled his way in, was being *paid to play baseball*, and the jig would be up any minute.

Bouton, despite a lack of height or an overpowering body, developed a straight-overhand delivery that maximized his strength. Year by year, his fastball became faster. His years spent fooling high school and college hitters with junk had developed in him a keen sense of control and mound finesse. An intellectual anyway, Bouton used his smarts to outthink hitters and slowly began to get noticed in the Yankees' organization.

Bouton's oddball ways always made him a bit of an outsider. He did not play cards and found his minor league teammates to be Neanderthals, but he did drink beer, was a great practical joker, and managed to fit in, at least a little bit. He gravitated to other collegians and blacks, who regarded the liberal white boy with suspicion until they realized his desire for interracial friendship was genuine. But both in baseball and in his Army service, Bouton was a conundrum. He made fun of "small-minded people," whom he found in both occupations, but still worked hard to please his superiors.

Bouton worked extremely hard. He ran until exhausted, built up his body, and insisted—often to the consternation of pitching coaches—on throwing more than was expected in between starts. When he was coming up, he was a kindred spirit with pitching coach Johnny Sain. Either Bouton was a disciple of Sain or happened to believe in Sain's approach before he met the coach. He had different ideas about training methods, which were mostly rejected when suggested, but Sain was open-minded. On the mound Bouton developed a "bulldog" reputation. He was a gritty competitor who never gave an inch. Against all odds in 1962 he made it into big league Spring Training camp, where he impressed everybody enough to eventually make the roster.

Bouton found himself in the starting rotation and, in his first big league game in May, threw perhaps the ugliest shutout of all time. He gave up hits and walks in bunches, constantly throwing out of the stretch, but made it anyway. After the game he was interviewed on the post-game show. Thrilled, he returned to the Yankees' clubhouse, where his teammates had made a row of towels to his locker, symbolizing a red carpet. Just as Bouton entered the clubhouse, he saw Mickey Mantle himself laying down the last of the towels. He had arrived.

In the broadcast booth, the Yankees featured Mel Allen and Phil "Scooter" Rizzuto. Allen was a homespun Alabamian, and in this regard part of an odd tradition of announcers from that most Southern of states. He and Red Barber announced in one of the most Northern of cities, New York. Nobody could ever remember Allen not fitting in. His awed, "How about that!" after a wondrous play is remembered to this day and has become, like many Yogiisms, a cultural touchphrase that covers all things of awe and wonder.

Rizzuto was from Brooklyn and had, against all odds it seemed, become a Yankee staple at the shortstop position. He was the quintessential little guy in the middle infield. Offensively, he bunted, hit-and-ran, and stole some bases. Defensively, he made every play that counted. He was the 1950 American League Most Valuable Player. There have been better shortstops, and if he had not been a Yankee, he would not have been as well remembered. But he *had* been and he was beloved.

Rizzuto was Catholic and superstitious. Spiders scared him to death. He famously excused himself from games in the seventh inning to beat the traffic out of the Stadium and cross the George Washington Bridge into Jersey. He was there, however, when Maris hit number 61, emphasizing it with his high-pitched, *"Holy cow Maris did it!"*

Mickey Mantle's high school and minor league record was the talk of the sporting press. Manager Casey Stengel built him up as the next great star center fielder to replace Joe DiMaggio. The pressure was intense.

In his rookie year (1951), the teenage switch hitter slumped and was sent to Kansas City. He called his father, telling him he was not good enough for the big leagues and wanted to come home. Mutt Mantle drove from Commerce to Kansas City, knocked on his son's hotel room door, and without sitting down demanded that the boy pack his bags before wasting any more time.

Mantle put up incredible numbers. As a second-year player in 1952, he batted .311 with 23 home runs and 94 runs batted in, leading what was now *his* team to a third straight World Championship in the first year of DiMaggio's retirement. In 1953, 1954, and 1955, his physical maladies kept him from reaching his full potential, either sidelining him entirely or slowing him down. He had been so good in 1952, combined with youth and obviously unmatched talent, that anything less than performances matching DiMaggio, Babe Ruth, or Lou Gehrig in their primes was met with some scorn.

In 1956 Mantle went out and did things on the field that shut all critics up. If 10 knowledgeable baseball people were to descend upon a sports bar and enter into a discussion based on the question, *Who had the greatest season ever?* Mantle's 1956 campaign is as worthy as any.

He earned the Triple Crown by leading the league in batting average (.353), home runs (52), and RBIs (130), not to mention an incredible .705 slugging percentage with 132 runs scored (all of this in a 154-game schedule). He was sensational in center field and added three home runs in a redeeming World Series win over Brooklyn. It was the perfect season.

Mickey followed that up with a .365 average in 1957, which incredibly did not lead the league because ancient Ted Williams batted .388. In 1958 he powered 42 homers with 121 RBIs. His two series clouts led New York to victory over the Milwaukee Braves in the World Series.

In 1960 frustration set in. Mantle hit 40 home runs and drove in 119, but batted only .275. He was spectacular in the World Series, slamming three homers while batting .400, but nobody cared because the club managed to lose an improbable seven-game slugfest to Pittsburgh. But what really tarnished Mantle's gold was Roger Maris, a newcomer from the Kansas City A's. Maris hit fewer homers (39) and drove in fewer runs (98) while batting .283, but the writers awarded this lesser player with the Most Valuable Player award that should have been awarded to Mantle for the third time (he had won back-to-back MVPs in 1956 and 1957).

Stories of Mantle's carousing were now out in the open. The 1957 incident at the famed Copacabana nightclub had opened the lid on Yankee party habits. Hank Bauer and Billy Martin had gotten involved in a fight, and Martin was scapegoated by the club. But the New York newspaper scene was becoming more like the tabloid press we see today. A gossip columnist named Dorothy Kilgallen took to detailing Mantle's escapades around Manhattan—Jilly's, Toots Shors, P.J. Clarke's, the Latin Quarter—with veiled references to beautiful women (not his wife) in his company. The club did not like it. Neither did Merlyn Mantle, the wife back in Texas.

In 1961 Mantle settled for a career-high 54 homers to go along with a .317 average and 132 runs batted in. For the second straight season, he was beaten out for the MVP award by Roger Maris, a fine player whose overall statistics, talent, and accomplishments were not of Hall of Fame level and certainly did not match Mantle's. But recapturing the World Series after a two-year drought made everybody happy. Mantle was now at the height of his fame and status as a true New York sports icon, a position in American and world society that surpasses Hollywood celebrity. Only such world figures as war heroes, astronauts, and political giants shone brighter.

Roger Maris was born in Hibbing, Minnesota, the hometown of rock legend Bob Dylan, in 1934. He grew up in Fargo, North Dakota. Few great athletes have come from North Dakota. Maris is by far the best. He was a fantastic all-around athlete. In the small town atmosphere of Fargo, facing country competition, Maris was a man among boys; his legendary feats on the football and baseball field inspiring awe among the locals.

Maris earned the 1960 MVP award with 39 home runs and 112 runs batted in. He hit two homers in the World Series loss to Pittsburgh. His home run total, while impressive, had been shortened by cracked ribs he suffered after having hit 25 through June 30. In 1961 he set the baseball world on its head by breaking Babe Ruth's all-time home run record, amid much controversy and angst, with 61 longballs in a 161 game schedule.

By 1962 Yogi Berra had been moved to left field, replaced behind the plate by Elston Howard. However, Berra went down in history as one of the greatest catchers of all time. Berra was also one of the luckiest, most improbable baseball stars ever.

Berra was born on May 12, 1925, in St. Louis, Missouri. He grew up in the Italian section of town known as The Hill. His best friend was Joe Garagiola, who went on to become the catcher for the hometown St. Louis Cardinals. Berra, like Garagiola, was a catcher. He was funny looking and seemingly unathletic, but blocked everything, threw runners out, and hit line drives all over the field.

One day a carnival rolled through The Hill. One of the circus performers was an Eastern character, a mystic known as a Yogi. Berra's friends said he looked like the Yogi and started calling him that.

Berra was a steady hitter who hovered at or near .300, usually hitting around 30 homers and driving in 100 runs. In 1954 and 1955 he won consecutive Most Valuable Player awards, giving him three before Mantle had won his first. But Elston Howard was on the rise. The Yankees, like the rest of the American League, had been slow to integrate. Their fan base was corporate, Wall Street, patrician pinstriped country club Republicans. The club was very careful that when black players wore the pin stripes, they not be "agitators." A talented black farmhand, Vic Powers, had been traded because he was flamboyant and liked white women.

In 1961 Berra hit 22 home runs, catching 15 games while playing 87 in the outfield. He was 36 years old when he reported to Spring Training in 1962.

Edward Charles "Whitey" Ford was born on October 21, 1926, in New York City. He attended Aviation High School in Queens, a Yankees fan since his first trip to the Stadium in 1938. For various reasons, New York has not produced many baseball stars. Great athletes more often than not come from the South or the West. In the Yankees' case, California—particularly the San Francisco Bay Area—was a breeding ground for the pinstripers. Ford, Phil Rizzuto, and Lou Gehrig were New Yorkers, but relative exceptions to the rule.

Throughout the 1950s, Ford's record was as consistent as any pitcher has ever been. Year in and year out, he won around 18 games, never 20. His earned run average was invariably below or near 3.00. He compiled a 2.71 World Series ERA, consistently winning key games en route to Yankee World Championships. His lifetime winning percentage was .690. In 1961, however, new manager Ralph Houk took an entirely different approach. With General Manager George Weiss gone, he did not hold Whitey back. Ford responded with the greatest season of his career, a sterling 25-4 (.862) record, a 3.21 earned run average, and the Cy Young award.

As the 1962 season played itself out, several things were made apparent. One was that Maris would not repeat his feat of 61 homeruns in 1961. Maris was wary of his place in the Yankee hierarchy. On the one hand, he had broken the record and was a two-time Most Valuable Player, highly paid, and a New York icon. On the other hand, he was not Mickey Mantle, and the carping about his play continued.

Maris was never a .300 hitter, or close to it, at least not since coming to New York. Mantle combined awesome power with a high batting average. Maris was an excellent right fielder, although not as good as Mantle, who, despite injuries, was a great center fielder. But his high salary and higher expectations made him a target, of both fans and writers. He was certainly not in a slump, but his home run pace was not Ruthian—or Marisian, for that matter. If he could have replaced the home runs with a .300 average, it might have made a difference, but the expectations were too great to overcome. He looked like he did in 1960, which back then was worthy of the MVP, but now earned him boos and desultory press.

Mantle also did not look like he was going to match his 1961 performance. In previous seasons he had missed games because of a tonsillectomy, a cyst, an abscess, and injuries to his right knee, right thigh, right shoulder, and right index finger. A photo of Mantle on crutches with highlights of where on his body he had suffered debilitating injuries looked like a war map.

Despite the fact that Mantle's pace looked to be about his average, or even by his standards a little below his average, he was granted a pass. He was by now a true New York sports icon of the first order, a legend every bit as hallowed at Yankee Stadium as Babe Ruth, Lou Gehrig, or Joe DiMaggio. He could do no wrong and was simply idolized.

The season was summarized by Whitey Ford, who said, "We always figure we'll win the pennant." The Yankees handled their competition in businesslike fashion, like a banker shoring up his portfolio. There were no surprises, no key series, no moments of great tension. It was not the 109-win explosion of 1961, but no challenger emerged as Detroit had the previous season.

"There was a sense of inevitability to the 1962 season, even as the Yankees got off to their customary slow start," wrote Glenn Stout in *Yankees Century*. A doubleheader loss to Cleveland on June 17 was their fourth straight loss and seventh in eight games, pushing them three back of Cleveland. Still, the club was "laughing it off and the Indians were almost on their knees apologizing," wrote Leonard Koppett in the *New York Post*.

"We got 100 games to play," said Houk. "We ain't gonna quit." Ford missed some starts—and his chance to repeat as a 20-game winner—with a muscle strain, and Mantle suffered a torn hamstring on May 18. He also pulled ligaments behind his left knee as he tried not to fall. Only Mantle could sustain a second injury while trying to avoid a first. At age 30, his injuries were annual affairs.

"All I have is natural ability," he said. Writers started to note that chronic injuries such as those to his joints could be caused by dehydration, a common result of alcohol abuse. When he played, his legs were wrapped like a mummy, but he never backed off, playing hard every out.

In August, the Yankees stumbled and lost five straight to Baltimore. Nobody blinked. "Don't bet too much against us," said Houk. "We ought to get caught up on things in September."

Howard gave Ford his nickname "Chairman of the Board," which was also Frank Sinatra's nickname. Stengel had called him his "Banty rooster." "It's amazing how many outs you can get by working the count to where the hitter is sure you're going to throw to his weakness, then throw to his strength instead," said Ford. He threw a three-hitter in his first game after his injury and won nine of 10 decisions.

Mantle may have come back too soon. "They [the Yankees] say I can't hurt it anymore by playing," he said, so he played. When Mantle injured himself and was recuperating away from the team, general manager Roy Hamey asked him to return. "Maybe the players will feel better if he's around," he reasoned. Upon Mantle's return, Bobby Richardson approached him.

"I just walked up to him and shook his hand," he remarked. "It's hard to explain, but just seeing him gave me a lift."

When Mantle limped back into the starting lineup on June 22 after another nagging injury, his teammates started calling him "B&G" (for "Blood and Guts"). Ten days later the Yankees were back in first place. With Mantle out of the lineup, the club trolled along at a .500 pace but upon his return won 12 of 18, in the process lifting the team batting average from .248 to .265. Mantle played right field for the first time since 1954, and New York continued to win, capturing 29 of 40 games to put the pennant away.

With Mantle establishing himself as the clear star and team leader, the press simply could not acknowledge that Maris was also a key component. He always suffered in comparison to the Mick.

"One really can't compare him to Mantle in real value," wrote Koppett. Maris was even benched in September, mainly an effort to rest him but seen by his detractors as proof that he was a lesser player. "Maris didn't seem upset by this. In a strange sort of way he feels a kind of vindication. [He] has always insisted he isn't a 'superstar' [and] has resented being treated like one."

Houk had a "take no prisoners" attitude about the regular season that Stengel did not. If "the Major" did not see blood, he expected his charges to play, so if Maris sat then it must be viewed as indicative of his weak character, or so said the "Knights of the Keyboard," as Ted Williams derisively dubbed the press box know-it-alls.

The early key was Tresh, who made the All-Star team as a shortstop on his way to Rookie of the Year honors. When Kubek returned from the Army, Tresh moved to the outfield.

"We felt he was a big league hitter, but no one expected that he'd develop that kind of power from both sides of the plate," said Houk. When Tresh moved to the outfield it portended the end for Yogi Berra, who hit only .224 with 10 homers and 35 RBIs in limited action. Berra never complained.

"I figure I still got enough to help the Yanks win another pennant," he said.

"It's a home run outfield, yet all of them can cover ground and throw," Houk said of the Tresh-Mantle-Maris triumvirate after the season. "That outfield is very strong. Mantle is a very young 31, Maris is 28 and Tresh, at 24, looks as though he'll be around for a long time."

Tresh's switch to the outfield was a cause for some alarm with journalists, who wondered whether it was wise to tinker with success. "I never considered that a gamble," said Houk. Tresh had youth, speed, a strong arm, and the ability to get after fly balls. "You could tell that by the way he got a jump on those Texas League pop-ups."

By 1962 not only had Mantle filled DiMaggio's shoes, but the argument could also be made that he was better than both Joe D. and Willie Mays in the pantheon. He certainly had surpassed Duke Snider, the third New York center fielder, who had been destroyed by the L.A. Coliseum's dimensions.

Mantle hit .321 with 30 homers and 89 runs batted, statistics that failed to match some of his better years in the past but that were slightly skewed by injury. His place on the team, his position as a leader, however, was secure, as was his place in the glory halls of Yankee Stadium. After having lost the MVP award by four points to Maris in 1960 and three points in 1961, Mantle beat out Richardson for the award in 1962.

"I thought Bobby would win," Mantle said modestly, as if there were any chance of that. "I'm happy to receive the award, and I'd like to be the first Major Leaguer to win it four times."

Up until that time, Mays had won it only once (1954). Begun by the Baseball Writers Association of America in 1931 (the MVP had been awarded in inconsistent manner prior to that), Jimmie Foxx, Joe DiMaggio, Stan Musial, Roy Campanella, and Yogi Berra had each won it three times. Mantle could easily have had five, and there seemed a good chance he would capture it again in future years.

Now 34 years old, Whitey Ford did not match his fabulous 1961 Cy Young performance, but he remained the Chairman of the Board. The "red-faced" Ford had in 11 seasons "grown chubbier, wiser, wittier, and more impressive," wrote Bill Wise in the *1963 Official Baseball Almanac*. Blending control, curves, and guile (which included using his wedding ring to throw mean cut fastballs), Ford went 17-8 with a 2.90 earned run average.

"If I could get away with it now, I'd throw nothing but fastballs," the 5-10", 182-pound southpaw said. "No matter how fast you throw it, the fastball doesn't put real strain on your arm because the motion is natural. But you can't get a big league hitter out on fastballs alone, no matter how hard you throw the ball."

Still pitching on the four-day rotation that Houk had instituted beginning the previous season, Ford remained remarkably free of strains and muscle pulls. "I've taken good care of myself and I've been lucky," he said. "It's got to end sometime, but I want to win 200 first."

"When he thinks about it, which is often, 28-year-old Roger Maris realizes he has finally found a shadow he can't escape," wrote Bill Wise in the *1963 Official Baseball Almanac*. In 1962 Maris "met his match," when by hitting 33 home runs and driving in 100, "the moody, temperamental outfielder" demonstrated that he was not only not as good as Mickey Mantle and Babe Ruth, but "not as good as Roger Maris and probably never would be."

"Even when he hit 61, Roger knew he wasn't that good," one anonymous Yankee said. "He's a fine ballplayer, but when people know you've done it once and they're paying you $100,000 to do it again, they expect perfection."

Maris rebelled against perfection beginning in Spring Training. He dealt with dismal slumps; worried, as was his custom; and lashed out in an angry explosion against the New York press. He was called a "problem ballplayer" and "the most unpopular Yankee." He announced a moratorium on interviews. His silence did not improve his batting average. Hitting around .200 at midseason, he was being booed unmercifully at home and on the road. The media destroyed him.

"After a while I just tried to forget about everything and everybody and just try to salvage something out of the season," he said. In the second half, Maris finally found his stroke, raising his average to .256. His 33 homers and 100 RBIs were better than Mantle and led the club.

Bobby Richardson improved from being a solid second baseman to a genuine star in 1962. His fast start kept the club afloat when it struggled, Maris slumped, and Mantle was hurt. Playing in 161 games, he batted .302 and finished second in the MVP balloting.

"With our big sluggers not hitting the homers the way they did last year, there is no denying that Bobby's steady hitting, especially with those timely two-baggers, played a tremendous role in putting us over the top," said Houk.

Ralph Terry, who became a new father, learned to control his emotions and became the staff ace, winning 23 games. Tom Tresh, the All-Star and Rookie of the Year when he successfully transitioned from shortstop to left field, hit .286 with 20 home runs and 93 runs batted in (four more than Mantle).

Luis Arroyo slumped after his great 1961 campaign, but Jim Bouton announced his presence with authority, going 7-7 with a 3.99 ERA. He also took to the Yankee lifestyle in a big way, particularly enjoying the Johnny Grant parties when the team visited Hollywood. At one shindig, he "tread water in the swimming pool, stripped to my underwear holding a martini in each hand while shimmying to the theme song from *Lawrence of Arabia*," he recalled.

Marshall Bridges was 8-4, Jim Coates was 7-6, Bud Daley was 7-5, and a new rookie from Trenton, New Jersey, named Al Downing was briefly called up from Richmond. Rollie Sheldon finished 7-8 and Bill Stafford was again 14-9.

Reliable John Blanchard baptized Bouton with a beer shower when he won his first game, but hit only .232. Elston Howard was firmly in control of the catcher's position, playing great defensively while hitting 21 home runs with 91 RBIs and a .279 average. Clete Boyer improved with the bat to .272. Tony Kubek batted .314 after returning from the Army. Outfielder Hector Lopez batted a creditable .275.

As a team, the Yankees led the league with a .267 mark. Their 199 home runs were second to Detroit's 209 but better than Minnesota's 185. The Yankees, as usual, eschewed the stolen base and had only 42. The league batting champion was Pete Runnels of Boston (.326), followed by Mantle at .321. Bobby Richardson's .302 placed him among the league leaders.

Mantle's .605 led the league in slugging percentage. Harmon Killebrew of the Twins led in homers (48) with Maris tied with Jim Gentile for fifth (33). Killebrew also led the league with 126 RBIs. Mantle's 122 walks set the pace as did Richardson's 208 hits. Bobby scored 99 runs and had 38 doubles, too.

On the mound, New York's team ERA was 3.70, third behind Baltimore and Los Angeles. Ford's 2.90 earned run average was third behind Detroit's Hank Aguirre (2.21) and the veteran Robin Roberts (2.78), now toiling for Baltimore. Terry's 23 wins led the AL, and he was the league workhorse with 299 innings pitched.

In addition to Tresh's Rookie of the Year and Mantle's MVP honors, both Richardson and Mantle won Gold Gloves.

The early season prognostications featured Detroit, winners of 101 games under manager Bob Scheffing, as their chief rival. If Maris saw a drop-off in production, it was nothing compared to Tigers first baseman Norm Cash. It has never really been proved, but many suspect cash corked his bat in 1961 when he hit .361. In 1962 his average fell to an abysmal .243. He would enjoy a creditable career, but the Hall of Fame potential of his early years never materialized.

But what killed Detroit's chances was a shoulder injury suffered by pitcher Frank Lary. He went from 23 wins in 1961 to 2-6 in 1962. Hall of Fame outfielder

Al Kaline was headed for his best year when he broke his collarbone and missed 61 games.

Defensively, the Tigers—especially without Kaline—looked like they all had clubfeet, which outfielder Rocky Colavito actually had. Colavito had come over from Cleveland in 1960 and continued to hit for power, but he struck out far too much. The Tigers resembled the 1947 Giants, a team that set the all-time home run record but finished in the middle of the pack. In June an anticipated battle between contenders turned into a marathon when New York prevailed, 9-7, in a 22-inning, seven-hour drag. Detroit never seriously contended and finished 85-76, 10.5 games back of the 96-66 Yankees, tied for fourth place.

THREE

A Midsummer's Dream

"'Tis better to have loved and lost than never to have loved at all."
—*Alfred Lord Tennyson*

On May 4, 1962, the Sunset Strip of Los Angeles was hopping with Mexican festivities for Cinco de Mayo. Bo Belinsky, a rookie left-handed pitcher for the second-year Angels, was scheduled to pitch the next night. Never one to favor rest and preparation when he could make the scene, Belinsky ventured to the strip, where he met a lovely brunette. They spent the evening at her pad. Belinsky departed with dawn's early light, but this encounter inspired him. He asked for her phone number and meant it.

"I'll see you again," she assured him. Belinsky told her he was leaving tickets for that night's game against Baltimore and insisted she make it, because "You're my lucky charm."

"I never saw her again," Belinsky told writer Pat Jordan in 1972. "It was like she was my lucky charm and once she was gone that was the end of that."

Eventually, maybe, but first Bo Belinsky skyrocketed to the heights of Hollywood fame and glory. That evening he threw a no-hit, no-run game against his old team, the Baltimore Orioles.

Nineteen sixty-two was not supposed to be a memorable year for the Los Angeles Angels. An expansion team in 1961, the Angels were a creditable 70-91 in their first year, playing at dilapidated Wrigley Field in south-central L.A., at the corner of 42nd Place and Avalon Boulevard. In '62, they rented Dodger Stadium from

Walter O'Malley, who nickel and dimed them with surcharges on just about everything and relegated their ticket booth next to a storage shed in a remote part of the stadium. The Dodgers were the toasts of Hollywood. The Angels, a combination of castoffs and kids, were tenants who played before family and friends. The first Angel to receive attention was Belinsky. The Angels thought he would attract female fans (he did). Another rookie, Dean Chance, was an emerging star, winning 14 games. Former Giant Leon "Daddy Wags" Wagner hit 37 home runs and knocked in 107 runs.

Belinsky started the year living in Ernie's House of Surfas with Laker wildman "Hot Rod" Hundley, but apparently Belinsky's consumption of women and alcohol was too much even for the Rodster. Belinsky then moved his act to the Hollywood Hills, where some adoring girl almost killed herself trying to climb a tree into his bedroom window. When Belinsky was not wining and dining Tina Louise and Ann-Margret, he was winning games. By August, an early-morning run-in with the LAPD and escapades with the Hollywood crowd had slowed his win total down, but the man had put the club on the map.

On July 4 Los Angeles was in first place in the American League. Bill Rigney and Fred Haney were shrewd baseball men. Rig had been schooled under Leo Durocher in New York. Haney had developed the great Milwaukee Braves' pennant winners of 1957–58. The Angels played them tough, finally succumbing in the dog days of late August and September. Their 86-76 record earned Rigney Manager of the Year honors. Haney was named Executive of the Year. Chance was the best rookie pitcher in the game. Movie stars like Cary Grant and Doris Day cheered them on.

Belinsky had garnered his 15 minutes of fame holding out for the enormous sum of $8,500. Writer Bud Furillo captured some of Belinsky's choice comments about women, sex, and hustling pool on a slow news day.

Fred Haney tired of negotiating with Belinsky over the phone. He sensed that if he were brought out to Palm Springs, it would create needed publicity in the shadow of the mighty Dodgers. He was right.

"He was the greatest thing to ever happen to us," said publicity director Irv Kaze. Kaze showed up at the airport and, without having to ask, immediately recognized Belinsky, oozing charisma in an open-collared shirt, sportscoat, long, slick hair, and "the biggest pair of sunglasses you've ever seen."

"Damn," said Belinsky when Kaze introduced himself, "I expected [owner Gene 'the Singing Cowboy'] Autry."

Belinsky was immediately driven to the Palm Springs Desert Inn, where Kaze arranged for a poolside press conference complete with a full bar and strategically placed bikini-clad girls lounging about. For a couple of hours the ballplayer regaled them with stories of his pool-hustling exploits, in which he was made out to sound like Minnesota Fats.

His sexual descriptions were explicit. Nobody had ever heard anything like this guy's stories, and in reality nobody has ever heard anything like them since. As a kiss-and-tell artist Belinsky put Jose Canseco, Derek Jeter, even Joe Namath to shame. The bizarre poolside scene—part carnival act, part "true confessions," part striptease show—was "the greatest thing I'd ever seen," recalled Kaze. All of this was over between 1,000 and 1,500 1962 dollars for an unproven career minor leaguer who said he would not sign "unless Autry begged me personally."

When Belinsky threw his no-hit game on May 5, immediate rewards were proffered. His contract was increased to the promised $8,500, along with a lipstick red Cadillac, a gift from the club. Bud Furillo assumed the role of Belinsky's social director, introducing him to Beverly Hills attorney Paul Caruso, who in turn introduced him to the controversial gossip columnist and movie voice, Walter Winchell.

Winchell had moved to Hollywood, hoping to start over. He had been booted from New York in the wake of McCarthyism. When Furillo introduced Belinsky to the show biz crowd, the Belinsky-Winchell relationship became a marriage made in Hollywood.

"I know every broad who matters," Winchell told the ballplayer. Winchell arranged through his publicity contacts for every aspiring model and actress in L.A. to date Belinsky, alerting the press to each liaison so that it could all be dutifully recorded in the trades.

Gilligan's Island beauty Tina Louise; actress Connie Stevens (and her younger, blonder sister); Dinah Shore; Queen Soraya, the divorced ex-wife of the Shah of Iran; a DuPont heiress; and *Carnal Knowledge* star Ann-Margret—Bo squired all of them and many more to every haunt on the Sunset Strip: Peppermint West, Barney's Beanery, Dino's, Chasen's, LaScala, the Rainbow, Gazarri's, and the Whisky.

He found himself invited to party with the Beautiful People: Jane Wyman, Merle Oberon, Maureen O'Hara, Frank Sinatra, and Lionel Hampton. In New York he was feted by Toots Shor and given tables reserved for celebrities and mobsters at the Copa, the Forum of the Twelve Caesars, and 21.

In Washington, Belinsky and Dean Chance were told that FBI director J. Edgar Hoover wanted to meet them.

"Jesus Christ, they're turning it into a Federal case," exclaimed Chance, who thought Hoover's invite was an inquest into some kind of illegal interstate activity. Hoover just wanted to meet them.

"J. Edgar?" Belinsky later told Pat Jordan. "Man, he's a swinger. He let Dean and I shoot Tommy guns at FBI headquarters."

The club tolerated Belinsky because the publicity was good for business, the team was winning, he was still effective, and Autry admired his style. But a 5:00 AM incident on Wilshire Boulevard brought everything to a boil. Belinsky and Chance went out for a night on the town, picking up two girls. Belinsky's was some kind of showgirl, or so she said. The four of them piled into Belinsky's Caddy.

"Now we are tooling down Wilshire Boulevard and everything is fine," Belinsky recalled. "Well, one thing led to another, and this girl starts mouthing off about she loves me and will stay with me and wants to cook breakfast and all that bull. I'm really in no mood for that, so I tell her to keep her big mouth shut or I'll throw her out."

According to Belinsky, the girl kept yakking, so he pulled the car over to a side street, demanding she get out. She resisted. Belinsky tried to force her out. In the process she smashed her head against a window, cutting herself and causing her to start screaming bloody murder.

Just then, an LAPD squad car pulled up. Chance, who had a pregnant wife back in Ohio, made a run for it but was caught. Arrests were made and it all hit the papers, to the great consternation of Haney and Rigney.

The girl decided not to press charges on the condition that Belinsky stay with her for a week, but later she found an attorney and sued the ballplayer, forcing him to pay her off. "You just can't trust broads," was Belinsky's assessment.

"You *can* play for the Mets. If you want rapid advancement, play for the Mets. We've got the bonus money. We'll even buy you a glove.

So join us. Take the bonus money. Play a year or two.

Then you can go back to school."

—*Casey Stengel*

Charles Dillon "Casey" Stengel was the perfect choice to manage the fledgling 1962 New York Mets. He *was* New York baseball. He had played in the World Series with both Brooklyn and the New York Giants. An outfielder for John McGraw, he batted .400 in the 1922 World Series victory over Babe Ruth's Yankees. He was a fan favorite and showman, with sparrows flying from his hat, always a practical joker.

The 1962 Mets were a force of nature. If there is any possible truth to George Burns's statement in *Oh, God!* that the 1969 Mets were his "last miracle," then the '62 version was somehow struck by supernatural forces, too. It was a comedy of errors, of flukes, of crazy plays, players, and situations, almost defying logic, therefore lending credence to the notion that the deity got involved. Never has a team played so badly, and never has failure been so loved.

Certainly Brooklyn's "Daffiness Boys" were popular, but Dazzy Vance was a Hall of Famer, Babe Herman a line drive impresario. It seems completely improbable that a bad team could be received so well in New York City. Today it would not happen. This is a town built on excellence. The George Steinbrenner mentality, the Donald Trump way of thinking, has completely overshadowed the old concepts. But with the Dodgers and Giants gone, with the Yankees resembling a shark in a tank full of minnows, somehow the whole thing played.

That spring, Stengel's explanations of his team were classics of baseball humor, even though it seems the "Ol' Perfessor" was deadly serious in his analysis. After announcing that "Chacon" was batting second, he got into a *tête-à-tête* with *New York Post* columnist Leonard Schecter and a few others.

"Chacon?" asked Schecter.

"Mantilla," said Stengel. It sounded liked like *scintilla*. "I mean Chacon. I mean I said Chacon, but I meant Mantilla. . . . I don't know who to hit third. If it's a right-handed pitcher, which it is, I might go with Bell in right field. . . . You asked me for a lineup and I can't give it to you. . . . I got two center fielders. Christopher and Smith."

Christopher was in the minors.

"Christopher?" inquired Schecter.

"Ashburn," said Casey. "Smith and Ashburn. Whichever one I play I'll put leading off."

This contradicted previous Stengelese about Neal leading off, Mantilla hitting second . . .

"Didn't you say that Neal was going to lead off?" asked Schecter.

"Well, put Neal third and Mantilla second," he replied, as if Schecter were making the decisions and Casey now just offering advice.

From there: "Let's see. You can put Hodges fifth. No, put Bell fifth. Hodges sixth." He looked at a reporter's notebook. "Better write it down so I'll remember it." Now the scribes were his secretaries. "And put [Jim] Marshall along with Hodges. Maybe I'll put Hodges in for a while and then Marshall."

"Batting fourth?"

"Thomas. That's right, Case?" a writer inquired. "Thomas in left field batting fourth."

"That's right," assented Casey, followed by some discussion of Don Zimmer hitting seventh and playing third.

Schecter: "One more thing. Who's the catcher, Landrith or Ginsberg?"

"It's Ginsberg or Landrith," replied Casey. "Ginsberg caught him [it turned out to be Roger Craig] pretty good. I'll decide when I get there."

"This was the process by which Casey Stengel made up his lineup every day," Schecter, whose bright ideas became *Ball Four* in 1970, later recalled.

Perhaps Stengel talked like this when he was with the Yankees, maybe even made out his lineup that way—although when you have Mantle, Berra, Howard, and the like it tends to make itself—but the Mets, as Robert Lipsyte pointed out, were a *feature story*, not a sports story. The press coverage looked for this angle and played it up. Still, there were comedies that went beyond seeming coincidence. The names of players certainly had a ring.

There was "Butterball" Botz, who apparently was one of the "youth of America" Casey invited to try out—and fail. It was like the old Dodgers of the "Daffiness" era, updated now to "Choo Choo" Coleman and "Marvelous Marv" Throneberry.

The opener told the whole story in a nutshell. According to legend, *nine Mets got stuck in an elevator*, making them late for the first game in St. Louis, an 11-4 loss. They dropped their first nine games and celebrated the first win, behind Jay Hook at Pittsburgh, as if the Series had been won.

Casey on Don Zimmer, who had a plate in his head after having been beaned: "He's the perdotius quotient of the qualificatilus."

Stengel told Zimmer he would "love the left field fence." He meant the left field fence at Cincinnati's Crosley Field. Zim had just been traded to Cincinnati but had not been told so yet.

In May, Stengel got back on the "tryout" bandwagon. This time there was a little more reasoning behind his invitation for young folks to come out and play for the Mets because you "*can* play for the Mets. If you want rapid advancement, play for the Mets. We've got the bonus money. We'll even buy you a glove. So join us. Take the bonus money. Play a year or two. Then you can go back to school."

It was like an Army enlistment commercial, but old Stengel was smart despite his contortions of language. His enticement of college money applied to pitcher Jay Hook, an engineer out of Northwestern University who certainly was academically inclined. It would later resonate with the likes of Tom Seaver, who signed with the Mets based on specific guarantees that they would pay for him to continue at USC. Then there was his Fresno High teammate, Dick Selma, in 1962 being scouted by everybody. The draft was a few years away. A high school or college prospect like Selma was a free agent who could choose the team he might sign with, rather than subject himself to the vagaries of a wide-open draft. Selma had choices within the pro and college ranks but went for the Mets because he could advance, which he did, all the way to the big leagues. When Seaver was waiting to see whether the Phillies, Indians, or Mets would draw his name out of a hat in 1966, he rooted for the Mets for the same reason: rapid advancement.

The lyrical stories of the early Mets did not become so famous by accident. They were in New York, the media capital of the world, and the writers in that city were the most talented. Aside from Jimmy Breslin, Jimmy Cannon, Red Smith, Maury Allen, and many others, a self-professed "nonprofessional" named Roger Angell was assigned the *New Yorker's* version of the "baseball beat". A highbrow arts and leisure magazine, it seemed the last place great baseball writing would come from, yet Angell had a knack for it.

A huge baseball fan who mourned the loss of the Dodgers and Giants, Angell viewed the Yankees from a pedestrian's point of view. He wanted color, humanity; the essence of the "Bums" from Brooklyn, of Willie Mays's cap flying off. The Yankees just shut everybody up, like the time at Ebbets when the crowd hooted and hollered at Mickey Mantle incessantly. Then Mick hit a gargantuan home run that mockingly bounced and caromed and broke windshields and dented car doors belonging to Dodgers' fans outside the park.

Angell resisted the Polo Grounds in April and May 1962 despite frequent invites to see "those amazin' Mets." But by late May, Angell was fascinated with the team's strange habit of actually leading in late innings before blowing games. The 1962 Mets are thought to be the worst team of all time, but despite the numbers, this may not be accurate. They lost by a landslide often enough, but not every time. They often lost in crazy ways. Among their 40 wins in 1962 were some impressive performances, including a series of come-from-behind efforts. After they swept Milwaukee in a doubleheader on May 20, Angell made it to the Polo Grounds for five days until June 2.

He bought his seats instead of taking a press pass, sitting in the stands with his 14-year-old daughter and 197,428 fans who came to see the Mets take on the Los Angeles Dodgers and San Francisco Giants. The villains had returned to the scene of the crime.

The Dodgers utterly destroyed the Mets. It was like O'Malley was a Roman general ordering his legions to crush the rebellion. Angell's daughter compared it to the "fifth grade against the sixth grade at school."

Some old Dodgers were wearing "LA" caps, and other old Dodgers were wearing "NY" caps, plus there were a few new stars in the Los Angeles constellation. Amid everything the stomping fans started to chant, "Let's go, *Mets!* Let's go, *Mets!*"

Angell was stunned to find goodwill in the air, not bitterness. The next day the Dodgers had to scrape for a win, but New York pulled off a triple play. After Los Angeles completed the sweep, San Francisco ran New York's losing streak to 15 with a lopsided four-game explosion of power and pitching. The losses to Los Angeles and San Francisco surprised nobody; after all, the 1962 Dodgers and Giants, respectively, were two of the best in each team's storied history.

But Angell fell in love with the Mets. Apparently so did "The 'Go!' Shouters," as he titled his *New Yorker* piece, later published in *The Summer Game*.

"The Mets' 'Go!' shouters enjoyed their finest hour on Friday night, after the Giants had hit four homers and moved inexorably to a seventh inning lead of 9-1," wrote Angell. "At this point, when most sensible baseball fans would be edging towards the exits, a man sitting in Section 14, behind first base, produced a long, battered foghorn and blew mournful blasts into the hot night air. Within minutes, the Mets fans were shouting in counterpoint—*Tooot!* 'Go!' *Tooot!* 'Go!' *Tooot!* 'GO!'—and the team, defeated and relaxed, came up with five hits that sent Billy Pierce to the showers."

It was all "exciting foolishness," of course, since San Francisco won the game going away. Angell thought about the demographical possibility of New York City producing "a 40- or 50,000-man audience made up exclusively of born losers—leftover Landon voters, collectors of mongrel puppies, owners of stock in played-out gold mines—who had been waiting for years for a suitably hopeless cause."

This was a Friday night in June, with the sensory pleasures of the New York bar scene beckoning in "a city known for its cool," but these people had no place they would rather be. Angell wanted to know what was going on. Two apparent Yankee fans sitting next to him derided the Mets in snide tones, going over the lineup and announcing that each was a player who would not even make the Bronx Bombers. Angell determined that it was not bitter, anti-Dodgers or anti-Giants sentiment. Rather, these people and this team were the *anti-Yankees*, who Angell had no love for.

The Giants won, their impressive stars—Willie Mays, Willie McCovey, Juan Marichal—all shining, but Angell observed that the Mets were "like France in the 1920s," with a "missing generation between the too-old and the too-young." He determined to see the Mets "as a ball team, rather than a flock of sacrificial lambs" and called Stengel "an Edison tinkering with rusty parts." He noted the receding stars of Felix Mantilla, Charlie Neal, Frank Thomas, Richie Ashburn, and Gil Hodges; the eager, opportunistic, oft-dumb base-running antics of Rod Kanehl and Choo Choo Coleman; Stengel's "bowlegged hobble" walking style; Elio Chacon's hesitancy costing an out; a pitching staff of Hook, Jackson, Anderson, and Roger Craig ("the Mets' own Cyrano"), delivering glimpses of competence, even brilliance, before falling apart.

San Francisco won a Sunday doubleheader. Angell departed to write what was not merely a brilliant story, but perhaps the most telling explanation of the early Mets and their fans. There was prescience in it, too, in describing some youth with promise that seven years later made him a small-time prophet of sorts.

On June 17, Marv Throneberry was at first base when the Mets caught a Chicago base runner in a rundown between first and second. Throneberry ran into the runner without the ball in his possession and was called for interference. Chicago scored four times after that. When Marv came to bat in the bottom half of the inning, he hit a drive to the right field bullpen, pulling into third with a triple just as the umpire called him out at first for having missed the bag. Stengel came out to argue but was rebuffed by news from his own bench that Throneberry also missed second. In July the Mets were 6-23.

Throneberry had some power and four times hit a sign for a clothing company, who awarded him a $6,000 sailboat. Richie Ashburn was also given a boat for winning the team MVP award. Judge Robert Cannon, legal counsel for the Major League Baseball Player's Association, told Throneberry not to forget to declare the full value of the boat.

"Declare it?" Throneberry asked. "Who to, the Coast Guard?"

"Taxes," Cannon replied, as in the IRS. "Ashburn's boat was a gift. He was voted it. Yours came the hard way. You hit the sign. You earned it. The boat is earnings. You pay income tax on it."

At season's end, Jimmy Breslin visited Throneberry in his hometown of Collierville, Tennessee.

"In my whole life I never believed there'd be as rough a year as there was last season," said Throneberry, who, believe it or not, at one time was considered a prospect with the Yankees. According to most accounts of his career he was, if not a really good player, not a terrible one; not the "worst player who ever lived," or whatever moniker has been attached to him.

The "worst ballplayer" never made the Major Leagues, or even signed a professional contract. If such a player existed in the big leagues he lasted one day, one inning, like the midget Eddie Gaedel. He did not pick up big league paychecks for the better part of a decade, as Marv did. "Terrible" Mets pitchers like Roger Craig (10-24), Al Jackson (8-20), Jay Hook (8-19), and even Craig Anderson (3-17) were not that terrible. Roger Craig was in fact a very good pitcher, Jackson a genuine talent. The truth is, a man cannot last long enough to *lose* 20 games if he is that bad; he would be drummed out of the corps long before given the chance to compile such a record.

Throneberry's home in Collierville was at least 100 miles from anything resembling a *sporting waterway*, and the man was never going to be part of the "skiff off the Hamptons crowd," wrote Breslin.

"And here I am, I'm still not out of it," said Marv. "I got a boat in a warehouse someplace and the man tell me I got to pay taxes on it and all we got around here is, like, filled-up bathtubs and maybe a crick or two. I think maybe I'll be able to sell it off someplace. I think you could say prospects is all right. But I still don't know what do about the tax thing."

It was that kind of year.

"We get to the end of the season, and I might need a couple of games to finish higher and what am I going to get?" Stengel said. "Everybody will be standing up there and going, whoom! Just trying to win theirselves a nice boat while I'm sittin' here hopin' they'll butcher boy the ball onto the ground and get me a run or two. I don't like it at all."

General manager George Weiss hired Hall of Famer Rogers Hornsby, an irascible sort who could not stay hired in his post-playing gigs, to scout Major League games, looking for players the Mets could use. Hornsby lived in Chicago and attended White Sox games, played at night in Comiskey Park. He spurned Wrigley because their day schedule interfered with his horse track pursuits.

"They say we're gonna get players out of a grab bag," he said. "From what I see, it's going to be a garbage bag. Ain't nobody got fat off eating out of the garbage, and that's just what the Mets is going to have to be doing. This is terrible. I mean, this is really going to be bad."

Stengel celebrated his 73rd birthday in a private party room at the Chase Hotel in St. Louis. He ordered a Manhattan.

"I've seen these do a lot of things to people," he said of the Manhattan. He smoked cigarettes and let his hair down, so to speak, with Jimmy Breslin. He spoke with trepidation of the Mets' initial visit to the brand new Dodger Stadium. "We're going into Los Angeles the first time, and, well, I don't want to go in there to see that big new ballpark in front of all them people and have to see the other fellas running around those bases the way they figured to on my own pitchers and my catchers, too. [Maury] Wills and those fellows, they start running in circles and they don't stop and so forth and it could be embarrassing, which I don't want to be.

"Well, we have Canzoneri [catcher Chris Cannizzaro] at Syracuse, and he catches good and throws real good and he should be able to stop them. I don't want to be embarrassed. So we bring him and he is going to throw out these runners.

"We come in there and you never seen anything like it in your life. I find I got a defensive catcher, only he can't catch the ball. The pitcher throws. Wild pitch. Throws again. Passed ball. Throws again. Oops! The ball drops out of the glove. And all the time I am dizzy on account of these runners running around in circles on me and so forth.

"Makes a man think. You look up and down the bench and you have to say to yourself, 'Can't anybody here play this game?'"

Hours later, "the bartender was falling asleep and the only sound in the hotel was the whine of the vacuum cleaner in the lobby," wrote Breslin. "Stengel banged his empty glass on the red-tiled bar top and then walked out of the room."

Casey walked to the lobby, stopping to light a smoke.

"I'm shell-shocked," he told the guy working the vacuum cleaner. "I'm not used to gettin' any of these shocks at all, and now they come every three innings. How do you like that?"

No answer.

"This is a disaster," he continued. "Do you know who my player of the year is? My player of the year is Choo Choo Coleman, and I have him for only two days. He runs very good."

"This, then, is the way the first year of the New York Mets went," wrote Breslin, an old-time scribe whose clipped style was reminiscent of Ring Lardner (and Mark Twain before that), in *Can't Anybody Here Play This Game?* "It was a team that featured 23-game losers, an opening day outfield that held the all-time Major League record for fathering children [19—"You can look it up," as Casey would say], a defensive catcher who couldn't catch, and an overall collection of strange players who performed strange feats. Yet it was absolutely wonderful. People loved it. The Mets gathered about them a breed of baseball fans who quite possibly will make you forget the characters who once made Brooklyn's Ebbets

Field a part of this country's folklore. The Mets' fans are made of the same things. Brooklyn fans, observed Garry Schumacher, once a great baseball writer and now part of the San Francisco Giants management, never would have appreciated Joe DiMaggio on their club.

"'Too perfect,' said Garry."

Bill Veeck announced that the 1962 Mets were "without a doubt the worst team in the history of baseball," claiming that he spoke with authority since his St. Louis Browns were the previous "title holders."

Technically, statistically, and by the record, he was right, but the '62 Mets were not the worst. Veeck's Browns had no-name players, nobody worth remembering. The Mets had former big names like Ashburn, Hodges, Craig, Gene Woodling, and Frank Thomas. Over the hill, yes, but there is something not quite right about saying a team with so many one-time stars was the worst ever assembled. Ashburn batted .306; Thomas hit 34 homers and drove in 94 runs. Then again, sometimes they sure looked terrible. In June, Sandy Koufax struck out the first three Mets on nine pitches, finished with 13 Ks, and a 5-0 no-hit win.

Certainly no team nearly that bad has been analyzed and talked about so much. Being in New York was part of that. Casey Stengel was part of it. But it went beyond these obvious factors. Sportswriter Leonard Koppett said it was part of a larger social revolution, embodied by the new, youthful President John F. Kennedy; the young taking over from the old.

"The times they are a-changin'," sang Bob Dylan.

The players poked fun at each other. There was much self-deprecation in the Mets' clubhouse. When Ashburn won the team MVP award, he said, "Most Valuable on the worst team ever? Just how do they mean that?"

He made fun of Throneberry, but the big ol' country boy took it in stride. The fans picked up on their humble, comical ways and ate it up. Strange, confusing things happened to that team that somehow did not happen to others. They had two pitchers named Bob Miller: Robert G. Miller, left-handed, and Robert L. Miller, right-handed. Robert L. made 21 starts with an 0–12 record and was preferred among the two.

One day Stengel called to the bullpen.

"Get Nelson ready," he told the bullpen coach.

"Who?" was the reply.

"Nelson," Stengel said. "Get him up."

The bullpen coach looked around. There was no Nelson. Nelson was broadcaster Lindsey Nelson. But Robert L. Miller knew that when Casey called for Nelson, he meant him, so he warmed up and went in the game. Later the Millers appeared on the TV quiz show *To Tell the Truth*. When the MC called, "Will the real Bob Miller please stand up?" both did so to confused delight.

Stengel would occasionally call on some past star of the Yankees or Giants to go into the game. He confused Jim Marshall with John Blanchard, a Yankee reliable of the 1950s. In a strange twist of coincidence, when his protégé, USC's Rod Dedeaux (who played for Casey at Brooklyn) grew old (sometimes showing up late for games after attending a cocktail party), he reportedly would call out, "Lynn, get your gun," or "Seaver, get loose." These were references to past Trojans like Fred Lynn or Tom Seaver who had graduated 10 or 15 years earlier.

Banners and placards made their appearance at the Polo Grounds, possibly for the first time. Certainly, the existence of this kind of fan signage began a trend. "Marv." "Marvelous Marv." "Cranberry Strawberry We Love Throneberry." "MARV!" "VRAM!" ("Marv" spelled backward.) The Mets responded with a team sign of their own: "To the Met Fans—We Love You Too."

Stengel called it all "Amazin.'" "Come out and see my 'Amazin' Mets,'" he said in an open invite to the public. "I been in this game a hundred years but I see new ways to lose I never knew existed before."

Stengel got into a taxi with several young writers and inquired whether they were ballplayers. They said they were not.

"No, and neither are my players," said Stengel.

Of the Northwestern engineer Jay Hook, Stengel said, "I got the smartest pitcher in the world until he goes to the mound."

When Yale's Ken MacKenzie entered a game Stengel advised, "Now just make believe you're pitching against Harvard."

Throneberry was "Thornberry." Casey never came close to Cannizzaro's proper pronunciation. Gus Bell was an established player, yet Casey never got a handle on who he was.

"And in left field, in left field we have a splendid man, and he knows how to do it," Stengel said. "He's been around and he swings the bat there in left field and he knows what to do. He's got a big family [six children, including future big leaguer Buddy Bell] and he wants to provide for them, and he's a fine outstanding player, the fella in left field. You can be sure he'll be ready when the bell rings—and that's his name, *Bell!*"

"About this Choo Choo Coleman," Casey told Dan Daniel of the *Sporting News*. "Is he a catcher or an outfielder? . . . Watch this carefully."

First baseman Ed Kranepool, a native of nearby Yonkers, spent most of 1962 in the minor leagues but got called up and hit .167 in his brief stint. He was only 17 years old.

Infielder "Hot Rod" Kanehl, a one-time Yankee prospect, hit .248. Married with four kids, he was one of those "record breaking" fathers of multiple kids, supposedly something the '62 Mets had more of than any other team.

"He can't field," George Weiss told Casey.

"But he can run the bases," Stengel replied.

"But Weiss always wanted to get rid of me, and now he couldn't because I had become a hero in New York," said Kanehl. "All of New York was asking, 'Who is this guy?' and the front page of the *Daily News* had a picture of Stengel pulling me out of a hat like a rabbit."

Kanehl was one of those strange hybrids of baseball—a Yankee farmhand who never made it there, but became a household name, still fondly remembered, because he played for the Mets. It did not last long. A few years later he was playing for the Wichita Dreamliners against USC's Tom Seaver, then pitching for the Alaska Goldpanners.

"Even though we lost, we were still upbeat," said Kanehl. "And so was Casey, who was leading the parade down Broadway. A lot of people identified with the Mets—underdog types, not losers—quality people who weren't quite getting it together.

"In May we beat Cincinnati, and we beat the Braves at home, we were playing well, but then we went on the road and lost 17 games in a row. We sure could dream up ways to lose."

When the Mets were mathematically eliminated from the National League pennant the first week of August, Casey called a meeting.

"You guys can relax now," he told them.

The season ended, appropriately enough, with a triple play and a worst-ever 40-120 record. More than 900,000 fans attended Mets games at the Polo Grounds, a significant improvement over the attendance of the New York Giants, a team featuring such stalwarts as Willie Mays, playing at the same park in their last year (1957).

"It's been a helluva year," Casey remarked.

FOUR

There's No Business Like Show Business

"If you build it, they will come."
— "The Voice," Field of Dreams

Indeed, Walter O'Malley did build Dodger Stadium, and Hollywood came calling. Sports and Hollywood were already a natural fit in Los Angeles. Marion Morrison, a football player for coach Howard Jones at the University of Southern California, quit the Trojans when he injured his shoulder surfing in Newport Beach and went to work for Fox Studios. He became a big star using the name John "Duke" Wayne. USC built their program in large measure on the recruiting advantages of nearby Hollywood, which was an advantage unavailable to the likes of Iowa or Alabama.

According to a late 1990s edition of Los Angeles magazine, Wayne arranged for the USC team to satisfy the insatiable sexual appetites of silent screen it-girl Clara Bow on Saturday night orgies at her Hollywood Hills mansion. A search of the Internet, however, reveals that while this rumor has lived for decades, it is false.

Wayne did arrange for USC players to be used for the football scenes in a movie about the Naval Academy called Salute. His college teammate, Ward Bond, was his film sidekick in many movies, including The Quiet Man. Bond was often the friendly priest or rival for the affections of a lady who would get in knock down, drag out fisticuffs with Wayne and then, when it was over, share a shot of whiskey with him.

UCLA quarterback Bob Waterfield became a star with the Los Angeles Rams but was never a bigger name than his girlfriend, the busty actress Jane Russell, who starred in the infamous close-up-on-her-breasts shot in Howard Hughes's *The Outlaw.*

But the cross-pollination of film and sports never reached greater heights than when the Dodgers arrived. It reached a crescendo in 1962, the year Dodger Stadium was unveiled to bravura reviews.

Hollywood and the entertainment industry were on the verge of major change in 1962. The studio system was still in place, but it was only a few years before Gulf & Western would nearly shut the doors at Paramount; United Artists would begin a slide toward dissolution; and the 1960s generation would shun old-style movie fare in favor of edgier stuff.

The postmodern architecture of the 1950s, which manifested itself in the ranch 'n' kitsch style embodied by homes in the Hollywood Hills, began to find its way into art forms. Jackson Pollack's paintings led to Andy Warhol's new pop art exhibition in New York. Out of Greenwich Village, the folk-revival movement offered *The Free-Wheelin' Bob Dylan.* On Broadway, audiences shocked to the acid-tongued *Who's Afraid of Virginia Woolf.* Vladimir Nabokov's *Lolita,* which dared to explore forbidden love between a middle-aged man and an underage girl, was made into a controversial film by director Stanley Kubrick, starring James Mason and Shelley Winters. *To Kill a Mockingbird* (Gregory Peck), developed from the Harper Lee novel, dared the South to change its racist ways.

One Flew Over the Cuckoo's Nest by Ken Kesey was published, as was the stimulating *Sex and the Single Girl* by *Cosmopolitan* editor Helen Gurley Brown. Traditional fare still had its place, in the form of *How the West Was Won,* a standard Western of epic proportions, with a stirring soundtrack.

ABC debuted a color cartoon, *The Jetsons. Perry Mason, Andy Griffith,* and *Candid Camera* were all still black-and-white. Other popular programs included *Wagon Train, Bonanza, Gunsmoke, Rawhide, Lawman, Maverick, The Rifleman, Danny Thomas, My Three Sons, Dennis the Menace,* and *Dick Van Dyke.*

The Beverly Hillbillies hit home with Los Angelinos. Starring Buddy Ebsen as Jed Clampett—"a burly mountaineer . . . barely kept his family fed" who gets rich on oil and "loaded up the truck and moved to Beverleee . . . Hills, that is . . . swimmin' pools, movie stars"—it struck a nerve with the public. America was fascinated with *the life,* which was the world of movies, money, and moguls, all with some nice window dressing in the form of scantily clad young lovelies. People enjoyed living vicariously through Hollywood, like a married girl who enjoys hearing about the sexual dalliances of a single girlfriend.

Dodger Stadium's opening had a similar effect. Color photos and footage depicting the "Dodger blue" uniforms, the green grass, the red, white, and blue stands, and the blue skies were panacea to cold Easterners shivering in front of their TV sets with wintry conditions outside. This phenomenon played itself out in football, too. New Year's Day viewers were in awe of the Rose Bowl, a sunsplashed panorama in the dead of winter. The USC Trojans and UCLA Bruins became the glamour teams of college football for the same reason—fans in beach attire on sunny days, pretty cheerleaders, and gladiators in colorful uniforms doing battle on the green plains below.

Sports and entertainment were fused by television. The fan in the stands might, and often did, see celebrities at Dodger Stadium, but the TV camera caught them up close and personal, where they could be interviewed, their clothes and maybe even dates scrutinized in tabloid style.

The Dodgers solved their colorless infield problem using movie methods. Heavy rain rendered the field thin and pallid prior to Opening Day in 1962, but Walter O'Malley followed the advice of his good friend, film director Mervyn LeRoy, who suggested green dye. That solved the problem. The Stadium Club was packed with celebrities for the opener, including Frank Sinatra, Jack Warner, and Jimmy Stewart. The opener against Cincinnati came at the same time as the Academy Awards. "*West Side Story* Sweeps Oscars," read the *Los Angeles Times*, above the fold.

Hollywood had already played a big role in getting the Dodgers to L.A. in the first place. In 1957 comedians Jack Benny, Groucho Marx, and George Burns hosted a telethon in support of a land referendum to build the proposed Dodger Stadium. Ronald Reagan, president of the Screen Actors Guild, lobbied for the stadium to be built in the downtown area, close to the action.

"For years we have been watching golf courses and other recreation areas destroyed to make room for subdivisions and factories," stated Reagan. "Where is a baseball stadium to go, in the suburbs, away from the freeways?" The five-hour telethon was a critical Dodgers success.

In the Coliseum years, Gene Autry, Lauren Bacall, Spencer Tracy, and Nat King Cole were regulars. Celebrity all-star softball games became popular fare, with lineups that included Phil Silvers, Dinah Shore, Doris Day, and Mickey Rooney. Local radio celebrities also got involved. Actor Edward G. Robinson "mowed down" an umpire with a mock Tommy gun in 1960.

The celebrity events were even more popular at Dodger Stadium, when Dean Martin, James Garner, and Nipsey Russell became regulars. Two ex-ballplayers were also popular actors. Chuck Connors was a former Dodger, now the star of *The Rifleman*. John Berardino had played at USC and for the Yankees and was now a soap opera star on *General Hospital*.

"Jack Benny used to sit with Walter O'Malley almost every night," recalled general manager Buzzie Bavasi. "I gave Danny Kaye a key to my office and my private box. Rosalind Russell really loved the game. Fred Astaire and Bing Crosby were there a lot, and Randolph Scott, Milton Berle, and Cary Grant were real fans."

"Cary Grant was probably the most glamorous regular—and he was a very good fan," said Vin Scully. "He was not coming to the ballpark because it was *de rigueur*, the thing to do. Cary came because he really loved baseball."

"Once, when I was going to pitch the second game of a doubleheader, I was sitting next to him and he asked me, 'Is there any chance sometime that I could go into the clubhouse?'" recalled pitcher Joe Moeller. "So I took him in with me and he was so excited to be there—like a little kid. Believe me, the players were just as much in awe of him."

Movies loved to include shots of Dodger Stadium. *That Touch of Mink*, starring Grant and another baseball fanatic, Doris Day, featured scenes of game action. "At that time, a lot of films included shots of the park. It seemed as if the producers, directors, and writers were going out of their way to incorporate Dodger Stadium in their movies."

Like USC and UCLA football players for years before them, many Dodgers played small roles in movies. "Most of the time, we just did cameos, playing ourselves," remembered pitcher Stan Williams. "That way, we didn't have to join the actors' union." Williams, Larry Sherry, Sandy Koufax, Ed Roebuck, and Vin Scully appeared as themselves on the detective show *Michael Shayne*. Williams and Sherry appeared in *The Tom Ewell Show*. Sandy Koufax gave pitching pointers on an episode of *Dennis the Menace*. Don Drysdale, whose rugged good looks and caramel-rich voice were made for the screen, appeared frequently. He went beyond cameos, playing cowboys on *The Rifleman* and *The Lawman*. He had a fairly big role in *The Millionaire*, and appeared in variety shows with Red Skelton, Groucho Marx, and Steve Allen. Big D also appeared on screen with Jack Webb and Robert Mitchum in the comedy *The Last Time I Saw Archie*.

Drysdale was on *The Donna Reed Show* twice and appeared as himself in an episode of *Leave It to Beaver*. In "Flashing Spikes," an episode of the *Alcoa Premiere* anthology series, Drysdale played a fictitious baseball player in a show that included Jimmy Stewart, Jack Warden, and Edgar Buchanan, all directed by the great John Ford.

The Giants and Candlestick Park also got involved. Famed director Alfred Hitchcock had long made San Francisco a backdrop for many of his films. The movie industry followed suit by utilizing its vistas, skylines, and bay. *Experiment in Terror* was a thriller starring Glenn Ford, Lee Remick, Stefanie Powers, and Ross Martin (later Robert Conrad's sidekick in the TV program *The Wild, Wild West*). In it, a murderer kidnaps a young woman. The climax occurs at Candlestick during a Giants-Dodgers game.

"They told us they were going to film the game that night," recalled San Francisco pitcher Mike McCormick, a Los Angeles native. "We all had to sign releases and were paid $50 apiece for being in it. They just said to go play and not even think about what they were doing.

"I pitched a complete game win that night, so I was on the post-game show in the clubhouse when they brought Lee Remick down and we were introduced. I signed my cap and gave it to her. Then she left because they were setting up to shoot other scenes.

"All the shots with fans in the stands were done after the game. They were there until three or four in the morning. We had no idea what it was all about until we saw the finished film in '62."

Director Blake Edwards (*Peter Gunn*, *The Pink Panther*, *10*) shot additional close-ups of John Roseboro, Wally Moon, and Drysdale back in L.A. Vin Scully's play-by-play was integrated into the film. Henry Mancini's score provided a stunning soundtrack.

Andy Carey of the Dodgers parlayed his journeyman career into a photography business. A business-savvy fellow who wore three-piece suits to the park after having conducted meetings beforehand (he was also a stockbroker), Carey began a side business called "Hero of the Day."

"I'd always been an avid photographer and I had my own portrait studio," recalled Carey. "So one day I brought my Polaroid camera with me to the park and thought if I took some shots it'd loosen the guys up. Well, we won the game and the next night we won again and I took another 'Hero of the Day' picture. After a few more wins, it kinda got to be old hat just taking pictures with the guys in their uniform, so I went to John the clubhouse man for help."

John "Senator" Griffin, the clubhouse man, was an old-school guy with a Hollywood twist. He would wear outrageous garb like grass skirts, flowered hats, loud ties, and kimonos, leaving the respective items on as long as the Dodgers continued to win. He had more props than a costume designer—hats, gag glasses, moustaches—and let Carey borrow them for his pictures. Players had photos taken wearing wigs, cigars, shaving cream, and other clown acts. The team went on a winning streak, and Carey's "assistants"—Daryl Spencer and Lee Walls— helped him take pictures after wins all year. At season's end *Life* magazine ran the best of them.

A recording by "The Dodgermen" was released, featuring songs such as "The Dodger Song" and "Dodger Calypso." Danny Kaye sang a song that made good-natured fun of O'Malley. Kaye and his wife, Sylvia Fine, collaborated with Herbert Baker to perform a five-man musical drama about the team, which did brisk sales. The music was played over the PA system during batting practice.

"We all thought it was pretty amusing," recalled catcher Doug Camilli.

Art Rosenbaum of the *San Francisco Chronicle* wrote that O'Malley was offended by the song's premise, which was that he was less interested in victory and more so in sellout attendance.

"That's absolutely false," said Bavasi. "We sold the record at the park all summer. It was a big item at the concession stands. Besides, Danny sat with me almost every night."

Other musical hits of the year included "Hully-Gully," "Watusi," and "Monster Mash." Dance tunes were Little Eva's "Locomotion" and the "Peppermint Twist" by Joey Dee and the Starliters. Young America was seized by a dance craze.

But O'Malley was upset by the relationship between 29-year-old black shortstop Maury Wills and 38-year-old lily-white actress Doris Day. On top of the interracial issue, Wills was married and had a family in Spokane, Washington.

Rumors were rampant, although Wills did not speak of it with teammates. Both were asked about it repeatedly, yet denied it. Some 30 years later, however, Wills wrote in his autobiography, *On the Run*, "We had a mutual need for one another. We were in love—as I understood it at the time. I only had so much love for another human being because I was so much in love with baseball. As much love as I had, it was extended to her, but it was too much for me. I couldn't handle it. I was a baseball player."

Other Dodgers dated starlets and singers, although none as conspicuously as the Angels' Bo Belinsky. Aside from actresses, the town was filled with beautiful girls. The sexy clothing styles of the West Coast were in, and players met young lovelies at the beach, in bars, nightclubs, restaurants, the stadium, and everywhere else. It was an adult Disneyland.

O'Malley did not like that. He knew the boys would be boys and could not prevent them from playing the field. He was no moralist himself, but the team's core image and fan base were family oriented. The club went to great lengths, just like Disneyland in Orange County, to sell a wholesome image. Groupies, one-night stands, and the many results thereof—venereal disease, abortions, broken marriages, blackmail—were to be kept to a minimum.

Hollywood was always a potential distraction. For Wills, it had definitely become one, so he would "pull the shade and block it all out when I got to the park." In May, Marilyn Monroe appeared at Dodger Stadium. She was said to be involved with Bo Belinsky, but it was just a rumor, probably stirred up by Bud Furillo or Walter Winchell. Albie Pearson of the Angels was tasked with escorting her on the field and later said that he saw "desperation" in her eyes. She had recently sung her notorious "Happy Birthday" song to JFK, but the aftermath had been toxic politically and emotionally for her. The Christian outfielder wanted to talk to her about Jesus and salvation, but the opportunity did not present itself. She would soon be dead, either by her own hand, by accidental overdose, or worse. Hers was a cautionary tale in Tinseltown: "All that glitters is not gold."

FIVE

Los Angeles

"Pull up a chair."
—*Dodgers announcer Vin Scully's common pregame
invitation to radio listeners*

Dodgertown, the Vero Beach, Florida, Spring Training home of the Los Angeles Dodgers, was in its day the finest facility in baseball. It was a self-contained village that met most every need the players had. In part this was because Florida was, as late as 1962, still not hospitable to black players. Built out of old U.S. Navy barracks, Dodgertown had over the years been modified to become a shelter of sorts for Jackie Robinson, Roy Campanella, and other black Dodgers.

By 1962 racial conditions had not improved. The Dodgers had some hip, mod black guys like Maury Wills who were not one bit happy about this. Unlike many quiet black players of past years—or even quiet teammates like Junior Gilliam—Wills thought it was time for the world to wake up. John Roseboro was not a big talker, but in a less public way he, too, was fed up with racism. How could they be treated so well in Los Angeles, and most of the country, and so poorly in Florida? Why did the Dodgers have to train in Vero Beach anyway? Wills was asked why he did not bring his family to Vero Beach.

"There's no good accommodations for wives of Negro players down here," he replied. "I really hope to see the day when the Dodgers train in the West so [my wife] has a decent place to stay."

The black wives were not able to enjoy the Florida sunshine like their white counterparts, among them Ginger Drysdale, Beverly Snider, Sally Sherry, and Sue Perranoski.

Black Dodgers ventured out of Dodgertown with caution. They could not play on the golf courses, had to sit in black balconies at the movies, could not drink out of "whites only" drinking fountains, and often were refused restaurant service. Fishing boats were not rented to them, auto rental agencies refused them service, and Roseboro was so badly cut by a barber trimming his sideburns that it caused a severe infection, requiring a doctor's care. The black players took to cutting each other's hair.

But O'Malley was committed to Florida. The club had this great facility. They were not going to abandon it. O'Malley outfitted Dodgertown with an Olympic-sized swimming pool and volleyball, shuffleboard, tennis, and badminton courts. He had a practice golfing green laid out.

The club built a theater and showed first-run movies. There was a day room with a TV, table tennis, a library, and further entertainment options. The rec hall featured lively billiard games. Jim Gilliam was a shark with a pool cue.

Besides, the move west did not deter many New Yorkers from rooting for the team. The Florida location allowed many of the Dodgers' old fans to see them in Spring Training, which was a financial and public relations bonanza that made them a national team. By the 1960s half of Brooklyn had seemingly moved to Florida anyway.

O'Malley was determined to make his club the classiest in baseball. For years he had taken a backseat to the New York Yankees. Now, in his fifth year in Los Angeles, he was ready to move his franchise past even the vaunted Yankees in every way. His team trained in the best facility in baseball. It was ready to move into a stadium that was the best in the world. For all of Yankee Stadium's tradition, it was not close to the spanking new Dodger Stadium. The Dodgers had played at the Coliseum, which was at least as famous and filled with tradition as Yankee Stadium, but they knew all too well that ghosts and past glories could not replace a state-of-the-art palace.

O'Malley sensed as the nation did that Los Angeles was the city of the future, and he was cresting this wave like a surfer on a wild ride. All was in his favor—the stadium, the weather, the Beautiful People, and of course his team, which was favored to win and looked fabulous. But he had one more ace up his sleeve, and when *Elektra II* was introduced, that was the kicker. The Dodgers had their own plane. Not even the Yankees had their own plane, a "hotel in the sky." While O'Malley was the architect of Dodger opulence, his son Peter, a graduate of the prestigious Wharton School of Business at the University of Pennsylvania, was more active in the daily operations of the club than ever before.

While Junior Gilliam may have been a billiards ace, he was no match for manager Walter Emmons Alston. The two developed a friendship that would last for years, with Gilliam becoming the first black coach under Alston, in large measure because of the hours they spent shooting pool.

Alston was beginning his ninth year at the helm. He was less than a marginal player and had been a rube in the eyes of many, especially in sophisticated New York. His hiring inspired the headline, "Walter Who?" in the *New York Daily News*. Born in 1911 in Venice, Ohio, Alston's father was an automobile worker who owned a farm. Alston's early nickname was "Smokey" because he was the fastest pitcher on the town team (Alston would play semipro ball for fun until he was 60).

He played at the University of Miami (Ohio) but dropped out to get married. During the Great Depression he found no work so he returned to school, borrowing money from a local church and taking odd jobs to help with tuition. He was the captain of the baseball and basketball teams, earned a bachelor's degree, and signed with the St. Louis Cardinals. But the big club was loaded with stars like Johnny Mize, Enos Slaughter, and Stan Musial, so advancement was a problem.

In his single Major League at-bat with St. Louis in 1936 he struck out. He was returned to the bushes and never returned as a player. His break came when Branch Rickey took over the Dodgers. Rickey knew him from his days as general manager in St. Louis. They had a lot in common. Both were midwesterners, very religious, and had gone to college in an age in which college men were not the norm.

Alston's managerial career began with the Portsmouth Red Birds of the Mid-Atlantic League. To supplement his income Alston taught biology and mechanical drawing while coaching in the off-seasons at a local Ohio high school. He managed in the Dodger farm system for 13 minor league seasons. Eventually, Alston took over the club's triple-A farm club at Montreal, where he gained the reputation of a man who could manage black players.

When the Dodgers hired him prior to the 1954 campaign, one sportswriter wrote, "The Dodgers do not *need* a manager and that is why they got Alston." The team he inherited, the 1953 National League champions, had so many veterans that few had any minor league association with him.

From the beginning, Alston seemed to constantly fight an uphill struggle. He took over from Charley Dressen in 1953. Dressen had demanded a multiyear deal and was summarily shown the door. Alston was happy to sign a one-year contract, so the message was clear from the get-go: "No multiyear deals." It took a certain kind of man to accept that premise, especially when it kept repeating itself. Alston had been hired less because of his merits and more because of personal— not on-field—dissatisfaction with the previous man. Winning recognition in his own right would prove to be the Great White Whale of his career. Because he was not a "baseball Ahab," Alston would some day achieve what an Ahab could not.

After two straight National League pennants, the 1954 Dodgers under Alston lost to the New York Giants, who featured the return of Willie Mays from Army service. Right off the bat, Walt Alston had produced results that failed to match his predecessor. To make matters worse, the Giants under Leo Durocher won the World Series, the "wait till next year" goal that seemed unattainable, no matter how close the club so often had come to attaining it.

Nineteen fifty-five might have been the Great White Whale, and it certainly was "next year," but in the eyes of many, while Alston was given credit, he was seen as skippering a luxury cruise liner across placid seas. *Anybody* could have managed the 1955 Dodgers to the Promised Land. True, they started out hot, and true, they ran into a rough patch in which Alston's calming influence was credited. But capturing a seven-game World Series from the New York Yankees, *that* no Dodger manager had done before. The world gave credit to the fabled *Boys of Summer*, the title of Roger Kahn's book.

If the Dodgers had stayed in Brooklyn and Alston had done there what he did in Los Angeles, he would have eventually become an iconic figure. Of course, he may not have survived some of his biggest trials if he had been forced to do it with the New York press as opposed to the relatively friendly L.A. media. But the

1955 World Championship earned Alston much goodwill should he face tough times, and he would need every inch of it.

"With a year under his belt, Alston became a better manager," said Duke Snider, who was never president of the Walt Alston Fan Club.

In 1956 the Dodgers again won the pennant, but the Series was lost. Alston and Jackie Robinson had no love for each other. Robinson was injured and Alston suspected he was malingering. When Robinson announced to the media that he was healthy and ready to play, Alston continued to bench him. Alston took him on for taking the internal matter to the press. A shouting match ensued. It got so bad that Alston "invited" Robinson into the manager's office, telling him, "Only one of us is gonna come out."

Robinson backed off. It was a tactic Alston, who at 6'2" and 210 pounds with huge hands and forearms, employed on a few select occasions in his career. He was quiet, religious, and unassuming, but if he got "backed up," watch out. Robinson was adept with his fists; his courage was undisputed, but he also knew, as he had told Branch Rickey way back when, that "I can turn my cheek." Later, when Robinson got into an argument with an umpire, Alston failed to come to his defense, and that meant more bad blood.

When Robinson refused to accompany the team on the Japanese exhibition tour at season's end, that was the last straw. He was traded to the Giants, the ultimate insult. Robinson's real problems were with O'Malley, who resented his great love for Branch Rickey, a man O'Malley despised. Instead of accepting the trade, Robinson retired.

The Alston-Robinson feud caused some in the black press to accuse the manager of racism, but that charge had no merit. Alston had been hired by Rickey in large measure because he wanted to replace some of the racists who *were* managing in the organization, principally to pave the way for his grand "emancipation" plan. Alston's rise through the system was largely based on his good performance with young black players. Roy Campanella, Don Newcombe, and Jim Gilliam were given special care by Alston in the 1950s. They respected him.

In 1957 the team performed below its usual expectations. The players were beginning to age. Alston's homespun demeanor was not considered ideal for the move to Los Angeles in 1958. More pizzazz would have been preferred, but he was what he was. After the club's seventh place finish in L.A., Alston was frustrated at how many over-the-hill veterans he was forced to keep on the roster in order to attract fans. Some, who felt that the club had only one chance to make a first impression, considered the first year in California a disaster. Walt was on the hot seat. He knew the team needed a youth overhaul but was not allowed to make the moves he wanted to. The club wanted aging yet big names to sell tickets, but Alston knew they were costing him victories that the talented youth were not allowed to deliver.

Despite having argued for youth, Alston was universally blamed for the use of veterans. Dressen was brought back as a coach. According to some reports, Dressen had no loyalty except to himself, lobbied behind the scenes to take over his old job, and nobody made any effort to dissuade the notion. Alston was charitable and said Dressen was a good baseball man and he appreciated having him around.

Again, he reached into his bag of tricks and produced an improbable World Championship. The 1959 Dodgers won a mere 88 regular season games. They were a hodgepodge of the old, the young, and the cast-off. However, enough of Alston's young charges were allowed to play and it paid off. They played in a football stadium, and nobody could quite figure out how to strategize the Coliseum, to make it an advantage. Against the odds, Alston led his team to a comeback. After San Francisco fell apart, the Dodgers scored a playoff win over Milwaukee and a six-game Series victory against Chicago. It was the first time a team had ever ascended from seventh place to a World Championship the next season. Dressen was let go. So was Bobby Bragan, another high-profile ex-manager hired by the club as a coach.

At that point, Alston should have been the "king of L.A.," a crown later worn with glory by the likes of John McKay, Pat Riley, and Pete Carroll. He well could have been accorded near-Hall-of-Fame status. Instead, he was made fun of, still not respected.

On top of that, Alston's character was impugned in that, despite his reputation with black athletes in Montreal and Brooklyn, some people still viewed him as a racist and anti-Semite. His disagreements with Robinson had led to tensions with the younger black players. In 1961 the Dodgers featured two young Jewish pitchers, Larry Sherry and Sandy Koufax. One night Alston caught the two of them coming in late after curfew. Alston became so enraged that he banged their locked door down, breaking his World Series ring. He was a lit fuse who took the lack of respect often accorded him only for so long before exploding. He could be mighty ornery.

Alston and Koufax took years to get on the same page. To Walt, a baseball player chewed tobacco; was vocal in his dugout exhortations of teammates; and loved, ate, and breathed baseball. Koufax was quiet. He did not yell and scream or use swear words as a sign of "toughness." His interests included classical music and fine dining. Alston could not relate to that, even though he was not a yeller or a foulmouth. But Koufax's development was a long time coming. To Alston, it was a sign that the pitcher lacked competitive fire. His efforts at reaching Koufax, to get him to meet his expectations, were mistakenly taken by some as disparagement over the fact Koufax was a Jew. There was in the early 1960s a growing divide, in which people felt only "hip" whites from the East or West Coast could relate to minorities of any kind. Alston was neither hip nor from either coast.

When Los Angeles lost the 1961 pennant to Cincinnati, Buzzie Bavasi gave Alston no vote of confidence. Bavasi said finishing second behind the Reds was "no disgrace," but when asked if that meant Alston's job was secure, he replied, "I didn't say that," which must have made the manager feel warm and fuzzy all over. Alston was allowed to twist in the wind. Public votes of confidence for Alston never served the purpose; they seemed to have the opposite effect.

"The Dodgers never plan to fire Alston," said one observer. "They prefer to torment him."

Enter Leo "the Lip" Durocher and the beginning of Greek tragedy, or comedy, L.A.-style. Fired by the Giants, Durocher had moved to Beverly Hills. It was typical of Durocher that he had not moved to Santa Monica, or Woodland Hills, or Pasadena, or any of the other comfortable locales where successful Los Angelinos tended to live. No, he moved to Beverly Hills, where *Frank* and *George* and *Dino* (Sinatra, Raft, Martin) lived. He was *not* a sympathetic figure. This was a guy who said he would knock down his own mother to win a game. Babe Ruth beat him up when, as his roommate, Durocher stole his watch. He was a gambler, a hard drinker, a womanizer who cheated on his wives. He ordered his pitchers to throw at the opponents, often to outright hit them. He wanted spikes flying, did not mind if the other guy got hurt. He probably used a spy in the scoreboard to flash signals to the Giants, giving them an edge in 1951. He went for every advantage—legal, illegal, or immoral.

He was a backstabber, a "table for one" guy who played politics, went after the other fellas' job, position, wife, girlfriend, sister, friend. Durocher had an exclusive Hollywood tailor, a mansion, drove a Caddy. Alston lived modestly, went back to Darrtown in the winter, and wore clothes off the rack. Durocher had guys in the press do his dirty work. He made fun of people on a lower pay scale ("My dry cleaning bills are bigger than his salary"). His endorsements were for cigarettes and beer. He smoked, got in guys' faces, reeked of tobacco. The umpires felt his spittle on their faces, his shoes "accidentally" kicking them during arguments. He had a deal with Schlitz beer, an appropriately ugly name for an ugly man. Durocher was no matinee idol, but he could "dirty talk" a woman into bed.

"Always try to get her in the sack the first five minutes of a date," he advised. "That way if she says no you've got time to score another broad. You'd be surprised, there's a helluva lot of famous broads who say yes quick."

Durocher bragged of his sexual conquests, mostly lying, not caring if he spread rumors or impugned the reputation of an actress in the tabloids. He was from Massachusetts, seemed like he was from the Bowery, but thought of himself as Beverly Hills or Park Avenue. He cultivated big shot friends like Frank Sinatra, the Rat Pack, George Raft, New York Mob boys, gang hitters. It was always "Frank called" and "Frank's comin' by," and most everybody looked at each other and rolled their eyes in disbelief.

He thought money was class, a fancy car defined you, a gold watch, a big ring. He was like the Alec Baldwin character in *Glengarry Glen Ross* who waves his expensive timepiece at poor Ed Harris and says, "My watch is worth more than your car. That's who I am, pal."

Branch Rickey fired him for immoralities, using the cover of his gambling suspension of 1947. What an odd couple *those two* made. Durocher and Walter O'Malley got along. Not surprising. Strangely, the word that most appropriately suits Durocher is not *immoral*, but *amoral*. He was not evil. If the right thing was convenient, that was okay by him. If anything good could be said of him, it was that he was not a racist. Maybe an anti-Semite, probably used the N-word, but for effect more than anything. He gave Willie Mays his chance, stuck with him when Willie needed a friend. It was a shining moment for "Mista Leo," and he deserves credit. Famed Los Angeles sportswriter Mel Durslag wrote there was a "good Leo" and a "bad Leo," which was better than just a "bad Leo." When he was dying he appealed to God during an interview, expressing hope that his sins would be forgiven and Heaven opened for a wretch. John Wayne did a similar thing.

Beyond all other considerations, Leo Durocher was a winning baseball man. He was a Yankee in the team's heyday, a member of the St. Louis "Gashouse Gang"—winners—and resurrected losers into winning outfits in Brooklyn, New York, later Chicago, even in Houston, for a while at least. He was Billy Martin before Martin, cut out of the same cloth. He always wore out his welcome but left his mark wherever he went.

Durocher was old school, brother. His starters went every fourth day, and they went nine innings. His regulars did not beg out, take days off, sit out the nightcap of a twin bill, a day game after a night game, or with hangovers, hang-nails, or hangdog attitudes. They played through injuries and pain. Durocher played to win. If the season was lost he would dog it, not care, let his work ethic slide, but he did not tolerate it in others. If the pennant was still on the line, he was relentless. He did not care about second place money, which some players and coaches needed in those days. He had his, probably got dough from his actress ex-wife, keeping him in style. Maybe he did a little gigolo work on the side.

Mel Durslag was a modern Iago, Othello's disturbing "friend." He had a reputation for writing arbitrary columns advocating the position of selected patrons. Los Angeles Lakers owner Jack Kent Cooke would use Durslag to spread nasty rumors about players in order to gain the upper hand. Durocher advocated his cause through Durslag, too.

After his firing and move to L.A., Durocher did some commentary on nationally televised baseball broadcasts, but he was not very good at it. His place was in the dugout, managing. He was not built to be a second fiddle to anybody. Durocher approached Durslag and had him write a national article he called "an explanation to my friends," which was as self-serving as it sounded. In it, Durocher made it clear that the fact he was not managing was not his idea. He intimated that he had been "blackballed" by baseball. Durocher made it clear he wanted to manage, and since he lived in L.A., well, Durslag managed to make Durocher look sympathetic; no mean feat.

It was around this time that the expansion Angels came into being. With Dodger Stadium not yet built, and the club struggling after the 1959 title, O'Malley decided to add some spice to the mix. Durocher was hired as a "celebrity coach."

"Though Alston had nothing to do with Leo's appointment, he was solicited to make the official announcement," wrote Durslag in an article penned for *Look* magazine called "Manager in a Hair Shirt." "After a flight from Darrtown to California, he had the privilege of revealing to the world the newest candidate for his job."

Durslag pointed out the obvious differences between the two: Alston's "comfortable but modest home" as opposed to Durocher's $150,000 mansion; Alston's hobby of woodworking versus Durocher's of women and gambling; Alston's Mercury and Durocher's Cadillac; and finally, Alston's off-the-rack clothes and Durocher's exclusive tailor with celebrity clientele.

Alston preferred to "carry a beef" until cooler heads prevailed, while Durocher preferred to handle disputes in the here and now. When Durslag rebuked Alston in print over a dugout berating of Durocher, Alston confronted the writer and snapped, "You're pretty sensitive about Durocher's feelings, but you don't seem to care much about mine."

Alston demonstrated thin skin on this and other occasions. A strange Kabuki theater with Durocher, the press, and the club was in full swing in 1962. Alston was on his usual one-year contract status. In later years, Alston's tenuous position with the club was recalled with a certain amount of historical revisionism.

"Walter knew he had a job as long as I was there," recalled Buzzie Bavasi. "He was the type of person you liked to have running your business because you knew where he was all the time. If you needed him, you'd call his hotel room and he'd always be there."

By contrast, Leo Durocher could be anywhere: the racetrack, a bar, or incognito with somebody else's wife. Alston was "a quiet, strong and honest man who never makes excuses—I have always felt he should have rode shotgun through Indian territory in the old days," broadcaster Vin Scully said of him. He "manages as he lives . . . and he has done it almost without your noticing it."

But the Los Angeles writers always wanted more. By 1962 a talented core of sports scribes included the likes of Bud Furillo and Mel Durslag of the *Los Angeles Herald-Express*, and some excellent writers at the *L.A. Times*: Jim Murray, John Hall, and Mal Florence. This was Hollywood, and they wanted color, some tabloid flare. Every sports story was a feature. New rules were being written when it came to the coverage of athletics.

Over at USC, young coach John McKay held court at a nearby pub called Julie's. Twirling his cigar, drinking whiskey, and dispensing Irish wit, humor, and vitriol in one entertaining package, he was a sportswriter's dream. Every time he opened his mouth it was story time, and they wanted something similar from the other coaches and managers in the L.A. constellation. There was no shortage of interesting characters on the L.A. sports scene: Bo Belinsky and Dean Chance, Bill Rigney, "Hot Rod" Hundley. UCLA football coach Red Sanders was still fresh in their minds, too. Sanders was one of the all-timers, a whiskey-drinking, skirt-chasing Southerner who died in flagrante delicto in a Sunset Strip brothel just a few years earlier.

Naturally, the writers gravitated to the fast-talking Durocher and found Alston boring. From the standpoint of selling newspapers, his honesty was not the best policy. *Sports Illustrated*'s Robert Creamer called him, "Whistler's Mother with a scorecard in his lap."

"If you were to meet Walter Alston, you'd come away convinced you hadn't been introduced," another writer wrote.

"I appreciate a good shotgun," Alston said. "I appreciate a good target rifle. I appreciate a good pool table. The fancy clothes and big dinners don't appeal to me much. Any time a man tries to be something he's not, he's only hurting himself."

"He played the game by the book," recalled catcher John Roseboro. "He knew baseball as well as anyone, but he missed some opportunities because he didn't see them soon enough and seize them fast enough. He didn't want to be second-guessed by the press and the public and didn't want to be criticized by the front office."

"Alston's greatest ability was to do nothing—having confidence with the guys to say, 'Don't let me screw things up because your talent will come out somewhere during the ballgame,'" said first baseman Ron Fairly. "His patience allowed our abilities to eventually surface."

Alston loved "little ball," a style of play he had to adapt when *The Boys of Summer* departed, the power supply was depleted, the Coliseum demanded a new style, and the club moved into pitcher-friendly Dodger Stadium. He platooned, double-switched, ordered intentional walks, and always seemed to know in the third inning what to expect in the eighth, a sign of a hardworking manager. Alston's quiet ways meant that when he did have a temper outburst, it had an effect, as opposed to the blustery Durocher, who always seemed steamed about something.

"He was a man's man and when he talked to you, he looked you straight in the eye," recalled pitcher Ron Perranoski. "But you just didn't want to fool around with Walter. He could physically break you in two and was capable of doing so till the day he died."

An example of Alston's physical strength came when he arm-wrestled mammoth Frank Howard, one of the biggest, strongest baseball players who ever lived—and won.

"We didn't let those gray hairs on his head fool us into thinking he couldn't take any of us on," recalled Fairly. Once or twice a year, Alston would call a closed-door meeting, and if his ire was up, "he'd have a rough time lighting his cigarette," said Fairly. Alston would go around the room, pointing accusatory fingers, laying it all on the line. But these were rare. His normal method was to wait a day, until tempers—probably his own more than anybody's—had died down, and then have a private meeting with a player.

The Alston-Durocher controversy built up in the spring of 1962, when Durocher arrived at Dodgertown and was assigned Spartan quarters in the single men's barracks. Durocher immediately tried to move "off base," where he could utilize his maid and cook from Beverly Hills, but team rules allowed only married men to live off base. When word of that leaked out, Durocher was inundated with marriage proposals from local women willing to make him eligible for the married men's housing allowance. But Durocher upgraded his accommodations with lavish touches, then personally oversaw his meal preparations. He ate specialty dishes while the rest of the club ate what was offered them.

The writers, who got zero from Alston beyond platitudes and baseball cliches, went to Durocher. Alston accepted the situation. He knew his "celebrity coach" was a colorful figure and insisted there was mutual respect. Alston quietly coached his players, trying to instill confidence. Durocher's style was to belittle. He was like the devil, using psychology to get in his players' heads, and had an endless storage of knowledge about them that he used to inflict maximum effect. He knew inside stuff about players' parents and their personal lives and used it to embarrass or discredit. The singled-out player would endure teammates' nervous laughter. Anybody could be next.

Pitcher Johnny Podres said, "There was conflict because Leo wanted Walt's job—he wanted to manage the Dodgers." Alston's dislike of Durocher was hard to hide. He never liked him, going back to the two years when they managed against each other in New York.

During Spring Training, Durocher held court in the Dodgertown rec room, where he dominated pool games. Durocher was a pool hustler from way back. One day he was dominating all comers with loud quips and wisecracks. His excellent play and domineering personality filled the room, making him look larger than life among the Dodgers. He was already a legendary baseball figure who had roomed with Babe Ruth, slept with "every actress who counts," and knew "anybody who's anybody." Alston was unknown until 1954, when Leo was at the height of his fame.

On one occasion, Durocher's pool exploits created a major commotion, causing Alston to peek his head in. When he saw it was Durocher holding court, Alston wanted nothing to do with this scene. It was not one he was designed to thrive in, so he turned to leave. Maury Wills saw him and urged him to join the game. Reluctantly, Alston entered the room. A palpable tension suddenly filled the air.

Durocher looked up and saw Alston. Silence replaced the wild boasting and cheering. The two men squared off and "it was like a scene from *The Hustler*," recalled Wills. "There was a burning desire by both men to beat one another—a personal vendetta."

Alston was on top of his game, building a big lead while Durocher stood in a silent corner, seething. "Hey Leo, you're losing," one of the players said. The silence, in contrast to the previous boisterousness, was deafening. Durocher fancied himself a pool expert, seeing the game as an extension of his manhood, but Alston was a master at it. Durocher rallied and took a brief lead, but Alston sunk two difficult shots and the game was tied.

"Staff meeting at 8:30," Alston suddenly announced, looking at his watch.

It was the best move Alston could make. If he beat Durocher in front of the team, his coach would lose face and there would be hell to pay. If *he* lost then he would lose a notch in the pole of respect. Alston probably could have won the game, but sacrificed victory for team unity. Durocher silently realized his rival had spared him embarrassment and went along without protest. Alston's benevolence, however, did not lead Durocher into Alston's corner. After all, "nice guys finish in last place," as he had been saying for years.

Maury Wills's partner in crime was Jim "Junior" Gilliam. He was the ultimate team player and, in the view of many, the ultimate symbol of the Dodger way. He was adept at bunting, the hit-and-run, working the count. Gilliam hit second in the order behind Wills and often protected Wills by swinging at pitches he might otherwise have taken. On many occasions, he took pitches in order to let Wills get his steal.

"Sure, I've laid off the ball intentionally," the switch-hitting Gilliam stated. "Sometimes the ball will be right down the middle, too. But I'm in no hurry to hit. You hit one pitch and I'm in no hurry."

"I know Jim sacrificed his own personal gains many times to help me," said Wills. "When he's batting left-handed, he obstructs the catcher's view of first base. Jim doesn't pull the ball, so it's impossible for fielders to play him in any specific manner. This gives me a great advantage in keeping the shortstop and second baseman honest. He isn't a first-ball hitter and doesn't jump around going for bad pitches. Before a pitcher finishes with him, usually he has to throw five or six pitches, and that's all I need to pull a steal."

Bavasi felt that Gilliam was responsible for half of Wills's stolen bases. Gilliam had incredible peripheral vision and could see out of the corner of his eye whether Wills was stealing. Gilliam had the ability to foul a ball off intentionally, an old Negro League trick that is virtually a lost art today.

Gilliam started playing in the Negro Leagues when he was 16. They called him Junior because he was so young, and the name stuck. "I'm one of the lucky ones," said Gilliam in 1969. "I was born at the right time. I'm lucky because I got a chance. Ever hear of Josh Gibson? If they came to Josh Gibson today and he were 17 years old, they would have a blank spot on the contract and they'd say, 'fill in the amount.' That's how good Josh Gibson was."

He made $275 a month in the Negro Leagues. At the age of 17 Gilliam played for the Baltimore Elite Giants, then moved on to the Nashville club before Brooklyn purchased his contract for $11,500, along with pitcher Joe Black. He toiled for two years at Montreal.

"I think of the old days often," he told sportswriter John Wiebusch. "I think of the games we played at Bugle Field in Baltimore. And how rough it was. I think of the guys who made it—the Roy Campanella's, the Monte Irvin's, the Larry Doby's, the Willie Mays's . . . the Junior Gilliam's."

"Then I think of Josh Gibson and the others. And Satchel Paige and the barnstorming days and the guys who played for the New York Black Yankees and the Homestead Grays."

The 1953 Rookie of the Year enjoyed the musical stylings of Ray Charles, time with his wife and four kids, playing golf, and of course pool. Alston felt he was as valuable a player as any of his stars, stating, "I would rather see Gilliam up at bat with a man on second base and no one out than anybody I know." Alston told Vin Scully that Gilliam never missed a sign, never threw to a wrong base, and, incredibly, never made a mistake.

Gilliam played anywhere he was needed: second base, third base, or the outfield. Year after year, hotshot rookies came along to take his job, but if one position was taken, Gilliam had three gloves for three different positions and found himself in the lineup at one of them every game. Charlie Neal, Randy Jackson, Dick Gray, and Don Zimmer came and went. Gilliam was a constant.

"A young fellow taking my place can't be good for two days or two weeks," he explained. "Baseball is an everyday game." In 1962 a promising rookie named Larry Burright came along. Instead of shunning him, Gilliam worked with Burright. "He's a real great guy," Burright said.

Gilliam's only complaint was flying. He came up when it was still a parochial game. The subway could get him to 11 road games a year at the Polo Grounds, and trains could handle the mostly East Coast schedule. Now he played for a team that had to travel more miles than any other.

John Roseboro apparently had his problems with Gilliam. Perhaps this was the result of the "old school" (Gilliam) running up against the "new breed" (Roseboro). Roseboro was sensitive about his civil rights, whereas Gilliam was happy for the opportunity and not about to make waves.

Roseboro's nickname was "Gabby." Roger Craig called him that because he was so reticent. Ed Roebuck said that Roseboro was "on the same wavelength" with the pitchers but did not need to talk a lot. "You know what sign the guy's gonna put down before he puts it down," said Roebuck. If Roseboro thought a pitcher was not bearing down, he would fire a heater right back at his solar plexus, a practice that Mets catcher Jerry Grote later employed. Roseboro's hands were so dark-skinned he needed to wear tape during night games so his pitchers could see the signs.

"He knew every pitcher and what they were capable of doing," said Ron Perranoski. "He never got mad. He was an even-tempered individual, a strong, quiet man. He seldom came out to the mound; I had to call him out if I needed him. And then he'd crack a little joke to take some of the pressure off. Sometimes I'd see him smile at me through his mask."

Roseboro "had more courage than any catcher I ever saw," said Bavasi. "On a close play at home, nobody'd ever score because he'd block the plate with his entire body. He was the 'Rock of Gibraltar.'"

Roseboro, like Alston, was from Ohio. He came up with Brooklyn as Roy Campanella's backup. "I think I was as close to Campy as any man I've ever known, except my father," said Roseboro. When Campanella was paralyzed prior to the first season in Los Angeles, young Roseboro was the starter. Roseboro immediately assumed a leadership role.

On a team of speedsters, Roseboro was the fastest-running catcher in baseball at that time. In 1962 he hit 11 triples and stole 12 bases in 15 tries. He beat out infield hits.

In his autobiography, Roseboro confessed that the life of a big league ballplayer can be a real eye-opener for a shy, innocent Ohio lad. He had little experience with women, but when he got to the Major Leagues a teammate introduced him to groupies who made themselves available to the team, performing sexual feats that Roseboro had never known existed, much less fantasized about. As he matured, Roseboro became "the 'Iviest' guy in the league," said Vin Scully. "On road trips, if John Roseboro isn't at a movie, he's at a laundry," wrote Jim Murray. "He has more wardrobe changes than Loretta Young."

"When the Swift Set sits in a hotel lobby, everyone marvels at its splendid sweaters," wrote *Sports Illustrated* in reference to the clothing styles of Wills, Roseboro, and the others.

Roseboro's backup, Doug Camilli, was the son of former big leaguer Dolf Camilli, the 1941 National League Most Valuable Player with the Brooklyn Dodgers. The 25-year-old resident of Santa Rosa, California, had played 19 total big league games prior to the 1962 campaign.

First baseman Ron Fairly was one of those guys who was born to be a Dodger. A native of Long Beach, he prepped at Jordan High School and in 1958 was the best player in college baseball, hitting .348 with nine homers and 67 runs batted in for Rod Dedeaux's National Champion Southern California Trojans. He signed with the brand new Los Angeles Dodgers and made his debut that season. In 1959 Fairly played 118 games for the world champions and was living the dream, but he did not establish himself as a regular until 1961, when he hit .322. A left-hander all the way, the 5'10", 180-pound Fairly was a defensive whiz who could also play left field, but he was s-l-o-w. He was a handsome, personable collegiate type.

Maury Wills was fast. Willie Davis was faster. A *lot* faster. "Going from first to third, there was never anybody who ran as fast as Willie," recalled Dodgers broadcaster Jerry Doggett. (Mickey Mantle was the only player faster.)

"The best play in baseball was to watch Willie Davis run out a triple," said Bavasi.

When Alston first laid eyes on the wide-open Dodger Stadium outfield, he knew Davis was his man.

Born in Arkansas, Davis moved with his mother and brother to east Los Angeles when he was still an infant. He ran a newspaper stand as a kid and stayed out of trouble. Davis went to Roosevelt High, the same school that produced

Heisman Trophy winner Mike Garrett of USC, and lettered in basketball and track. Baseball was not his best sport, but his speed made him a prospect. Scout Kenny Meyers signed him to a Dodger contract for $5,000. Vin Scully said he was "manufactured . . . everything else was taught to him."

Davis was a product of the refined and processed Dodgers' farm system, which at that time was the model for success in player development. Meyers worked endlessly with Davis, making the most use of his speed. Another scout, Harold "Lefty" Phillips, was also instrumental in turning Davis from a right-handed-hitting high school first baseman into a left-handed-hitting big league center fielder and one of the very best outfielders of the decade.

Davis lit up the minor leagues before arriving in Los Angeles to stay in 1961. He was cocky and sure of himself. The press loved the local angle. "He looks like a decade of World Series checks," the L.A. Times raved. Filmmaker David Wolper did a documentary called Biography of a Rookie. Featuring Davis, it was narrated by Mike Wallace. Batting coach Pete Reiser glowed over Davis.

"We had him on the post-game show after his very first game," Vin Scully recalled. "At the end of the night, there was a fly ball to center with the bases loaded and two out. He stood almost at attention and caught the ball with a 'ho-hum' kind of attitude. So I asked him how he could be so relaxed in his first game in the big leagues. Well, Willie has a voice that's as low as the ocean floor. He replies in that rumbling, deep tone of his: 'It's not my life—it's not my wife—so why worry?'"

Davis had come out of the 'hood and now was a Hollywood star of sorts with "the foxes hanging all over me," he recalled. The Dodgers offered the self-described "swinging man" money if he would settle down and get married. Davis took Buzzie Bavasi up on his offer, and "I've been a happier player since."

Tommy Davis also worked with his friend to improve him as a hitter.

Maury Wills was high-strung, for sure, but he also helped alleviate tensions by orchestrating his "Dr. Frankenstein" act. The team would gather in the clubhouse. Wills and 6'7", 250-pound Frank Howard had a routine. Wills would take an imaginary phone call from Walter O'Malley, answering that he would handle the request for more offensive power.

"I'll build you a monster," Wills would say.

He would then bark out batting orders to the stiff, robotic Howard, who followed each instruction just like Frankenstein's monster. Swinging the bat, Howard would suddenly go crazy until his "master" (Wills) ordered him to stop. Wills would then "call" O'Malley and inform him that his monster would be playing right field that day, wearing number 25.

"He wasn't born—he was founded," wrote Jim Murray of Howard. "He answers to the nickname 'Hondo' because he's the only guy in the world outside of organized baseball who could call John Wayne 'Shorty.'"

Howard came out of the legendary Ohio State basketball program, which in the late 1950s and early 1960s was, in those pre-UCLA dynasty days, the best in the nation with John Havlicek, Jerry Lucas, Larry Siegfried, and Bobby Knight. An All-American in basketball and baseball, Howard signed an enormous $108,000 bonus with the Dodgers in 1958. In 1959 he was voted the *Sporting News* Minor League Player of the Year, and he followed that up with Rookie of the Year honors in 1960.

In short order, Howard became a player of legend, his long-distance home runs being of a Paul Bunyan quality. Off the field, he was also an All-American—religious, honest, no swearing.

"He would 'yessir' you to death," recalled Al Campanis.

"He was such a courteous young man that you'd feel kind of silly," said pitcher Stan Williams. "It was like meeting a 12-year-old boy who was nine feet tall. He'd call everybody 'Mister,' then shake your hand and almost tear your arm off."

"Because he was so polite, other players teased him, and he was often the butt of jokes," said Vin Scully. "But he was very good-natured, thank goodness, or he would have dismantled the clubhouse."

Howard would polish off three steaks in one sitting. He was said to have eaten six airline dinners during one flight, but claimed he ate only four.

As great an athlete as Howard was, his size made him prone to strikeouts and he was also not a fundamental base runner, which stood out on a team of base-running experts. He had one of the best throwing arms in baseball but lacked accuracy. He was ahead of his time, with the designated hitter not coming into existence until 1973.

The league figured Howard out in 1961. "You just keep teasing him with bad pitches and changes of speed, and you can forget about Howard," said St. Louis pitching coach Howie Pollet.

"You drill him day in and day out, and finally you think you've got him straightened out and then all of a sudden he's swinging at balls he couldn't reach with a 10-foot bat," said batting coach Pete Reiser. "One of these days, the pitcher will throw over to first and Frank will take a cut at it."

"The tragedy of Frank Howard was that one day he could hit a 500-foot home run and the next day strike out five times," wrote Bill Wise in the *1963 Official Baseball Almanac.*

"All I can do is try," said Howard. "Maybe if I just keep working at learning the strike zone, I'll surprise a few people."

"All Frank ever needed was to put his many assets together," said Alston. "If he makes contact enough, he'll break every home run record whether he's trying or not. Frank had a bad habit of hitting off his left foot and overstriding. He corrected that in '62. By 1964 he should break the home run record. All he needs is a little more experience and confidence."

"If Howard gets better, he could break every home run record around," said Solly Hemus of the Mets.

The short left field at the Coliseum got the best of Howard, and Wally Moon played ahead of him, but he was expected to provide much-needed power at Dodger Stadium in 1962. By mid-June Howard regained the right field job and went on a tear, driving in 41 runs with 12 homers and a .381 average over 26 games. He also improved his throwing accuracy, nailing 19 runners to tie the great Roberto Clemente for the lead in assists with 19. Howard elicited oohs and aahs from the Dodger Stadium throngs.

The man Howard replaced, Wally Moon, was a fan favorite whose "Moon shots" made him a legend in Dodger annals.

On the field, Alston had some decisions to make. Moving out of the Coliseum would hurt 32-year-old Moon, who had batted .328 with 88 RBIs in 1961. Duke Snider was 34 and had hit almost .300. Theoretically, Dodger Stadium would help him; after all, anything was better than the Coliseum for a left-handed hitting slugger. But Tommy Davis, Willie Davis, and Frank Howard were young talents who needed to play. So was Ron Fairly, who could handle first base or left field. Offensive considerations gave way to defensive ones, and in that respect Willie Davis needed to be out there. The left-center field gap at Dodger Stadium would have to be covered. There was no more playing singles off the screen.

Moon and Snider were given symbolic send-offs of sorts. On May 7 Moon was honored by his home state of Texas when the Dodgers traveled to Houston. Moon, who earned a master's degree from Texas A&M, was given the key to the city while an annual school trophy was named after him.

Snider was made team captain, an honor he took seriously. He told the writers that the club had young players who had heard of him growing up, and "I think they will listen to me when I make suggestions."

Now 35 at the beginning of the 1962 campaign, Edwin "Duke" Snider was already a Dodger legend and sure Hall of Famer. In 1958 he was still only 31 when the club moved to his hometown of Los Angeles, but his career out west never approached the greatness of the Brooklyn years, when he was known as the "Duke of Flatbush." As it had been for another Los Angelino, Don Drysdale, the Coliseum was more or less his undoing. In Snider's case, he was not young enough to overcome it when the club finally moved to Dodger Stadium. He was a key player on the 1959 World Championship team, but after that his career whittled down. He was none too impressed with Alston, who increasingly benched him.

Snider was cursed at an early age, "robbed of the gift of perspective," according to Michael Shapiro in *The Last Good Season*. Growing up, he was "that most envied and exalted of young men: the best ballplayer around."

His father worked at the Goodyear Tire plant and gave Snider the "Duke" moniker, which fit perfectly from the beginning. He earned 16 letters at Compton High School, was popular, and met his future wife in their junior year. He never knew adversity.

Signing with Brooklyn at age 17, he did a short stint in the Navy and then came back to rise through the ultracompetitive farm system to debut in 1949. His lifetime of success did not prepare him for big league failure, but Branch Rickey recognized his potential. He was also an excellent teammate for Jackie Robinson. On a team of southerners, midwesterners, and East Coasters, it was good for Robinson to have a fellow Californian. Snider had grown up watching Robinson play football at the Coliseum. Robinson, a veteran by the time Snider arrived, helped hone the youngsters' competitive juices, understanding that failure was a natural part of baseball.

It was a team of veterans, led by the strong personalities of Robinson and shortstop Pee Wee Reese. Roy Campanella, a three-time MVP, was the star player. But as the 1950s played out, Snider emerged as the team leader. Comparisons with New York's Mickey Mantle and the Giants' Willie Mays became inevitable. By the middle of the decade, there was no truly discernible difference among the three.

Carl Erskine told a story about a group of Dodgers riding from Brooklyn to the Polo Grounds for a game against the Giants. Pee Wee Reese was stopped by a cop, but when he told the policeman he was with the Dodgers, he was let go. The next day Snider drove and was stopped. He volunteered that he played for the Dodgers.

"I don't like baseball," said the cop.

"I don't like cops," Snider replied. "Gimme the ticket."

Snider's breakout year was 1950, when he hit 31 homers with 199 hits, 107 runs batted in, and a .321 average, but Brooklyn lost on the last day to Dick Sisler and the Phillies.

Snider tailed off toward the end of the 1951 campaign along with the rest of the club but still had 101 RBIs. From 1952 to 1954 he batted over .300 each season. He hit 40-plus home runs from 1953 to 1957 and drove in 100 or more from 1953 to 1956.

Snider's roots were deep in Brooklyn, and even though he married a California girl, he had misgivings about Los Angeles. He also had problems with Alston's "youth movement," which eventually reduced his playing time. In a classic photo in Glenn Stout's *The Dodgers: 120 Years of Dodgers Baseball*, Snider is shown wearing a crisply tailored suit with a tie clasp. Two young lovelies wearing Dodger caps and tight shorts are with him, Snider's arm around the brunette's waist while the blonde smiles at him adoringly. His hair is slicked back, and he is indeed the Duke in all his glory. The three pick chocolates out of a giant box, so that the empty slots spell "Los Angeles is Sweet on the Dodgers."

The enormous Coliseum dimensions in right-center reduced him to 15 homers in 1958 and caused Willie Mays to tell him, "They're killin' you, man."

Snider hit .308 with 23 homers and 88 RBIs in the world title year of 1959, but it was his last hurrah. Alston finally got his way, moving the old out in favor of the new. In 1960 Snider hit .243 and played only 85 games in 1961.

Aside from Don Drysdale and Sandy Koufax, the Dodgers' pitching staff still consisted of talented professionals. They were a rough, veteran group—with some youth mixed in—who enjoyed drinking together.

"We'd go to dinner together, have drinks together, and talk baseball together," said Ron Perranoski. "We were a very close-knit pitching staff."

"Playing at home in L.A., we used to sit around in the clubhouse an hour and a half after the game, have a couple of beers and talk about baseball," said Johnny Podres. "When we went out, it was pretty much just us. We generally didn't let too many of the other guys come along. It was a pitchers' fraternity."

Whatever they did the night before, it did not seem to affect their control the next day.

"I loved to catch those guys because they could all throw to spots," said Roseboro.

Their good control only made their occasional brushbacks more effective. They followed the lead of Don Drysdale, the leading "barber" of the era.

Perranoski came to the club from the Chicago Cubs. A native of Patterson, New Jersey, he signed a hefty $30,000 bonus in 1958, played a couple of years in the minors, then came to L.A. in the Don Zimmer trade of 1961. He was one of the first young pitchers ticketed for the bullpen from the beginning. After starting one game as a rookie, he went to the bullpen and never left it. With few exceptions, relief pitchers were usually castoffs who were not good enough to start, but Perranoski became a closer.

"I don't care if I never start another game as long as I live," he stated. "I can't wait to throw the ball when I get in there."

Perranoski had a hard sinker and good curveball that was slow enough to throw hitters off stride. His control was impeccable, plus he was courageous and smart. In 1962 Alston used him on a very regular basis.

"I loved it," he said. "The more work I got, the better it felt. I had the type of arm it never bothered me to throw every day, and if I threw four out of five days, I would have better stuff and better control on the fourth day than I would on the first."

In 1961 Perranoski was used against both right- and left-handed hitters as opposed to his 1961 role against lefties. He also replaced Larry Sherry as the ace of the bullpen corps.

That actually worked out for Sherry. He was an effective short relief pitcher, but thought of himself as a starter and never adjusted to the limited work. When Perranoski assumed that role, Sherry went to long relief, giving him a chance to work longer periods. He threw seven shutout innings in one extra-inning victory over the Cubs.

Born in Hollywood, Sherry and his brother Norm went to Fairfax High School. Unlike Koufax, Sherry was combative. Born with two clubbed feet, Sherry made up for it with a competitive attitude.

"He was a little troublemaker, always fighting," recalled Norm. "If he didn't like the way a game was going, he'd break the bat."

Eventually, Sherry grew to be 6'2" and 205 pounds. He had piercing dark eyes that resembled the actor Sal Mineo. He was a typical Dodger pitcher who employed the brushback, even knocking down brother Norm in a 1959 Spring Training intrasquad game.

"Larry was a guy who would enter a ballgame and take over," recalled teammate Ed Roebuck. "He would knock you down if you didn't play his way." Roebuck gave him a nickname: "the Rude Jew." Instead of taking offense, Sherry considered it a badge of honor.

It was in 1959 when Sherry established his name forever in the Dodgers' glory halls. A rookie that year, Sherry was the winning pitcher in the first playoff game against Milwaukee. Then he won two games and saved two others in the World Series triumph over the White Sox, earning the MVP award. Three days later he appeared on *The Ed Sullivan Show*.

"I had to go out and buy a suit for that," Sherry said. "I didn't own one. I didn't even make the minimum salary that year."

In 1960 Sherry compiled 13 wins in relief, but he had a sore arm in 1961. He complained to Alston that he should be a regular starter, but the staff was so loaded he could not break into the rotation. In 1962 he nursed shoulder troubles but was still effective.

Ed Roebuck started with the Dodgers in the World Championship 1955 season. By 1962, at the age of 30, he was the dean of the staff. Scout Kenny Meyers helped Roebuck rehabilitate his arm after suffering a shoulder injury in 1961. He threw "long toss" and repeated the repetitive process of throwing against a fence until the adhesions in his arm somehow fused and got better.

Dr. Robert Kerlan, the Dodgers' respected surgeon who later revolutionized treatment of rotator cuffs as well as the "Tommy John surgery," called Roebuck's recovery "miraculous." Roebuck was a sinker specialist who, like Perranoski, could throw on a daily basis.

Nineteen sixty-two was a tough year for him because in addition to coming back from injury, both his father and brother died and he suffered from insomnia. He "could not separate the reality from the unreality," but camaraderie with his fellow pitchers proved to be his saving grace.

He made 60 appearances in the year. "It was almost as if I was in a trance," he recalled. "I was making great pitches. I felt I couldn't lose—I didn't even care how or when they used me; short or long relief, starting—it just didn't matter."

Roebuck's next-door neighbor was Stan Williams. A few years earlier, Williams, Roebuck, pitcher Roger Craig, and first baseman Norm Larker had all built homes on the same street in suburban Lakewood, a pleasant community nestled in between Long Beach in L.A. County and Los Alamitos in Orange County.

But in 1961 Craig and Larker were lost in the expansion draft. Williams's family grew out of the house so they moved to Long Beach. Because Williams was the first of the group to become a father, he was given the nickname "Big Daddy." Later he was called "Big Hurt" because his pitching assignments often were tailored around the disabled list. Plus, a song called "Big Hurt" had come out.

The large, powerful Williams would sneak up on teammates and put a half nelson on them until the other guy screamed. "I guess I was kind of a playful giant with a lot of energy," recalled the 6'4", 225-pound Williams. Norm Sherry said Williams was the hardest-throwing pitcher on the staff; maybe his speed was not as great as Koufax's, but the bruises on the catcher's hand were bluer.

Williams's professional debut was dubious. Arriving late for his first game at Shawnee in 1954, he entered the dugout just as the umpire was turning to the dugout to throw out a player who had made a caustic remark. Mistaking Williams for the offending man, he tossed him before he had even arrived.

Williams won 18 and 19 games in separate minor league seasons, then hooked on with Los Angeles for good in 1960, when he was 14-10 with a 3.00 ERA, making the All-Star team. His 205 strikeouts in 1961 trailed only Koufax in the National League. He kept notes, was smart, and, like the rest of the guys, pitched inside, keeping track of batters he hit. He was strategically wild, just enough to intimidate the opposition. In 1961 Alston was concerned that he was working the count too deep. He took a lot of time in between pitches and his fielders were sometimes caught flat-footed. Alston thought he was frivolous.

"We were never very close," Williams said of his relationship with the manager. "I always had the impression he thought I was a big dummy, and even when I pitched well I didn't feel a lot of respect coming from him. I never cared a lot for Walter and I think he felt the same way about me."

In 1962 Williams was expected to have a breakout year, but his control problems made him inconsistent. During one monthlong stretch he did not complete or win a single game. In a relief appearance against the Mets, he walked eight batters in five innings. A week later against Philadelphia, however, Williams tossed a shutout with no walks in the second game of a doubleheader.

Johnny Podres started the season opener at Dodger Stadium but lost, and struggled all year, especially at home. In the first game of a July 2 twin bill, however, Podres won his first-ever game at Chavez Ravine, 5-1. He retired the first 20 Phillies and struck out a then–big league record eight straight batters.

The southpaw Podres was a native of New York State, where he was born in 1932. His mother had double pneumonia when he was born, and his father worked in the mines for $18 a week. Despite that, he enjoyed his childhood.

"A small town is the only place to live," he said. "I knew everyone and everyone knows me, but nobody bothers me. I can find more friends there in one day than in the rest of the world over."

His passions were ice fishing in the winter, baseball in the summer. Baseball paid better: a $6,000 signing bonus by the Dodgers. His father's encouragement kept his hopes up as he struggled through the low minor leagues and a back injury.

At the age of 23, Podres was a regular starter on the famed 1955 Dodgers' staff, winning game seven of the World Series, 2-0, over the hated Yankees. A carefree man about town, he liked to party and was the toast of Brooklyn, but other than that such pitching stalwarts as Carl Erskine and Don Newcombe overshadowed Podres. He was a good pitcher year in and year out, however. While Newcombe won the Cy Young and the MVP awards, he was the vanishing man in the World Series, whereas Podres stepped up.

"When something was on the line, I guess I rose to the occasion more than I did during other times during the course of the year," he said.

Podres was a "money pitcher," said Perranoski, with "one of the best change-ups in the history of baseball." Norm Sherry described it as a "pull-down-the-window-shade" change of pace. Buzzie Bavasi said if he needed one pitcher to win one game, he would pick Podres, and so would Alston. This on a team with Koufax and Drysdale!

Podres loved Los Angeles, particularly the nightlife and the ladies. Like Angels southpaw Bo Belinsky, he was renowned for his amorous adventures, and at 29 was still a bachelor and loving it. Podres enjoyed drinking with the other pitchers as well as playing the horses at Hollywood Park.

Alston, the malted milk drinker, did not like it, but Bavasi said, "I never thought malted milk drinkers were good ballplayers, and that's why I always had a soft spot for guys like John." Apparently, Podres abstained from alcohol and sex the night before he pitched, and was, like Whitey Ford, always ready to go. He adhered to the principle enunciated by another fun-loving guy, USC baseball coach Rod Dedeaux, who told countless Trojans, "No drinkin' before the game, but afterwards there's nothin' like a tub o' suds."

In 1961 Podres was 18-5, and his father died of lung cancer, probably the result of working in the mines. He missed a few September starts. At the beginning of the 1962 campaign Podres pitched poorly. Some speculated that the loss of his dad was still affecting him.

Joe Moeller was 19 years old in 1962, the youngest player in baseball. He was in only his second year of organized baseball. The previous season he won 20 games with almost 300 strikeouts in three different minor league stops. Despite plans for more seasoning, Moeller impressed Alston so much at Vero Beach that he made it to Los Angeles.

"Everything he throws jumps and moves," said *Sports Illustrated*.

Moeller had mixed success in 1962, getting sent back to the minor leagues before getting called up again. He was a local kid from the Manhattan Beach strand. Playing for the Dodgers was a dream come true.

"Two years before I signed, I was still getting players' autographs," he said. "I collected every article about the Dodgers, going back to when they were in Brooklyn. I got higher offers from other ballclubs, but I really wanted to play for the Dodgers."

On a pitching staff that liked to drink beer, Moeller was not old enough to tag along, and there was some resentment. The Dodgers always had the biggest farm system in baseball. Getting to the Major Leagues meant a lengthy process of "paying dues," but Moeller had avoided all of that.

Nobody even wanted to room with the kid, so he became one of the first Major Leaguers to have his own room, which made for a "pretty lonely existence." It was a tough experience for him, especially after having dreamt of it all his life, but Moeller dealt with his rookie woes as best as he could.

There may never have been a professional athlete more perfectly suited for the team he played for than Don Drysdale. He was the ultimate Hollywood athlete: a Los Angeles native with the looks of a matinee idol and a budding film career on the side. Even his name had marquee value, like John Barrymore or Errol Flynn. He made guest appearances on *The Beverly Hillbillies*, which featured a banker character also named Drysdale.

His background was straight out of Tinseltown, too. At Van Nuys High School, his classmates included the acclaimed actress Natalie Wood, already an international child star, and Robert Redford. Redford, known then as Bobby, was the star outfielder on Drysdale's baseball team. He was good enough to garner a baseball scholarship to the University of Colorado.

In 1960 Drysdale led the league with 246 strikeouts, had a 2.84 ERA, but in what would amount to the story of so much of his career, received little support in a 15-14 season. Los Angeles failed to repeat. In 1961 he was 13-10, but the Dodgers finished a disappointing second to the Reds. Drysdale hit 20 batters in 1961, mostly out of frustration.

Entering the 1962 campaign, Drysdale was the biggest name on the team, an established All-Star and fan favorite. He was the unquestioned ace of the staff despite Koufax's presence and emergence as a star after years of struggle. As good as he was, however, Drysdale's career had not taken off the way it should. The reason was the Coliseum. First the bandbox Ebbets Field, then the crazy Coliseum; Drysdale had been forced to pitch with a short left field fence.

"At the Coliseum his best pitch, a fastball on the fists, became a fastball into the seats," wrote Steve Gelman in *Sport* magazine. Drysdale complained long and loud about the Coliseum, stating, "I'll never win in this place as long as I live." The hometown hero even asked for a trade—anywhere. His blustery attitude engendered some boos in the Coliseum years. Finally, after the 1961 season, Dodgers pitchers came to the Coliseum and symbolically tore down the left field fence once and for all.

Now, at Dodger Stadium, he was in his element. He talked less, worked more, and pitched marvelous baseball, winning 11 in a row at one point. On August 3 he reached 20 victories for the first time.

Aside from his Hollywood gigs, Drysdale did public relations work for a local dairy and opened restaurants. "The Meanest Man in Baseball" donated hours to charity, dressing as Santa for a Christmas party at an orphanage, among many of his good deeds. He had it all. His wife, Ginger, was literally a beauty queen. The former Tournament of Roses princess told the writers that tough guy Drysdale helped around the house, waxing floors, doing dishes, and "I never have to ask him to do a thing."

"If you had seen Sandy Koufax the first time I saw him, you never would have imagined that he would become what he became—the greatest pitcher I've ever seen and possibly the greatest ever," recalled Duke Snider of his old teammate.

Koufax was 6'2", 210 pounds, with enormous hands, powerhouse legs, excellent jumping ability, dexterity, and strength that belied the notion of physical weakness that, perhaps out of some sense of anti-Semitism, has pervaded the Jewish stereotype.

Koufax did not play high school baseball until his senior year, when he was used at first base. He earned a basketball scholarship to the University of Cincinnati, where he scored 10 points per game for the freshman team. When the season was over, it was still winter and the weather was freezing cold. Koufax never liked the cold. He heard that the Cincinnati baseball team was planning a trip to New Orleans for a series of games against colleges there. Trying to finagle a free trip to paradise, Koufax approached the baseball coach during a practice held in the gymnasium. He was given a tryout as a pitcher. After warming up, he took the "mound," which was the free throw line with a catcher approximately 60 feet, six inches away. He wore basketball sneakers and had no elevation. Told to air one out, he wound up and delivered a blazing fastball. According to the legend, the impact of the ball caused the catcher to slide backward, the slickness of his sneakers sliding on the wood floor. It was like a scene from the comedy baseball movie *The Scout*, where the superhuman Brendan Fraser delivers a pitch that blows the catcher away as if by hurricane force winds.

Koufax won a spot on the roster and accompanied the team to New Orleans but was wild and ineffective. Nevertheless, word of the speed of his fastball spread like wildfire throughout baseball circles. The Dodgers' scouting staff included the likes of Buzzie Bavasi, Al Campanis, and Fresco Thompson. Here was an 18-year old Jewish kid from Brooklyn reputed to throw 100 miles per hour. He was a basketball star, not a baseball player. His family members were people of education, not sports. It was something out of novel. A legend. His religious background made him especially attractive to the Dodgers, since Brooklyn had the largest Jewish population in America. It made him less attractive to teams like St. Louis and Cincinnati, whose populations were not as enlightened.

The Dodgers figured they had best grab the kid now instead of leaving him available to another club. Koufax realized his financial potential and ran a hard bargain. Brooklyn was "forced" to sign him to a $14,000 bonus. Big league rules of the time required that he had to go straight to the Majors. A "bonus baby" had to be kept on the Major League roster for two years. He could not be sent to the minors. The idea was to prevent wealthy franchises—like the Dodgers and Yankees—from stockpiling talent. It could easily have been the undoing of Koufax. The agreement guaranteed the 19-year-old could return to college, and over the next few years there were many times when that appeared to be his best option.

After years of struggle, in 1961 he finally hit his stride, winning 18 games with a 3.52 ERA, striking out an incredible (and league-leading) 269 hitters with only 96 walks in 255⅔ innings. Again, however, the season ended in disappointment for the team, but the young southpaw finally had arrived.

"He'd throw his fastball that started at the letters, but by the time the batters would swing, the pitch was already out of the strike zone," said pitcher

Stan Williams. His curve dropped from shoulders to knees and was all-but untouchable. They often did not look like strikes but ended up in the strike zone. He learned how to change speeds. Using his natural intelligence, he was mastering the pitching arts.

"He shortened his stride on his front foot," said pitching coach Joe Becker. "That helped his control. Batters used to read his pitches. He showed the ball when he brought it up. Now he hides it and takes his time. . . . He'll be one of the all-time greats."

Entering the 1962 campaign, Koufax was a mature man of 26. His first start came on "Chinatown Night." Reeled in on a rickshaw, Koufax defeated Cincinnati, 6-2, for the club's first-ever win at Dodger Stadium.

Dodger Stadium, set to open in 1962, was built for Koufax and Drysdale, with its distant fences. Expectations for Koufax were sky high. The Dodgers played mostly night games, which worked to the pitcher's advantage. This included Saturday nights, a novelty but very popular as it gave fans a chance to enjoy their day and still make the game. The heavy smog of the era also worked to reduce well-hit balls.

Tommy Davis turned 23 years old during Spring Training in 1962. Like Koufax, he was a Brooklynite, born in the borough in 1939. The Bedford-Stuyvesant neighborhood he was raised in, which housed Ebbets Field, was by the time he reached high school a rugged area, infested with crime and drugs. Church helped keep Davis out of trouble, but he was street smart, too. He gravitated toward sports, starring in baseball and track at Boys High School. The big sport in Brooklyn among black youth, however, was basketball, and it was his first love. The problem was that "I couldn't shoot a lick, I was a garbage man," he said.

Davis was a 6'2", 200-pound right-handed batter with a natural line drive stroke. Before Charlie Lau taught hitters like George Brett to swing down on the ball, Davis was doing just that. His vicious drives reminded old-timers of Napoleon Lajoie, who hit balls that posed danger to pitchers, first basemen, and third basemen in the first decade of the twentieth century.

"Tommy was probably the best pure hitter I ever saw," claimed Dodgers broadcaster Jerry Doggett. In 1962 Davis learned how to hit to right field, but he got off to a slow start. Bavasi used financial incentives to get his charges to improve their production. Bavasi offered him $100 if he tried not to pull everything. Davis's hits to right and right-center would cost the general manager $3,500 ($100 per hit).

Maurice Morning Wills was the epitome of this aggressive style, stealing bases, taking the extra base, forcing errors on pick-off throws and outfielders trying to nab runners stretching out hits. He was, as Cobb had once described himself, a "scientific" player, a "thinking man's" ballplayer. At 5'11" and only 170, the wiry little shortstop needed to develop the skills he had—namely, speed and smarts—instead of focusing on what he did not have—power and a strong throwing arm.

Wills had seemingly come out of nowhere. Four years earlier he was unknown. The son of a Baptist preacher, born in Washington, D.C., in 1932, Wills was one of 13 children who grew up in a rat-infested government housing project. His father also worked as a naval yard machinist. His mother was an elevator operator and domestic. Wills had to care for himself. Constantly worried, he became a bedwetter, a big problem in a house in which children were forced to sleep in the same beds.

Wills was all-city in baseball, basketball, and football his senior year of high school. At the age of 17 he eloped. His new bride, Gertrude was 16. Their first child was born shortly after the marriage.

Nine colleges offered Wills athletic scholarships, including Syracuse and Ohio State, but with a young family he went for pro baseball. He entered as part of the wave of black and Latino players who came after Jackie Robinson, Willie Mays, and Roberto Clemente opened so many doors. Many were called, but few were chosen. He did not impress the people who mattered and spent years toiling in the minor leagues. Even his strengths were seen as weaknesses under the code of 1950s society. A light-skinned black, Wills was extremely smart, too smart for some of his white managers and counterparts, who called him a "clubhouse lawyer."

Wills played minor league ball from 1951 to 1959. It seemed he would never make it. He made no money, lived in squalid conditions, endured the vagaries of the South, and was separated from his family. In 1955 Wills broke the Texas

League color barrier. He ended up in Spokane, the Dodgers' triple-A farm club, and was there so long it became his residence.

Wills became a creditable Major League hitter, but what separated him from the competition was his penchant for stealing bases. He led the National League in that category in 1960 (50) and 1961 (35). From the lead-off position, Wills drew many walks, forced pitchers to throw a lot of pitches and pick-offs, while setting the table for the likes of Tommy Davis hitting behind him.

Alston allowed Wills to run whenever he wanted to. The manager had confidence not only in his star's ability to steal the base, but also in his sense of diamond intelligence. Wills was a field captain who new the game inside and out. His strategic mind was always working.

"I've never seen a better base runner," said Alston. "He knows when to take a chance, how to get a good lead, how to get the jump on the pitcher and how to slide."

Dodger Stadium crowds exhorted him with chants of, "Go, Maury, go!" Vin Scully called him the Roadrunner, after the popular cartoon character. Broadcasts made the "beep-beep" sound from the show whenever he stole a base. Wills stole the show in the All-Star Game, thrilling President Kennedy and Vice President Lyndon Johnson with daring-do on the base paths that fueled the National League's 3-1 victory.

SIX

San Francisco

"And it's bye, bye baby!!"

—*Giants announcer Russ Hodges's standard call of home runs*

In many ways, the story of Alvin Dark is the story of America: a nation's reconciliation, redemption, and new understanding, followed by sociopolitical restructuring. This describes how the American South struggled to find, as Abe Lincoln called them, "the better angels of our nature." In many ways, the South came to grips with new racial realities through sports, then saw the Republican Party husband the region "back into the Union" until it rose again not as a marginalized New Deal voting bloc, but as an economic and political powerhouse.

Al Dark was that walking conundrum of Dixie: a hardcore Baptist Christian burdened by racial prejudice. Through baseball, he was able to get out of the South and become a man of the world. It first led him to New York, where he starred for the 1954 World Champion Giants. There is a great photo of Dark and the black superstar Willie Mays, smiling in each other's company during the team's Broadway ticker tape parade.

The Giants of the early 1960s were one of the first truly integrated teams. Mays, Willie McCovey, Felipe Alou, Juan Marichal, and Orlando Cepeda were black and Latino stars of the first order.

Dark, who lived in Atherton, on the peninsula south of San Francisco, appeared at religious functions. The Holy Bible went everywhere with him and he read it religiously. The Giants were in contrast to the secular nature of The

City. Aside from Dark, the team had a large number of Christian players. The Latinos, in particularly, were strong Catholics. Mays and McCovey, while never known for being outgoing Christians, were from the Bible Belt and could not help but be influenced by their religious upbringing.

Despite his teammate's faith, Dark refused to make the Giants' clubhouse a church. "He had a rule against presenting his Christian testimony to any of the players while in uniform, a rule I was also to abide by," said Felipe Alou. "He told me he felt there was ample time to talk about my beliefs, but that while I was in the clubhouse and on the field I was to be dedicated to winning baseball games."

Dark was particularly careful about talking religion with the San Francisco press corps, which included Jews and Left Coast secularists. In Spring Training he did draw a parable, calling the cut-off play "just like the Bible. You don't question it, you just accept it."

Off the field he neither smoked nor drank. On the field he was aggressive, a gambler who "instilled an aggressiveness in that ballclub," recalled catcher Tom Haller. "He wanted us to play hard. Alvin loved to win, but hated to lose. And he did curse. He'd get hot under the collar and could get quite angry at times."

After screaming profanities to umpire Shag Crawford, he "confessed" to the *San Francisco Examiner* that "the devil was in me," that it was "not a Christian thing to do. Never before have I so addressed any man—and with the Lord's help, I hope to have the strength to never do so again." Dark could be a martinet, lumping the good in with the bad after a tough loss that embittered all.

Dark was born on January 22, 1922, in Commanche, Oklahoma, the son of an oil well engineer. The family moved to Lake Charles, Louisiana, where he grew up in a staunch religious household. Life in the Bayou state of his childhood was heavily Baptist, with strong racist and segregationist overtones. Laws against integration had been on the books since the Civil War era. When Felipe Alou played in Louisiana in 1956, he and a minority teammate were banned from future action by a law forbidding whites and blacks from playing with or against each other.

Dark's religious convictions were the shield against instinctive racism. His years in New York with black and Latino teammates certainly moderated him further. "Since I had been a kid, the ways I have used to express myself have been mostly physical. . . . I was not good at expressing my thoughts verbally or on paper," said Dark.

Dark was not alone in his interpretation of the Southern white's dynamic with African Americans. "I felt that because I was from the South—and we from the South actually take care of colored people, I think, better than they're taken care of in the North—I felt when I was playing with them it was a responsibility for me," he was quoted as saying in Jackie Robinson's 1964 book *Baseball Has Done It*. "I liked the idea that I was pushed to take care of them and make them feel at home and to help them out any way possible that I could playing baseball the way that you can win pennants."

Dark played football and baseball, but his love was baseball. At age 10 he played against 19-year-olds. He was all-state in football, captain of the basketball team. LSU beat out Texas A&M for his services. He played football and baseball for the Tigers. In 1942, his sophomore year, Dark was the running back along with Steve Van Buren, later a Hall of Famer with the Philadelphia Eagles.

Dark was in the Marines during World War II and was assigned to officer candidate school at Southwestern Louisiana State, where he earned football All-American honors. He played halfback on an overseas team in 1945 before going to China. Sports kept him out of major combat, as it did for numerous college and pro athletes. Despite being drafted by the NFL and the All-American Football Conference, Dark went for the Boston Braves, breaking into the big leagues in 1946. He played all of 1947 at triple-A, then at age 26 helped lead the Braves to the 1948 World Series.

The Braves' middle infield of Dark and Eddie Stanky was distinctively Southern. Stanky taught the youngster the intricacies of the game. Dark's .322 average earned him Rookie of the Year honors over Philadelphia's Richie Ashburn. In 1949 Dark and the Braves tanked. Manager Billy Southworth lost his son in an airplane crash in 1945 and thereafter drank heavily. Dark learned from South-worth things *not* to do. He and Stanky were too opinionated for the Braves, and both were traded to the New York Giants.

Leo Durocher loved Dark's fiery ways. When Dark turned down $500 to make a smoking commercial, Durocher paid him the money and made him captain. He thought of Dark as a player-coach, a manager on the field.

Over the years, Dark played for Gene Mauch, Charley Dressen, and Fred Hutchinson, all respected baseball minds. "You get the chance to learn managing from a Durocher or a Mauch—that's a pretty good education," he said.

Dark helped New York win two pennants and the 1954 World Series before he was traded to St. Louis. He later played for the Cubs, Phillies, and Braves. Whenever a new man joined teams Dark played for, the infielder would take him out to dinner, which was "something as a player that only one other man in baseball did to my knowledge," said ex-teammate Lee Walls, who played for the Dodgers in 1962.

In 14 years he had more than 2,000 hits and batted .289. In late 1960 Milwaukee traded him to San Francisco for shortstop Andre Rogers, and he took over as the team's manager in 1961.

"I never thought I'd say this about anybody," Willie Mays told writer Charles Einstein a few years later, "but I actually think more of 'Cap' [Dark] than I did of Leo. You know what he did when they made him manager? He sent me a letter, telling me how glad he was we were going to be back together again. How can you not want to play for a guy like that?"

Dark's hiring both fell in line with but deviated from owner Horace Stoneham's normal methods. On the one hand, the Stoneham family had hired former Giants players in the past—Bill Terry, Mel Ott, and Bill Rigney. They liked loyalty and tradition. There was a feeling that to be a Giant was something bigger than to be a Philly or a Red. But Stoneham also liked hail-fellow-well-met types with whom he could share a cocktail and camaraderie. Leo Durocher had not played for the Giants but was certainly not averse to drinking. Neither was the Irishman Tom Sheehan.

"Normally, Horace insists that his managers drink with him," recalled Bill Veeck. "It goes with the job. When he drinks, everybody drinks. Especially if he is paying their salaries."

Dark, 39, did not drink. He was loyal to Stoneham and would perform his job 100 percent, but he would not drink. Stoneham understood and did not press the subject. Dark's coaching staff, hired in 1961, came straight out of the great 1951 pennant winners: Larry Jansen (40), Whitey Lockman (34), and Wes Westrum (38). The coaches as well as Dark were all active players in 1960.

"He had a lot faith in our judgment," said Jansen. "Wes was a solid defensive catcher and a great guy. Lockman really knew how to deal with people, and I guess Alvin thought I knew enough about pitching to help him."

"I know what each of us can do," Dark told the media. "When I assign them their work at Spring Training, I can relax. I know the job is getting done because they know what I want done. And they do it."

Dark's temper was difficult for him to control in those days. "We were playing the Phillies and lost three straight games by one run," Dark recalled. "We had our opportunities, but couldn't score. After one of those ballgames I heard some guys at the other end of the clubhouse laughing. What they were laughing about, I don't know. It was probably something I should have found out before I got so mad. But it hit me all at once. How could anybody laugh in a situation like this?"

Dark picked up a stool and threw it with full force against a door. His finger had lodged into the chair, and he lost the tip of his little finger. On another occasion Dark turned over the food trays in Houston, ruining one of Willie McCovey's cherished suits. Willie Mac was a clotheshorse. Dark provided the first baseman with a check the next day to pay for a new outfit.

Dark had not been away from the playing field long enough to gain the proper perspective for managing. He wanted his players to play as he had and was upset at the "new breed" of athlete that was starting to emerge in the 1960s. It was not just a matter of race, although the game was rapidly changing its complexion, but the modern player was different, less intense, more worldly.

Great managers and coaches have always been identified as those who could change with the times. That was the key to John Wooden's success at UCLA, and Bear Bryant's at Alabama. Dark was old school. *San Francisco Chronicle* columnist Charles McCabe said that Dark's attitude was a "very dangerous thing," that the manager felt that he needed to "win every game himself."

Dark stood in the dugout "like Washington crossing the Delaware," one writer quipped. He did not have time for jokes or tobacco jawing, saying that he had seen too many managers let the games pass them by. He had no use for individual achievements, even though his team had some of the greatest individual stars in baseball. It was a challenge for him.

Dark immediately noticed at his first Spring Training that the team was divided between whites, blacks, and Latinos. He had equipment manager Eddie

Logan mix the cubicles so that blacks would be next to whites, Latinos next to blacks, and the like. "It went over like a lead balloon," Dark admitted.

Dark also had a sign posted in the clubhouse that read, "Speak English, You're in America." Dark had a meeting of the Latinos and said the others complained that they jabbered in Spanish. There were worries that they were telling jokes or hatching plots behind teammates' backs. But Orlando Cepeda called Dark's complaints "an insult to our language," and the Latinos kept talking in their native tongue.

Felipe Alou understood what Dark was trying to do—assimilate these players into the culture, into their new country, and with their teammates—but said it was forced. "Can you imagine talking to your own brothers in a foreign language?" he said, and he should know; his brothers Matteo and Jesus were also in the Giants' organization. Besides, many of the Latinos spoke poor English, so it was hard for them.

Dark, however, was not rigid. When he imposed an edict that did not work, he realized it and stopped the practice, as he did with the cubicle assignments and the English-only rules.

"My intentions were good but the results were bad, so I stopped it," he said.

Unlike Walt Alston, Dark was not a "by the book" manager, said pitcher Billy O'Dell. He thought out every move and had reasons for each. He liked using defensive replacements and went to his bullpen early by the standards of the day. He juggled his batting order, tried to apply defensive strategy based on his interpretation of the shifting Candlestick winds, and warmed up relievers just to bluff opponents.

"Alvin overmanaged, but even he admitted that," said writer Charles Einstein. The writers called him the "mad scientist." He had fake pick-off plays and other gadget maneuvers.

"I don't think I ever managed thinking some move was the 'safe' thing to do," said Dark. He said he wanted to "have some fun. But you only have fun when you win."

Dark was competitive at everything, including gin rummy (which he was taught by Leo Durocher, a master) and golf. He beat his players on the greens and used that to extract a psychological advantage.

Dark could play "little ball" even with the slugging Giants and had a grading system that awarded points to players whose obvious statistics were not comparable to a Mays, McCovey, or Cepeda. If a player moved a runner along 30 or 40 times in a season, Dark kept a record of it, and the players were able to use that in contract negotiations.

When Dark told the writers that third baseman Jim Davenport's plus/minus record was excellent, but that Cepeda's was "terribly minus," he asked that it not be printed in the headlines. The papers ran it anyway. *Look* magazine printed Cepeda's so-called minus-40 rating, and the sensitive first baseman sued for defamation of character. He lost.

In March 1962 the conflict between Cepeda and Dark took a turn for the worse when, after a brilliant 1961 campaign, Orlando held out of Spring Training for $60,000.

Dark's biggest concern entering Spring Training was the age of his pitching staff. Sam Jones and Billy Loes, both effective pitchers in the 1950s, had nothing left. Dark was relying on 32-year-old Don Larsen and 35-year-old Billy Pierce. Larsen was a hard drinker whose lifestyle made him a decade older. Pierce had been an outstanding pitcher with the Chicago White Sox, but in the Cactus League he was terrible. His spring ERA hovered around 16.00. He gave up numerous home runs.

Billy O'Dell held out, and Jack Sanford was an unknown quantity: maybe excellent, maybe a bust. Stu Miller was the bullpen ace. A host of untested young pitchers included Jim Duffalo, Bob Bolin, and Gaylord Perry. Mike McCormick, at 23, offered huge potential but was always seemingly troubled with arm injuries. Juan Marichal was worried sick about his girlfriend, Alma. Dominican dictator Rafael Trujillo had been assassinated, and violent extremists threatened to throw a bomb through the window of her family's home.

Marichal requested a leave so he could go to the Dominican Republican, marry Alma, and bring her to America. Dark did not hesitate. "He was terribly unhappy and needed to get that gal up here," he recalled.

Marichal was deeply grateful and wanted to do something for Dark. He asked Willie Mays for advice. "Win," said Mays.

Dark certainly could count on Mays to provide veteran leadership, hustle, and his usual brilliance. Ed Bailey was a veteran catcher. Tom Haller was a youngster. At 32, Harvey Kuenn could still hit. Jose Pagan would provide good defense. Jim Davenport was solid at third base. Chuck "Iron Hands" Hiller was the second baseman. Dark decided to make him a project in Spring Training, to improve him defensively.

"That showed me that Dark could be a teacher, and he made Hiller into a second baseman," said *San Francisco Examiner* sportswriter Harry Jupiter.

First base was a festering controversy, albeit an embarrassment of riches: Orlando Cepeda and Willie McCovey. After Cepeda finally signed, Dark needed to find a place for Willie Mac. Left field was the only solution, but his outfield was also full: Kuenn, the Alou brothers, and of course Mays in center.

Team trainer Frank "Doc" Bowman posted a sign on the clubhouse wall in Phoenix: "Work hard this year—and eat corn on the cob all winter." It did not make a lot of sense but its meaning was clear. They had potential, and if they made the most of it, a championship was theirs for the taking.

Felipe Alou, 27, averaged .274 in four previous seasons. When he was out with a sore elbow, the club lost six of eight. When he returned the team won eight straight. In June Alou was hitting .345, one point from the National League lead. "I just am hitting better through the middle than I ever did," he said. "I have no worry about whether I hit .170 or .300. I have great confidence since Al Dark play me regular. Don't worry. I just swing."

Batting fifth instead of first as in 1961, the 6'0", 195-pounder said, "This year I like where I am batting. I am too big for a leadoff man. I cannot try to get walks. I am a swinger, not a waiter."

Alou embarked on consecutive-game hitting streaks of 11, 10, 9, and 8 games in 1962. He was also very mature and a solid influence on moody fellow Latinos Cepeda and Marichal, as well as a pathfinder for younger brothers Matty and Jesus.

"Felipe was a very classy person, and a good team ballplayer," said Billy Pierce. "He led a great life and carried himself well. He would try to work with the guys. If some of the Latin fellows got a little excited, he would be the man to calm them down. I don't know if Felipe would ever swear about anything."

Alou carried his Bible with him at all times, and this helped him form a bond with Dark. He also spoke up to writers and was no "shrinking violet," according to writer David Plaut. When Dark kicked over the food table, Alou picked the food off the floor and ate it while staring at Dark. The message was clear: food was a gift from God. Born into poverty, Alou never wasted it.

Alou was born in the fishing village of Haina, Dominican Republic, in 1935, the eldest of four sons. His father, Rojas, was a blacksmith and, like Jesus of Nazareth, a carpenter. He made hand-carved bats for his sons, who practiced by hitting lemons.

In high school Felipe was a track star but played baseball in the summer leagues. At 16 he worked in a concrete mix facility and became a legend when he wrestled sharks with his bare hands. His grades were excellent, and he attended the University of Santo Domingo to study medicine. He played on the baseball team, coached by a Giants bird dog named Horacio Martinez. Alou's father lost his job, and Felipe quit school to support his family. He signed a $200 bonus for the Giants and went to Lake Charles, Louisiana, of the Evangeline League.

He was barred from the Louisiana League by his color and sent to Cocoa Beach, where he led the Florida State League at .308. He impressed the Americans by learning English and in 1958 made it to San Francisco. In 1961 he became a starter, even though pitchers could get him out on the outside corner.

He arrived at Spring Training in 1962 and closed up his stance. It paid off immediately. He hit .500 in the Cactus League and stayed hot in regular season play. He was moved from lead-off to fifth and displayed power. Alou went on a 12-game tear. His homer in Cincinnati shattered the letters on an advertisement atop the Crosley Field scoreboard.

He killed the Dodgers in an April series, prompting a Dodger fan to send a telegram to San Francisco: "Roses are red, violets are blue . . . we'll give our team for Felipe Alou."

He continued hitting well in the first half and made the All-Star Game. He had nine straight hits at one point.

For all of Alou's on-field exploits, however, his greatest contribution to baseball might have been when he saved Juan Marichal from drowning off the coast of Haina.

Jim Davenport made the National League All-Star team in 1962. He finally came into his own after years of injuries. He already was generally viewed as the best-fielding third sacker in the senior circuit. If he could stay healthy, he was destined for greatness. The press dubbed him "a man for all lesions."

His injuries were an anomaly, since he had been a college safety at Southern Mississippi without any health problems. Alabama originally recruited him, but 'Bama had a rule against married players. Since Davenport was wed, the scholarship was rescinded, and he ended up at Southern Miss instead. In his sophomore and junior years he led his team to upsets over the Crimson Tide. The losing quarterback both times was Bart Starr.

Davenport was an original 1958 Giant but suffered rib and ankle injuries. In 1959 it was an eye infection. On his 26th birthday he tore his knee up in a collision with then–Reds catcher Ed Bailey. Larry Jackson's pitch cracked his collar bone. Bleeding ulcers landed him in a Milwaukee hospital. He hurt his groin. His injuries made it tough to run and train properly. The lack of conditioning affected his stamina. The writers speculated that the missing ingredient between 1958 and 1961 was Davenport. Despite his injuries, he led the league in fielding percentage three years in a row.

"Here was a guy who was so quiet, and he never sought out publicity, but he is still the best fielding third baseman I ever saw," said Bob Stevens, a legendary baseball writer for the *San Francisco Chronicle* who eventually had the press box at Candelstick park named after him.

Second baseman Chuck Hiller, on the other hand, was a defensive liability who would lead the National League in errors in 1962.

"One time in Cincinnati, we went to see the very first James Bond movie," recalled Tom Haller. "At the end of the picture, it was discovered that the bad guy, Dr. No, had no iron hands. So poor Charlie got nailed with 'Dr. No' for awhile." That was interchanged with "Iron Hands."

Hiller had actually led two minor leagues in fielding after being signed by the same Cleveland scout who had inked Bob Feller. The Giants picked him up in 1959, and he hit over .300. Hiller was a talker who Cepeda called "Abner," as in Doubleday, because "he talked like he invented the game."

But Hiller began to press, and the more he pressed the more it affected his play at the plate and in the field. After spending 1961 at triple-A, Hiller was told by Dark he was the starter in 1962. Hiller spent the spring fretting over whether he would blow the opportunity, but when the season started and he was the starter, he was his old "Abner" self again. His fielding, despite the errors, was adequate, and he was adept at turning double plays. None of the Giants pitchers was a strikeout artist—certainly not comparable to Sandy Koufax and Don Drysdale—so they needed those twin killings.

Hiller's partner was Jose Pagan, who "has been making me look good on double plays," said Hiller in 1962. "When [he] gained confidence in me, we started to function as a combination. We're at ease with each other now."

Pagan was probably the least-publicized player on the team. He was a Latino on a team of high-profile, high-temper Latinos, but he remained quiet and reserved. "With big stars like Mays, Marichal and so many others, it's too bad Jose never really got the recognition he deserved," said Cepeda. "He was there every day, made all the plays and he could hit."

"You didn't have to worry about Pagan at all," said Billy O'Dell. "He was in the right place all the time. Some of the other guys, you might have wanted to move them a little bit, but not Jose."

Pedro Zorilla, credited with the Cepeda signing, had signed Pagan. He played five years of minor league ball and stuck in 1961, when he beat out Ed Bressoud for the job. Teammates called him "Humphrey," as in Bogart, because of his nonplussed facial expressions, which the actor effected on-screen.

When the club had a scare flying to Chicago in 1962, the cabin went silent until Pagan broke the quiet with a blessed joke: "I say we should take a vote. I'm for taking the bus." The remark eased the tension.

Pagan hit eighth but drove in a lot of clutch runs. His fielding percentage in 1962 led the National League.

Harvey Kuenn was a former American League batting champion. He had hit .300 in eight of the previous nine seasons. Kuenn graduated from the University of Wisconsin in 1952 and announced that he was accepting bids for his services, which came in. Detroit won the "bidding war," signing him to a $55,000 package.

After 63 minor league games the shortstop was brought up in September 1952. In 1953 he was named Rookie of the Year. The 21-year-old picked up the tab for a lavish team party at his hotel. He was barely old enough to consume the alcohol that flowed, and in some ways Kuenn was the first of the "new breed," college-educated, rich, and savvy.

He hit .300 every year, switched to the outfield, and was a perennial All-Star. On a team that included Al Kaline, he was the captain. His .353 batting average in 1959 won the batting title.

In 1960 a controversial trade sent Kuenn to Detroit for Rocky Colavito. Kuenn was booed, but he batted .308 and was the player representative. Cleveland fell below .500 after years of success and general manager Frank Lane traded him to San Francisco for Willie Kirkland and Johnny Antonelli. Harvey chewed Red Man on the field and smoked big cigars off it. *Sports Illustrated* did a piece on him. Writer Tex Maule said he kept the team loose, entertained, and united.

"I don't think there was anyone on the club who enjoyed life or playing in the big leagues more than Harvey," said Billy Pierce.

One day Mays arrived to find a gift-wrapped package in his locker. The box of candy was opened to reveal two dozen decoratively wrapped pieces of horse manure.

"I know you done it," giggled Mays at the laughing Kuenn. "I know you done it."

At midseason Kuenn's dad died, and the teammates rallied around their friend.

"He taught the younger players about hitting, volunteering his own time which was something Mays didn't do," said Bob Stevens. "He also became very close to Stoneham. He loved drinking margaritas with Horace during Spring Training."

Charles Einstein noted that Kuenn was effective "drunk or sober."

Matty Alou, the younger brother of Felipe Alou (and older brother of Jesus Alou) was born on December 22, 1938, in Haina, Dominican Republic. At 5'9" and 155 pounds he was much smaller than his powerful brother. He grew up with Juan Marichal and was part of the wholesale exportation of Dominican baseball talent to the United States that has become more than a cottage industry.

Matty played four Major League games in 1960 and 81 in 1961. He was a decent outfielder who threw and batted left-handed.

Carl Boles's only year in Major League baseball was 1962. He was called up from El Paso in midsummer. He would play the rest of his career in Japan. He had one distinctive trait, one reason for being memorable: he was a dead ringer for Willie Mays.

"It was really noticeable when we made a trip back to the Polo Grounds," said Boles. "Willie would get these huge ovations there. That night I came out through the center field bleachers before he did and the crowd thought I was Mays."

The Mets' fans gave him a standing ovation, until they noticed that his number was 14, not Mays's 24. Then they booed him. After games, fans wanting mays's autograph would mob Boles. Sometimes he would sign Mays's name as a joke. He got excellent service at restaurants and roomed with Willie McCovey, which further made people think he was Mays, since the two Willies from Alabama were linked.

Catcher Ed Bailey, 31, loved to talk about women, which is the favorite subject of most athletes anyway. His spicy descriptions of girls, alcohol, and his golf game earned him the nickname "Words" and "Mr. Clean."

"He loved to give guys the hot foot," said McCormick. Wes Westrum was his favorite target because he fell asleep on the team bus.

Hailing from Strawberry Plains, Tennessee, Bailey broke into the bigs in 1953 and developed into a three-time All-Star catcher. In 1961 he was traded to San Francisco to make room for Johnny Edwards in Cincinnati. The Reds won the title but Bailey was still happy to be in San Francisco. Cow-milking contests were occasionally held in big league stadiums, and the country boy Bailey usually won.

Just as Bailey had been traded to make room for catcher Edwards, he discovered a young catching sensation on his new team. Tom Haller, 24, had been a quarterback at the University of Illinois. Born on June 23, 1937, in Lockport, Illinois, he was the prototypical athlete/catcher. Haller was boyishly handsome, the All-American type, possessing great leadership skills, a first-rate throwing arm, and a powerful left-handed bat. He was 6'4", 195 pounds, and had been called up to play 30 games in 1961. He was the Giants' future behind the dish. Bailey was there in case he was not ready, but Haller was ready in '62.

"Alvin told us we were both going to play, but it's only natural for them to want to go with the youngest guy they've got and look to the future," recalled Bailey. "And Dark liked having me available to come off the bench."

Bailey was involved in several "pier six brawls" in his career. In 1962 he followed Cepeda after a homer, and Pittsburgh's Bob Friend went after him.

Catcher Don Leppert tackled Bailey. He and Friend exchanged shouts while being restrained. Then Bailey hit a 400-foot home run, giving rookie Gaylord Perry an 8-3 win, the first of his career. It started a 10-game winning streak.

Bailey and Haller provided 35 homers and 100 RBIs out of the catching position.

Billy O'Dell liked Bailey so much that the two operated without signals. Theirs was almost a telepathic relationship.

O'Dell was from Newberry, South Carolina; like Bailey, south of the Mason-Dixon Line. Baltimore signed him out of Clemson. Given the name "Digger" after the main character in *Life of Riley*, he never pitched in the minors.

He gained needed weight in the military and in 1957 made the bigs for good. He was an All-Star in 1958. Pitching for Baltimore in front of the Orioles' fans, he threw three scoreless innings in a 4-3 American League win but hurt his back the next year. O'Dell's back injury plagued him, and eventually he and Billy Loes were traded to San Francisco.

At first he and Dark feuded over how he was used. He was fined, and they had shouting matches. Dark wanted to put him in the 1961 expansion draft, but Stoneham insisted he be kept.

In 1962 Spring Training Dark told him he was the fourth starter "until you show me you can't do it." After an awesome spring he started game two of the regular season, beating the Braves with a four-hitter. The key was his relationship with Bailey. He was effective and consistent all season.

"He never really got credit for being a good catcher, but I thought he was a great receiver," said O'Dell.

Billy O'Dell's catcher was Ed Bailey. Jack Sanford's guy was Tom Haller. Sanford was 33 years old and won 16 games in a row in 1962, his best year in the big leagues by far. The 6'0", 196-pound right-handed pitcher from Wellesley, Massachusetts, had been the 1957 Rookie of the Year with the Phillies before a 1958 trade to the Giants.

"Jack wasn't the easiest guy to know," said Haller. Sanford was from the "wrong side of the tracks" in a rough Boston neighborhood. Like many Boston Irishmen, it seemed, he had to "battle for everything in his life."

He was not a prospect in high school, which in cold Massachusetts was not much anyway. The Red Sox rejected him in a tryout, but Philadelphia took a shot at Sanford. He spent eight years in the minors and even drove the team bus. He was the hardest thrower in the Philadelphia organization but could not control his emotions. He almost punched a club official when told he was being sent to the minors. When traveling secretary Johnny Wise told him he was being sent down on another occasion, Sanford tried to plead his case, but Wise just told him he had a bad attitude. Then the Army drafted him. He hurt his arm pitching in an Army game and developed a clot in his pitching hand after a fight. The Army wanted to operate and cut into his clavicle, which would have ended his pitching career. He got up and left.

Out of the service he came back, and in 1957, at 28, Sanford won Rookie of the Year honors with 19 wins and a 3.08 earned run average. But he had worn out his welcome in Philly and was traded to the Giants, where he was 40-35 over the next three years.

He was surly on game days, and his family avoided him. He maintained silence all through the pre game routine. He was a loner anyway. The clot made it hard for him to complete games, and he was called a "composer of unfinished symphonies." The weather at Candlestick did not benefit him, and he was known as a "six inning pitcher," a bone of contention during contract negotiations.

In Spring Training of 1962 Dark told the hard thrower to worry less about strikeouts. This and Haller's influence helped him reduce his pitch counts, maintain stamina, and pitch longer into games. He went less for the big strike and more for ground ball outs on the corners. He became one of the best pitchers in baseball, compiling his 16-game streak between June and September. He refused to celebrate it, however, calling it a "fluke." Rube Marquard of the Giants had won the all-time record of 19 straight, but Sanford just said it was "ridiculous" and that the record meant nothing to him. It was his nature to be surly.

Billy Pierce was already a veteran star pitcher by 1962.

"If he didn't win, it didn't quite cut him as bad as it did people like Sanford," said O'Dell. Perhaps that was because Pierce had never made a practice of losing much—not in Chicago, certainly not with the Giants, and not once at Candlestick Park in 1962. Twice a 20-game winner with the White Sox, he was a seven-time All-Star and helped the Chisox to the 1959 American League crown, only the second time since 1948 a team other than the Yankees won the flag. He lost a perfect game with two outs in the ninth inning against Washington in 1958.

The White Sox decided that at 35 his best years were behind him, and he found himself San Francisco–bound. Pierce wanted number 19, Dark's number. Dark said fine. In Spring Training, Pierce was awful, and the Giants had second thoughts. When the regular season started, however, Pierce won his first eight decisions.

Pitching coach Larry Jansen was convinced that the cool Candlestick weather was the key to Pierce's success. Chicago was brutally hot in the summer and could wear a pitcher out. Dark used Pierce as Casey Stengel used Whitey Ford, holding him out for homestands.

"And the results were about as good as I could expect because I won 13 in a row at home," said Pierce.

He missed a month of the season with a spike wound, but that made him fresh late in the year.

The player who came over in trade with Pierce was Don Larsen. He is a legend in New York because he pitched the only perfect game in World Series history, but the native of Point Loma, California, near San Diego, was a legendary drinker. His buddies were Billy Martin, Mickey Mantle, and Whitey Ford, major drinkers all. They called him "Goony Bird."

Mike McCormick said drinking was more common in baseball then compared to today, but said, "even I marveled at how much [Larsen] could consume."

After the perfect game, great things were expected of Larsen, but he never found his form in New York. He was traded to Kansas City then went to the minors. In 1961 Larsen was 7-2 at Chicago, giving life to his career. When the Pierce trade was negotiated, San Francisco insisted on Larsen's inclusion. He pitched effectively in 1962. Against Pittsburgh, Larsen came in with the bases loaded and none out, striking out the side on nine pitches. Larsen enjoyed frog hunting in the Sacramento Delta and cooked the delicacies.

Stu Miller never threw more than 85 miles per hour, but his junk was effective as a closer.

"Stu had the best off-speed pitch of anybody in the history of baseball," said Ron Fairly of Los Angeles.

Choo Choo Coleman went from the Phillies to the Mets in 1962. He said when he swung at a Miller pitch "the ball was THERE! I swung where it was. How could I miss it?"

They called Miller "the Killer Moth" because his pitches resembled the insect. Dark had felt in 1961 that the staff relied on Miller too much and forced pitchers to go the distance instead of bowing out in favor of the reliever.

Miller loved crossword puzzles. he and Mike McCormick, a native of Los Angeles with great promise, were the only former New York Giants on the staff. Bob Bolin was "the hardest thrower on the staff," according to Bailey. Gaylord Perry was a rookie from North Carolina. At 6'4", 205 pounds he was the younger brother of Jim Perry, who was a star pitcher for Cleveland.

Bob Garibaldi was a huge prospect from Stockton who had starred at the nearby University of Santa Clara, where he pitched the Broncos into the College World Series and earned Most Outstanding Player honors. At the time of his signing, he was considered "can't miss."

When the 1962 baseball season began, Willie Howard Mays had a chip on his shoulder. He had something to prove. The fact that he had something to prove was the reason he had a chip on his shoulder.

In 1951 New York manager Leo Durocher took Mays under his wing. He started 0-for-12 and begged "Mista Leo" to send him back to Minneapolis because he could not handle big league pitching. Durocher told him was the Giants' starting center field no matter what he hit, or did not hit. Mays broke his slump with a homer off of no less a star pitcher than Warren Spahn, whom he owned for all their parallel careers. The numbers for 1951 are relatively pedestrian: 20 homers, 68 RBIs, and a .274 average, but Mays's arrival in New York jumpstarted a moribund team that made the mother of all comebacks to win the National League pennant. When Bobby Thomson hit the "shot heard round the world," Mays was nervously waiting on deck. The press was agog over the feature story of the World Series; the rookie center fielders Mantle and Mays taking the spotlight from the retiring DiMaggio.

In 1954 Mays was the league MVP. In the World Series win over Cleveland he was credited with The Catch and The Throw. Not only did the Giants beat Cleveland, they beat them in four straight. It was nuts. Between 1955 and 1960 Mays led the league in stolen bases every year. While Mantle could have done it had his team and his body let him, Mays *actually* did it. He also led the league in triples three of four years from 1954 to 1956, including the 1955 campaign when he hit 51 homers, drove in 127, and batted .319, an even better year than his MVP-winning 1954 campaign.

Mays had home run power combined with the excitement of triples, hard-charging doubles, league-leading slugging percentages, and a consistently high batting average (.345 in 1954, .333 in 1957, .347 in 1958). He beat out infield hits, stole bases, took extra bases, and scored runs as if he were a leadoff man. He played baseball with an infectious "Say Hey," cap-flying enthusiasm that has never been equaled.

Then, the Giants moved to San Francisco, and it all changed. Not statistically. Not on the field, although adjustments had to be made. Mays continued to be a marvel, but The City did not take to him. In New York, Mays was a kid who played stickball in the Harlem neighborhood he lived in. The pictures of the nattily attired Mays playing with local black kids is richly nostalgic. By 1962 he was a superstar and a Hall of Famer, but he was in debt, dealing with a divorce, and not particularly happy with the way the San Francisco fans treated him. He was bound and determined to change things in '62

Orlando Cepeda and Alvin Dark feuded. It reached a simmer on August 19, 1962. After splitting the first two of a four-game series, the players woke up on Sunday morning at the Pfister Hotel in Milwaukee. The club had a double-header against the Braves. At 10:30 the team bus rolled up for an 11:15 departure. Cepeda was in the bus by 11. However, some of Cepeda's friends appeared. They were a Puerto Rican family who lived in Minneapolis. They knew him from his minor league days there. Cepeda had been very close to them. Cepeda was told they were in the lobby, so he went to look for them. When they found each other, Cepeda and the family meandered out toward the bus. The daughter of the family had a very light complexion. When they said good-bye to each other, Cepeda kissed the daughter. Dark saw it and flipped out, apparently disturbed that the Puerto

Rican player was kissing a "white girl" right in front of him. He ordered the bus to go. There are varying reports on what happened. According to one, Cepeda was forced to take a cab to County Stadium.

However, Mays told the bus driver to stop, and according to an alternative report, Cepeda was allowed to board. Dark says it never happened. Either way, that afternoon a rift occurred between player and manager. McCovey started, and Cepeda was scratched. Cepeda felt it was because of the hotel incident, but Dark later claimed it was because his legs were sore. A 1961 collision with John Roseboro of Los Angeles had reinjured the knee Cepeda hurt at age 15.

"My knees were in bad shape so many times, but I didn't tell anybody, and [Dark] jumped on me for not playing hard," said Cepeda. "He thought I was faking. I was afraid to say I was hurt. They always say I did not want to play, so I was afraid."

Dark never mentioned the knee to the writers that day. With Milwaukee leading 10-6, Dark passed over Cepeda in a pinch-hitting capacity. A double play killed the rally, but Dark called on Cepeda in the ninth inning with the game lost. Cepeda was peeved. He hit a grounder to second, threw the bat away, and walked off the field. Dark went ape and fined him.

Cepeda called the manager a "son of a bitch." Dark ignored the preacher's advice about backing men into corners. "I treated him very badly that day," he admitted. Dark eventually said he did not know about Cepeda's knee and later apologized. The next day Cepeda belted two home runs. He went on a hitting streak, slamming nine hits, four home runs, and eight RBIs in a three-game set with Philadelphia. Dark went out of his way to praise him.

The San Francisco press psychoanalyzed Cepeda, mainly favorably. The general consensus was that he was a huge talent with a bruised ego, and that the Latin players needed special handling. In that respect, it was a condescending view.

Cepeda's numbers dropped off from his 1961 season. Stoneham made a big point of talking about his salary. He was paid $47,000 but had asked for $60,000. The owner made it clear he had not earned what he received.

"If a guy hits .300 and knocks in a hundred, how can he be hurting the ballclub?" asked Mays in his defense.

"I think Orlando had more problems with [management] than the rest of us because he was more vocal," said Felipe Alou. "He was a better player and kind of the leader of the Latins, so the confrontation was there."

Art Rosenbaum of the *San Francisco Chronicle* speculated that Cepeda could be the Stan Musial of the Latino players. By 1962 Cepeda was a superhero in Puerto Rico. Despite the vagaries of a long Major League season, it was demanded of him that he play a full Winter League schedule, which he did. Cepeda arrived at Spring Training in 1962 haggard, mentally and physically. He had had no off-season and was tired. His problems with Dark, who criticized him for not taking time off, and his public commentary, led to his being booed for the first time by San Francisco fans.

Born on January 10, 1938, Willie McCovey grew up to be tall and powerful. At 6'4", 225 pounds he was known as "Stretch." Today, many big men play baseball at all positions. In McCovey's day a man of his gargantuan proportions was seen exclusively as a first sacker. At first, people thought McCovey was clumsy. He was criticized as a "bull in a China shop," a buffoon of sorts, and to add racial insult to injury, he was called a baboon because of his long face and ultrablack skin.

In 1959 he could not be denied. Sent back to triple-A Phoenix, McCovey, instead of sulking, put on a legendary hitting display that may have overshadowed the one Mays demonstrated at Minneapolis in 1951. In 95 games, McCovey hit 29 home runs, drove in 92 runs, and batted .372. He also had 26 doubles and 11 triples. Rigney and the club's development people could no longer keep him away from Seals Stadium. His abbreviated homer and RBI numbers would hold up as Pacific Coast League–leading totals.

At San Francisco, McCovey broke in with one of the all-time greatest starts in baseball history, slamming 13 homers with a .354 average in 52 games down the stretch. The Giants appeared to be headed to the World Series but inexplicably faded when the hated—and seemingly less talented—captured the flag instead.

McCovey and Cepeda were in a battle for the first base position. The "consolation prize" was left field. McCovey, like Cepeda, was very comfortable in San Francisco. While Mays dealt with a troubled marriage, Cepeda and

McCovey were swinging bachelors. McCovey enjoyed the club scene, the myriad jazz places dotting The City. Pretty black girls—not to mention other kinds of girls—made themselves available to him. He was loving life. It was certainly a long way from Mobile, Alabama. He was happy and popular, made easy friendships, and developed what would be a lifelong love affair with San Francisco.

As a young boy growing up in the Dominican Republic, Juan Marichal helped work the plantations. The tradition was for families to take turns working the various neighboring farms. The children were always fed first. They were also allowed to swim in the irrigation ditches for recreation. One day, after loading up on rice, Marichal went for a swim. He woke up six days later. He had gone into a coma. The doctor told his mother on the sixth day that if he did not wake up by 12.

In September 1957 Marichal signed with the Giants for $500. He was assigned to the Escogido club of the Dominican Winter League, which had an arrangement with the Giants. Before that, the U.S. Air Force tried to convince Marichal to pitch against a group of American barnstormers led by Willie Mays. Because of his contractual commitment to the Giants he was unable to pitch against the American club. Told that it would be his only chance to meet Mays, Marichal expressed confidence that "maybe I will get to meet him later."

In 1960 Marichal was elevated to triple-A Tacoma of the PCL, where he was 11-5 when, at mid-season and 21 years of age, he was elevated to the Major Leagues.

The only big league baseball he had ever seen "was on television, mainly the Cub games when I was playing with Michigan City," he recalled. He immediately felt right at home on a club that included childhood pal Felipe Alou, Cepeda from Puerto Rico, and within a year Felipe's brother Matty, Jose Pagan, and Manny Mota. Felipe Alou lived next door to "a wonderful grandmotherly woman named Mrs. Blanche Johnson, and she and her husband took me in as a boarder," Marichal recounted.

Marichal fell in love with San Francisco, and the town in turn loved him back. He quickly became Americanized, savoring barbecued foods and other treats of his new culture while staying in touch with his roots. Scouting director Carl Hubbell issued a standing order: "Leave him alone." Marichal was that rarest of pitchers, a fully formed package, a pure natural. He was born to pitch. There was virtually no learning curve. He instinctively knew what to do, even when pitching against the best Major League hitters.

Marichal was 13-10 in 1961, but San Francisco again fell short in the standings, finishing third behind Cincinnati and Los Angeles. He was an established big leaguer, tested in two pennant races and well versed already in the Giants-Dodgers rivalry, which at this time was being played out in the new Candlestick and the old L.A. Coliseum with the same intensity as in New York.

SEVEN

Death Struggle

"Man, that's what we're playing the season to find out."
—*Willie Mays, when asked who would win the 1962 pennant*

When Spring Training broke up, the Dodgers boarded their team plane for the flight west. They stopped for exhibitions in Las Vegas and San Diego. On April Fool's Day in Los Angeles, the annual Baseball Writers' Banquet was held at the Beverly Hilton Hotel. Danny Thomas hosted it. Comedian Bob Newhart and singer Gogi Grant performed. Maury Wills played banjo. He had already performed on Dinah Shore's show in Vegas. Then Koufax, Drysdale, and Tommy Davis did some crooning. Walt Alston stayed in his seat.

The cover of the Dodgers' 1962 media guide was the team plane. The minimum big league salary was $7,000; the average was $16,000 per year. A gallon of gas cost $0.21.

A crowd of 52,562 attended the opener at Dodger Stadium, won by the Reds, 6-3. San Francisco won their opener, 6-0, when Mays hit a homer on the first pitch of the season off Warren Spahn of Milwaukee.

On April 11 Los Angeles won its first-ever game at Dodger Stadium, 6-2 over the Reds behind Koufax. On April 12 Pete Richert struck out six straight to tie the big league record in an 11-7 win over Cincinnati. On April 16 the Giants won 19-8 over the Dodgers in their first meeting of the season. Mays, Alou, and Davenport homered. The next day Sherry pitched well in an 8-7 Dodger win, their first at Candlestick since March 1961. On April 24 Koufax struck out a

Major League record 18 (broken with 19 in 1969 by Steve Carlton, and 19 again by Tom Seaver in 1970) versus the Chicago Cubs at Wrigley, winning 10-2. On April 25 Ed Bailey hit a homer after a knockdown from Bob Friend, spurring the 8-3 win over Pittsburgh. Four days later, San Francisco defeated Chicago, sweeping two games of a doubleheader with shutouts by Pierce and Sanford, 7-0 and 6-0, respectively.

On May 4 an emergency forced the Giants to land in Salt Lake City, Utah, delaying their arrival into the Windy City until 6:00 AM. Groggy from a lack of rest, they still beat the Cubs in an afternoon game at Wrigley Field for their 10th victory in a row. On May 21 Los Angeles hammered San Francisco, 8-1, at Chavez Ravine behind three RBIs from Tommy Davis and a dominating 10-strikeout performance by Koufax. Back in San Francisco, the Giants swept the fledgling New York Mets, 7-1 and 6-5, at the 'Stick. On May 30 the Dodgers swept the Mets at the "scene of the crime," in New York, by scores of 13-6 and 6-5. Wills homered from both sides of plate. At the end of May the Giants were 35-15, the best record in baseball.

"Will the Giants, carving out a whirlwind, pell mell early pace, as usual in the first month of the season, go *kerplunk* in June, as has been their pattern the last five seasons, or are they going to prove the *bona fide* Yankees of the National League?" wrote Jack McDonald of the *Sporting News*.

They called it the June swoon. A cartoon in the *San Francisco Chronicle* newspaper depicted a smiling bride and said, "June Bride Happy—What About Giants?" On June 1 the Giants beat the Mets, 9-7, at the Polo Grounds behind two Willie McCovey home runs and a solo shot by Mays, but the Dodgers swept Philadelphia, 11-4 and 8-5, igniting an eventual 13-game winning streak. San Francisco's swoon started on June 6, when, after leading by two games over Los Angeles, the team lost six straight, then went 6-6 over a dozen games to fall out of first. Their sixth straight defeat was a crushing loss at the hands of the Cardinals, by a score of 13-3 in St. Louis. Jim Murray of the *Los Angeles Times* wrote a scathing piece about the seemingly annual June demise of the San Franciscans, stating that "a business executive is standing in his office looking down over the city and is chatting to his secretary. Suddenly, a falling figure shoots past the window. 'Uh oh,' says the man, glancing at his chronometer. 'It must be June. There go the Giants.'"

Giants manager Alvin Dark battled personal demons
as he dealt with minority players.

Don Drysdale mowing 'em down.

Drysdale and Sandy Koufax were a dynamic duo until Koufax was injured.

Sandy Koufax delivers
some L.A. heat.

Ralph Houk presided
over the Yankee dynasty
at its greatest heights.

Mickey Mantle was a
power hitter from the
left side as well as
the right.

Mantle may have been
the greatest talent in
baseball history.

Willie Mays played the game in "quicksilver" manner.

Mays smiled through a year of personal sorrow in 1962.

Maury Wills was constantly in pain from sliding into bases
in the course of his 104-steal year.

Don Drysdale was
the perfect Dodger:
a matinee idol in L.A.

Sandy Koufax was thought
to be too introspective for
greatness until he proved
everyone wrong.

Willie Mays adjusted to Candlestick's winds and shifted
his power to right-center.

On June 8 the Dodgers beat the expansion Houston Colt .45s, 4-3, on the road, ascending to the top of the National League standings for the first time all year. On June 12 San Francisco began a comeback, sweeping Cincinnati in a doubleheader, 2-1 and 7-5. (On that day, F. L. Morris and two brothers, John and Clarence Anglkin, used spoons to dig out of Alcatraz Federal Prison, located in the middle of San Francisco Bay. They were never found, probably drowned in the swirling, cold waters, their bodies likely swept out to sea.) Sanford began his 16-game winning streak with a 6-3 win over the Cardinals on June 17. The next day, Koufax and young Bob Gibson of St. Louis dueled for nine classic, scoreless innings in a game won by a Tommy Davis home run, 1-0 in the 10th inning. On June 29 O'Dell went 12 innings and struck out 12 in a 4-3 win over Philadelphia. On June 30, Sandy Koufax threw a no-hitter, striking out 12 in a 5-0 win over the Mets.

July marked midseason, and on the second Los Angeles swept Gene Mauch's Phillies, 5-1 and 4-0. Podres retired the first 20 batters he faced, setting a record with eight consecutive strikeouts (broken with 10 in 1970 by Tom Seaver). On the fourth of July both Los Angeles teams, the Dodgers and the surprising Angels, were in first place, but San Francisco, recovered from the June swoon, continued to hang tough. Two days later Juan Marichal's 12 strikeouts keyed San Francisco to a 12-3 over Los Angeles. On July 8 the two rivals played a classic October-style game. Koufax, with Don Drysdale coming on in relief, shut out San Francisco, 2-0. L.A. held a slim half-game lead at the first All-Star break. They would hold that lead until the last day of the regular season. On July 10 Maury Wills singled, stole bases, and scored twice in leading the National League to a 3-1 triumph over the American League. Marichal was the winning pitcher. On July 17 Koufax was forced to sit down when his mysterious finger ailment became too much for him to bear, but the Dodgers were hot without him.

In late July before the second All-Star break, the Dodgers led by one game. A crowd of 162,000 fans packed Dodger Stadium for a monumental three-game series that had the whole sports world buzzing with excitement and anticipation. Certainly, it appeared that Walter O'Malley and Horace Stoneham were geniuses, the move to California a 20th century success beyond all previous conception. Milton Berle joked that he was going to fly to San Francisco so he could watch the games on TV, avoiding the congestion but also getting in a backhanded swipe at O'Malley's no-home-games-on-TV policy. Frank "Hondo" Howard hit three home runs and drove in 12 runs as L.A. swept their rivals 2-1, 8-6, and 11-1. Howard was the hottest hitter in baseball, having driven in 47 runs since June 28. The Dodgers were a perfect 5-0 at home versus the Giants and had split the first six games in San Francisco, which accounted for their essential edge so far. On July 29 the Dodgers were threatening to pull away, now up by four games at the break.

The Giants were hoping that the dog days of August would favor them, that the cool summer weather in Frisco would refresh them while the desert heat would tire out their rivals.

"San Francisco isn't a city—it's a no-host cocktail party," wrote Murray. "It has a nice, even climate: it's always winter."

The onset of August had the effect of heightening pennant race sensibilities. First, it was impossible not to compare this with the 1951 drama, and the 1959 race was also fresh in the minds of all concerned. The players, the fans, and the media began to view the season in larger than life terms. With the Dodgers now playing in their new stadium, there was a distinct sense that 1962 was truly a "big league" season, a debutante ball of sorts for the West Coast. John Wooden's UCLA Bruins had not yet won an NCAA basketball championship, but in 1962 they had come close and were obviously on the verge of great things. The Lakers and Trojans were all the rage.

Los Angeles seemed to have everything that San Francisco lacked. The former Los Angeles area congressman, Richard M. Nixon, looked to be an obvious favorite over the old-style San Francisco pol, incumbent Governor Edmund "Pat" Brown. Nixon was the former vice president and standard bearer of the Republican Party. Democrat-heavy San Francisco hated the idea of losing to Nixon and voter-rich, still-Republican L.A.

The Giants were their last, best hope, and if they failed, a sense of inferiority would infect the "superior" San Franciscans with a sickness that would be hard to heal. The college teams, Cal and Stanford, were dominated by their Southern California rivals, and it had, for the most part, been that way for at least a decade. The north-south rivalry took on political and cultural overtones that surpassed the rivalry the teams had during the New York years. The papers, particularly the provincial San Francisco dailies, began to give the pennant race front page space alongside a huge stock market crash, the Israeli execution of Adolf Eichman, the Kennedy administration's obsession with Fidel Castro, and the Mercury astronauts.

"You can talk all you want about Brooklyn and New York, Minneapolis and St. Paul, Dallas and Fort Worth, but there are no two cities in America where the people want to beat each other's brains out more than in San Francisco and Los Angeles," said American League President Joe Cronin, a native of The City.

The writers started to get personal, with particular jealousy and vitriol aimed at the Southland by San Francisco's scribes. The *Chronicle's* Art Rosenbaum called the Dodgers "Smodgers," sniping that L.A. was a "city whose women would attend the opera in leopard shirts and toreador pants if indeed they attended the opera at all."

"Isn't it nice that people who prefer Los Angeles to San Francisco live there?" wrote Herb Caen, as bitter and spiteful a man as has ever abused the privilege of a free press.

The players could "feel . . . definite tension in the air," said Wills. "It reminds me of a homecoming college football game. Each time we face San Francisco, it's different than any other National League series."

Veterans taught youngsters like Ron Fairly, who already was imbued by a sense of north-south rivalry against California and Stanford from his USC days, to "hate the Giants more than any other team," he said. "I'm sure the Giants weren't too fond of us, either—and that's exactly the way we wanted it."

Jim Gilliam called Willie Mays "one of the best friends I ever had in my life, but there was no way we would talk to each other on the field. Not even hello."

"Against the Giants, you just tried that much harder," recalled Joe Moeller. "Even if the Giants had been in last place, we would've wanted to beat them worse than the frontrunners."

"I don't care how you play these games—the Dodger-Giants rivalry is always intense," said Al Dark, insisting it had not lost a thing on the West Coast.

"Usually, in the batting cage, guys on the other teams would come over and exchange ideas, say hi," Orlando Cepeda said. "When we played the Dodgers, we wouldn't talk to them."

"It was a special event that required a much greater level of preparation," said Felipe Alou.

"When you stepped off the plane in Los Angeles, you could *hear* the electricity," Willie McCovey recalled. "Even the skycaps at the airport were all wrapped up in the rivalry. It carried over to the hotel and finally the ballpark."

"It may not have matched the spirit of the New York days, but it was still a great rivalry," said Podres. "You always got fired up playing the Giants."

If the Giants thought they had a weather advantage in August that would manifest itself into their overtaking Los Angeles, they found that it was not to be. On the third of the month Drysdale beat the Cubs, 8-3, to become the earliest 20-game winner since Jim "Hippo" Vaughn in 1918. The no-man's-land nature of the race, in which both teams had a distinct advantage in their home stadiums, continued to keep San Francisco from catching up.

"It seems to be an incontrovertible fact that neither team can play well in the other chaps' ballpark," wrote San Francisco beat writer Joe King. "The Giants are sad sacks in L.A.; nobody may ever see a team drop dead like the Dodgers in Candlestick."

"We would go to San Francisco with our great pitching staff, and there were games where we'd get blown out, 12-3 or whatever," Perranoski said. "Then they'd come down to Dodger Stadium and we'd win low-scoring games by a run. The two ballparks dictated the action."

With Los Angeles maintaining an overall lead, the tit-for-tat nature of the home-and-home rivalry was not helping the Giants. Both teams built their advantages using dirty tricks that intensified feelings on both sides.

The Giants kept tall grass and a slow infield. The Dodgers used a roller to pack their dirt for their speedsters. The Dodgers sloped the third base line so that bunts by Wills, Gilliam, and Willie Davis would stay fair. Their grass was short. Much of it was meant to gain a psychological advantage over San Francisco more than an actual one. Al Dark instructed the Candlestick groundscrew to water down the paths in order to slow Wills.

On August 4 a "Miracle at Coogan's Bluff" celebration was held at Candlestick Park, with Bobby Thomson, Eddie Stanky, and Monte Irvin attending. San Francisco's own Joe DiMaggio was invited to attend all three games but had to cancel when his ex-wife, Marilyn Monroe, died on August 5. On August 9 L.A. beat Philadelphia, 8-3. On August 10 the Dodgers came to San Francisco (who had lost three straight at Chavez Ravine) with a five and a half game lead, their biggest of the year. At 5:30 AM Matty Schwab, Candlestick's head groundskeeper, dug a pit where Wills normally took his lead, filled it with water, sand, and peat moss, then covered it with topsoil. During infield practice the Los Angeles players noticed and brought it to the attention of head umpire Tom Gorman. Gorman ordered the pit dug up, but Schwab's crew replaced it with more mud than before. Schwab's wheelbarrow of sand, which was supposed to dry up the pit, contained all the old, hidden ingredients that had previously been dug up. It was worse than before. Wills said the whole episode "demoralized" him. Mays hit a homer with four RBIs and the Dodgers came unglued in an 11-2 loss.

The next day the Dodgers came out doing mock breastrokes and further high-jinx followed. A Dodger stole San Francisco's leaded bat. A Giant stole L.A.'s practice bat. Dark kept a straight face, saying that unless the infield is watered down, the three o'clock winds kick up the dust. Drysdale started with an 11-game winning streak. Tommy Davis, hitting .452 against Giants pitching, hit a three-run homer off of Pierce.

In the third Wills kept stepping out against Pierce to unnerve him, but when the umpire ordered him in Wills exploded about the field, calling the umpire "gutless." Wills shouted it again, and the man in blue thumbed him. San Francisco scored two runs in the fourth, and the Giants sensed that L.A. was psyched. Their comeback was on. Then the winds *did* start to blow. There were delays and the tension was thick enough to cut with a knife.

Clinging to a 3-2 lead, Drysdale allowed a Felipe Alou bloop double. Haller struck out, and Drysdale then hit Jim Davenport, causing him a hairline fracture. Despite Big D's reputation as a headhunter, it was not intentional. He was the go-ahead run. Drysdale apologized on the spot (and called him later; Davenport was out two weeks). Drysdale struck out Pagan, then McCovey pinch-hit for Pierce. Alston came out to talk it over with his ace. Willie Mac always wore Drysdale out and was "the only batter who could consistently destroy [him]," said Roseboro.

McCovey had homered off of Drysdale a month earlier, and a year earlier had hit a 475-foot shot, the longest to date in Candlestick history, off of him.

Alston had Perranoski up and ready but stuck with Drysdale. The count went full, then McCovey slammed a homerun and the place went crazy. Stu Miller preserved Pierce's 5-4 win, the 200th of his career. Wills was fined $50, and the Giants were back in it.

On Sunday afternoon, Juan Marichal shoved Dodger bats where the sun don't shine in a dominating 5-1 win. Los Angeles was now thoroughly discombobulated, finding excuses for their failings. Buzzie Bavasi called the Giants "bush" and vowed protests, but they were off their game and it would affect the race. Alston said the field was dangerous, that Mays could have broken his leg. Vin Scully called Al Dark "the Swamp Fox."

"One more squirt and the Red Cross would have declared a disaster area and begun to evacuate the Dodgers by rowboat . . . an aircraft carrier would've run aground," Murray wrote.

The Giants exhibited "the most disgraceful case of poor sportsmanship since Major League baseball came to the coast," wrote writer Sid Ziff.

Wills paid his fine in coins, dragging an 80-pound bag to National League president Warren Giles's desk in Cincinnati, turning it over, and letting them spill everywhere. He then asked them to count it and give him a receipt. Alston tinkered with his heretofore-successful lineup, putting Tommy Davis at third and veteran Wally Moon in left field. Frank Howard started to slump. The Dodgers were not a good defensive team anyway. Moon's presence made them worse. Also in August, the Alston-Durocher feud reached a head. Third base coach Durocher had been disregarding Alston's signs for a month.

"Forget the signs," Durocher wrote in *Nice Guys Finish Last*. "We had a manager who sat back and played everything conservatively. To hell with it. Alston would give me the take sign, I'd flash the hit sign. Alston would signal bunt, I'd call for the hit-and-run."

Duke Snider, relegated to the bench, led a cabal of "Leo's guys," all of whom were benchwarmers. Daryl Spencer called Alston "wishy-washy" and called Durocher a decision maker. Some veterans questioned Alston's decisions. The starters were Alston's loyalists. Against the Cubs, Durocher badgered young third baseman Ron Santo relentlessly, saying he was going to be traded to L.A. Tampering charges were made, and Bavasi said it would stop.

Alston called a team meeting and laid down the law, saying, "Leo, that means you." If Durocher missed a sign, Alston said he would be fined $200; the player an additional $200. A few days later Fairly missed a sign and Tommy Davis ran into his own bunt.

"Somebody oughta take some money from these kids," shouted Durocher.

Alston confronted him then and there. "You do the coaching, Durocher, and I'll do the chewing out and fining," Alston declared.

It did not stop there. Alston had to whistle three times to get Durocher's attention, and signs were still missed. Mel Durslag castigated Alston for embarrassing Durocher in front of the team. Alston screamed at the writer for his concern over Durocher's feelings. What about his?

"What about the times he has shown me up in front of the players?" Alston yelled. "How much of this do I have to take?" Alston and Durocher moved their cubicles away from each other and stopped sitting next to each other on buses and planes.

Internal dissension was not relegated to the Dodgers, however. After a frustrating loss on August 19, Dark and Cepeda engaged in a shouting match. San Francisco slumped but ended a six-losses-in-seven-games stretch with a 2-1 win over New York on August 23. On August 24 the Durocher-Alston feud took a strange turn. Durocher had a reaction to penicillin and, thinking he was having a heart attack, was placed on a clubhouse table. Alston rushed in.

"I think this is it, Walt," said Durocher, as if it were the "George Gipp scene" from *Knute Rockne: All-American*. "Go get them." Durocher was given dosages of vitamin B, however, and he was restored to full health. He was still absent from the team for two weeks.

Los Angeles won seven of eight and led by three and a half by Labor Day. On September 3 at Dodger Stadium the infield dirt was "as dry as Pharaoh's tomb," wrote Charles McCabe. The biggest crowd (54,418) of the season came out wearing feathers and doing duck calls. Three thousand duck call sounders were sold by the concessions. Two fans brought in a real duck and a chicken and threw them on the field. Dodger batboy Rene Lachemann had to remove them. The Giants came out for batting practice and saw a "gift" on their dugout steps: a watering can.

Over the loudspeakers Danny Kaye's popular "Hiller-Haller-Miller" song played:

Cepeda runs to field the ball
And Hiller covers first
Haller runs to back up Hiller
Hiller crashes into Miller
Haller hollers 'Hiller!'
Hiller hollers 'Miller!'
Haller hollers 'Hiller,' points to Miller with his fist
And that's the Miller-Hiller-Haller-Holler-lujah-twist!

The Giants had a 10-game losing streak at Dodger Stadium dating back to 1961. Dark shuffled his batting order, and Mays, hitting fifth, clubbed a three-run homer off of Stan Williams. Sanford walked none in a complete game 7-3 win, his 20th of the season.

After the game the Giants were guests at blond bombshell Jayne Mansfield's house. The evening included cocktails and a buffet by the swimming pool, but some Giants were disappointed. Half expected Jayne would be wearing a bikini and the party would be a full-scale orgy, with the actress satiating all their needs. Instead, she was not "anything like her image on the screen," said Pierce, which of course promoted that very fantasy. "She was pleasant, but very businesslike and proper. We knew she was a big baseball fan, but I think there was also some kind of promotion or commercial involved. To the ballplayers, this was a big deal. We went because we wanted to see Jayne Mansfield, her house, and that heart-shaped swimming pool." Wives and girlfriends had a hard time believing the truth, which was that nothing amorous happened.

The next night, perhaps still fantasizing about Jayne, the Giants lost 5-4 when Willie Davis scored from first on a single, Roseboro stole home, and Perranoski struck out Mays and Cepeda to end the game. On September 5 Mays doubled and singled in a 3-0 win, but Marichal, dominating Los Angeles, injured his foot on a play at first base, just as he had a year earlier at the Coliseum. X-rays revealed no fracture, but he would miss several starts.

Dark accused Marichal of "jaking" it. It was his 18th and last win of the season.

On September 6 the Armed Forces Radio Network conducted a live satellite call-in interview with the presumed World Series managers, the Yankees' Ralph

Houk and the Dodgers' Walt Alston. It did not escape Dark's attention, and he took exception to it.

That day McCovey killed Drysdale again with a single and a double, staking San Francisco to a 4-0 lead. Los Angeles rallied behind Tommy Davis's single and a Howard home run. Drysdale then knocked down both Willies with furious inside buzz. Billy O'Dell returned the favor, buzzing Drysdale when he came to the plate.

A volatile exchange ensued between umpire Ed Barlick and both managers. Tommy Davis's homer tied it, and 54,263 Dodgers fans went wild. Perranoski came on in the ninth. Hiller beat out an infield single. Davenport, back from the disabled list, laid down a sacrifice bunt, and Perranoski tried to get the lead run at second. His throw went into center field for an error, and Giants runners were now at second and third. Felipe Alou walked to load the bases. Mays tapped a force-out at home. Cepeda worked Perranoski to a full count, but the southpaw reliever just missed, walking in the go-ahead run. Perranoski sagged perceptibly. Harvey Kuenn doubled, and it was "Katy bar the door," 9-5, Giants.

"Certainly, it was the biggest hit of my career," said Kuenn, which was saying something. Larsen came in to protect the lead. Typical Dodgers fans rushed to the parking lot and their appointments with the Pasadena, Harbor, Golden State, Hollywood, and Santa Monica freeways. In front of growing numbers of vacant seats, L.A. loaded the bases for the "Giant killer," Tommy Davis, who already had two hits and two RBIs in the game. Stu "the Killer Moth" Miller came in. Davis's drive to left field looked to be a homer, but Kuenn speared it. Dark dropped to his knees in the dugout. A run was scored, but there were two outs. Howard, who hated facing Miller and had previously struck out four straight times against him, came to the plate. Miller got him to swing clumsily, but then laid one in there. Hondo hit a towering shot, barely foul down the left field line. Then Howard popped to Davenport, and it was over. Dark called it, "The most important game I've ever managed."

The Giants returned to San Francisco. It was now September, the best time of the year in the Bay Area. They trailed by a mere game and a half with three weeks left. San Francisco and Los Angeles had no more regular season games left with each other. As if giving thanks for "deliverance" after the Dodger Stadium dramatics, Felipe Alou invited his manager to the Peninsula Bible Church in

Palo Alto, where 2,000 people heard the outfielder's testimony on "what the Lord meant to me."

Among Alou's blessings at that time were hits in seven straight plate appearances and the fact that his club was as hot as a pistol. They stayed hot, sweeping Chicago and Pittsburgh to increase their winning streak to seven games. However, L.A., refusing to buckle amid the late-season pressure, demolished both of those clubs. Both teams left for their final road trips—10 for the Dodgers, 11 for the Giants. On September 12 it was hot and muggy in Cincinnati. Starter Gaylord Perry said the change from the moderate San Francisco weather to the Midwest humidity was "a jolt for everyone." Perry changed his shirt twice that night.

Mays was affected, but not just by the weather. The pressures of the pennant race, in which he was carrying his team on his shoulders, combined with his troubles—a contentious divorce, tax problems, debts, an unhappy personal life—came to a head after the long plane flight from the cool West Coast to the sweltering Queen City. To top it off, he ate junk food that day and it did not sit well with him.

Mays shortened his batting practice turns and struck out his first time at the plate. In the third inning he staggered and fainted in the dugout. Mays was carried by stretcher to the clubhouse and then transferred to Christ Hospital. He rested, felt okay the next day, and asked to rejoin the team. He was released after 24 hours of observation.

The San Francisco papers treated Mays's health in tabloid manner with rumors of venereal disease, a dugout fight, epilepsy, a heart attack, and even the influence of Kentucky gamblers supposedly slipping him a "Mickey Finn" to affect the betting line. He was simply emotionally, mentally, and physically exhausted. Later Mays was given a clean bill of health by a San Francisco doctor.

But the star's collapse was a blow to the club. The Giants lost two to the Reds, and their momentum was gone. Dark sat Mays some more to be sure, and they lost two straight at Pittsburgh. In the last 19 games Mays had missed, his team was 0-19. The Giants blew a 2-1 ninth inning lead to the Pirates when pitcher Earl Francis hit a homer to win his game. The next night the Pirates broke an eighth inning tie on Bob Bailey's triple.

Mays returned the next night and homered to send the game into extra innings, but Smoky Burgess homered for Pittsburgh to hand the Giants their fifth straight loss. The next night the Pirates beat Mike McCormick to sweep the series. Dark was furious, throwing food around the clubhouse. They trailed by four games.

The Dodgers had won seven straight but struggled. Stan Williams beat the Cubs at home but gave up a grand slam at Wrigley Field in a loss. He was pulled from the rotation and, with no explanation, never returned in regular season play. "It really hurt my pride that they felt I wasn't good enough to do the job," said Williams.

Los Angeles lost two of three in Milwaukee. In St. Louis, a meeting was held on Thursday, September 20, at the Chase Park Plaza Hotel. Traveling secretary Lee Scott assembled Alston, Snider, and the coaching staff. Walter O'Malley flew in. It was an off-day.

"Get tough, Walter," advised O'Malley. "You've got to ride herd on 'em. They're going to blow this thing, sure as hell, unless you can light a fire under them. Warn them that if they blow the pennant, they'll lose more than just the World Series money. It will be reflected in their salaries next year."

Alston preferred a vote of confidence. O'Malley responded that "These are not high school kids—they're professionals," insisting that Alston get tough and "make me the heavy."

Alston held his ground, but O'Malley told him that if the team lost, "some heads will roll." Snider told O'Malley not to worry. That night, oddly, the Dodgers attended the Giants-Cardinals game at the old Busch Stadium. The Giants had snapped their six-game losing streak when Tom Haller homered twice, but that night the Giants blew a 4-3 lead in the ninth on a balk and Ken Boyer's game-winning single, 5-4.

The Giants and Dodgers were both staying at the Chase Park Plaza at the same time. Perranoski told Felipe Alou after the game he would "see you guys next year," and "we win and you won't." On September 7 Wills broke the National League record, previously set by Cincinnati's Bob Bescher in 1911, with his 81st stolen base. "My sincere congratulations," wired league president Warren Giles, apparently willing to let Wills's "nickels, dimes and pennies" fine-paying incident go. "Now go all the way and break the record held by the great Ty Cobb."

Cobb had stolen 96 bases in 1915 and had died in 1961. Considered one of the best players ever to play baseball, he was a portrait of human contrast: a virulent racist who was also a believing Baptist and major contributor to black colleges in the South. One year earlier, Al Stump's article about Cobb had been published in *Look* magazine. It told the story of a bitter old drunk, estranged from friends and family, utterly unable to make sense of the new world he lived in.

Most incomprehensible to Cobb was the existence of blacks in the Major Leagues—not just as participants, but veritable matinee idols of sports. One of those very men, the symbol of the "new breed," Maury Wills was about to break his most cherished record. Cobb, wrote many a writer, was "turning in his grave."

But the day of the 154th game of the season, Commissioner Ford Frick did the same thing he had done to Roger Maris in 1961, stating that Wills had to break the record in 154 games for the mark to stand. Because of two ties, Cobb had played 156 games in 1915, two more than the regular 154-game schedule. Frick still insisted that the 154-game standard would apply.

"I wouldn't have minded so much had Frick made his ruling earlier," Wills said. "But why did he wait until the last day?" Wills could have broken the mark earlier had he sensed urgency. "Cobb got 156 games to set his record and I thought I would, too."

On September 16 Bob Buhl of the Cubs shut out L.A., 5-0. Koufax returned in mid-September. The team won 17 of 21 after his injury in July, opening the five and a half game lead of August 8, but there was little doubt that his absence had helped San Francisco stay in the race.

"If we'd had Koufax the whole season we would have waltzed to the pennant," said Norm Sherry. "His injury was the opportunity that gave us a chance to get back in the race," said Al Dark.

On September 23, O'Dell won his 19th game, 10-3 over the Colt .45s. On that same day, a classic Koufax versus Bob Gibson rematch of their earlier scoreless duel was in the offing, but Gibby fractured a bone during batting practice.

"There was this tremendous sigh of relief from the Dodgers because they hadn't been hitting, and now they wouldn't have to face this future Hall of Famer," said Scully. "Curt Simmons, who was very much nearing the end of his career, was rushed into the breach to pitch for Gibson."

"I could get out of bed in the middle of December and steal two off Simmons," said Wills.

But Koufax had nothing and gave up a first-inning grand slam. Now the score altered Wills's stolen base strategy. He could not afford to run the team out of a rally just for personal gain. In the sixth, with the Dodgers trailing 4-1, Wills walked and stole number 95. He then took off for third to tie the mark in the 154th game. He had it easily. At the last moment, Jim Gilliam laid down a totally useless bunt. He was thrown out, credited with a sacrifice that was a joke. Wills lost the stolen base. He had no further chances and St. Louis won, 11-2.

After the game, George Lederer of the *Long Beach Press-Telegram* asked Wills if Alston had called for a bunt. "Why don't you ask him?" Wills replied, pointing to Gilliam. Lederer went to Gilliam and repeated the question. Gilliam had had enough. He disliked Wills, was tired of playing second fiddle to him all year, and had obviously bunted to deprive him of glory.

"If looks could kill, Gilliam's expression would have struck the man dead," wrote David Plaut in *Chasing October*. "Mind your Godd--n business," said Gilliam.

"You must have seen that Wills had the base stolen," Lederer continued. "What was going through your mind?"

Gilliam had been caught red-handed, backed into a corner, and reacted angrily by threatening to punch the writer in the nose. Wills, however, wisely avoided stirring further trouble by repeating the company lie that Gilliam was trying for a base hit with a legitimate bunt try—an effort to spark a rally—not trying to screw up his record-breaking effort.

"I haven't asked anybody to sacrifice for me all season, and I'm not about to now," said Wills. The next night Podres and Larry Sherry combined for a 4-3 win, number 100. Wills did not steal a base. Game number 156 was against the tough Larry Jackson, the most difficult guy in the league for Wills to steal on.

In the third Wills singled and stole second for number 96, as the crowd cheered. But St. Louis went out to an 11-2 lead. Wills batted in the seventh. Alston told him to try for the record regardless of the score. Wills poked a two-strike single and the Cardinal crowd cheered him on. Jackson threw over to first half a dozen times. First baseman Bill White applied hard slap tags to Wills's skull.

Wills shortened his lead to indicate "that Jackson had me buffaloed." Jackson delivered home and the Cardinals relaxed. Then Wills took off for second—a delayed steal, which he never did before, but Al Campanis had suggested he try—sliding in safely. Catcher Carl Sawatski, who was in the process of throwing back to Jackson, had to make a hurried throw to second that bounced. Wills slid headfirst and had the record.

In the ninth Wills was presented with the bag. Later, Frick backed off his 154-game edict, saying the mark would stand without an asterisk in the official records after all.

Hall of Famer Max Carey, a one-time practitioner of the base-stealing arts, had watched Wills closely all year, stealing home, rattling pitchers, and changing the dynamics of the game. "It does me good to see a fellow operate like that," he said.

"I didn't see how I could ever improve on that," Wills said of the club record 50 bases he stole in 1960. "I was even more sure of it the next year, when I only stole 35." Even that was good enough to lead the league.

Wills set a goal of 50 in 1962 but got there by July 27. "I didn't think of the record until I had upped my figure to 72 by stealing three against the Mets on August 26," he continued. "Then, for the first time, Ty Cobb's record of 96 look-ed possible."

Whenever Wills reached first, fans chanted "Go! Go!" giving him renewed strength and confidence despite the raspberries, fatigue bordering on physical exhaustion, pulled hamstrings, and internal bleeding.

On September 29 San Francisco visited Houston's brutally hot Colt Stadium, home of the Colt .45s before the Astrodome was built and the team became the Astros. Flies said to be as large as a man's fist buzzed about. The Giants won on Friday night, 11-5. On Saturday Miller was wild, and Sanford was brought in for a rare relief appearance. Roman Mejias stroked a hit past a drawn-in infield to beat the Giants. They trailed by four with seven games left. It seemed to be over. On Sunday they kept hope alive with a victory but had gone 3-8 in their disastrous last road trip.

Los Angeles was 100-56. The Giants, at 97-59, trailed by three. On Monday both teams rested. Both were at home to finish the season. Giants booster Bud Levitas threw a backyard barbecue, and it felt like a farewell party. Dark made a speech about never giving up. His Christian faith—not to mention the experience of 1951 that he shared with three coaches, Willie Mays, announcer Russ Hodges, owner Horace Stoneham, among others—was the rock he used to maintain strength.

"We're gonna catch these damn Dodgers and we'll beat 'em in the playoffs," Dark exclaimed.

"Everybody thought he was nuts," said Carl Boles.

The Dodgers—Snider, O'Malley, Bavasi, Scully, Leo Durocher—also remembered 1951. But Orlando Cepeda claimed that Dark told him if the club failed to finish second (Cincinnati was pushing and would win 98 games) he would not support the players' contract demands. Dark denied having said that, certainly not if "we had any mathematical chance to win."

Dark apparently did tell Billy Pierce he had "pitched enough this year" and was free to go home early "as soon as we're out of this thing." Pierce made some flight reservations, but events that week forced him to keep changing them and finally cancel them altogether. By the third or fourth call the airline reservation clerk knew him by name.

EIGHT

Beat L.A.!

"What the hell are they saving me for? The first spring exhibition game?"
—*Don Drysdale's reaction to not being named the starter in
the second 1962 playoff game*

On Tuesday and Wednesday, San Francisco beat St. Louis twice while
L.A. split with Houston. On Thursday, Gene Oliver's homer sparked the
Cardinals to a 7-4 win at Candlestick. In the sixth, Mays lost track of how many
outs there were, an unbelievable reversal from his regular baseball instincts,
which were flawless. Cepeda struck out, and Mays casually walked away from
third. The catcher tossed to Ken Boyer, tagging the stunned Mays out while the
crowd booed. It got worse when he proceeded to strike out with two men on.

That night, Koufax tried to clinch it at Chavez Ravine. He had good stuff at
first, retiring 11 straight with four strikeouts. In the fifth he still led Houston 4-2,
and the Dodgers could taste it. But he was tired, and Alston went to the bullpen. Roebuck, Sherry, and Perranoski were shelled in an 8-6 loss. They still were
up by three, but blowing Koufax's lead to an expansion team was devastating to
their psyches.

"That loss was the turnaround game," Perranoski admitted.

L.A.'s Daryl Spencer had been with St. Louis in 1961. He said the Cardinals
loved the Hollywood nightlife. "There was quite a bit of chasing around out there
with some gals," he recalled with a smile.

With nothing to play for, incoming Cardinals players hit the Sunset Strip
and hung out until four in the morning. They were loose, the only visiting team
to post a winning record at Dodger Stadium in 1962.

"They made pitches that they might not have thrown if they'd gotten a good night's rest," said Ron Fairly. "And that's how they got us out."

In game one, St. Louis won, 3-2 in 10 innings. The tension in the Los Angeles clubhouse was thick and heavy, what with Wills and Gilliam on less than friendly terms, Alston and Durocher mortal enemies, Drysdale complaining, Koufax's courage questioned, and Tommy Davis giving the evil eye to anybody who looked at him askance.

On top of everything, the specter of 1951 hung over them like a ghost. The Dodgers hit incessant grounders to shortstop. It got so bad that they laughed, in gallows-humor style, as if to say hungover St. Louis needed only a pitcher, catcher, shortstop, and first baseman to beat them. The fans were apoplectic, the media aghast. Doom. Creeping terror. It was 1951 redux.

On Friday a rare September rain canceled San Francisco's game. On Saturday afternoon, Houston's Joey Amalfitano, a talkative native of San Pedro, which serves as the Port of Los Angeles, asked Willie Mays if the Giants "could score a run." Mays just stared at him. Amalfitano told Mays that Los Angeles *could not* score anymore, so all the Giants needed was to score and the pennant was theirs. He was not far from wrong.

In the opener, San Francisco scored 11. Cepeda, McCovey, and Haller provided the offense behind Sanford and Miller. L.A., playing that Saturday night, looked on at the televised game in abject desperation. Marichal started the second game of the doubleheader. His foot still hurt him. X-rays showed no fracture, and Dark distrusted the "Dominican Dandy," thinking he was weak-minded and could not handle the pressure of the pennant chase.

"He said very little, but the look in his eye told me that he thought I was trying to quit under pressure," recalled Marichal.

Marichal pitched in pain, but it affected him in a 4-2 loss. After the game, the Latin players gathered at his cubicle. Marichal was hurting and his teammates—friends—felt Dark had risked his career pitching him, but the X-rays of 1962 had mysteriously not caught any fracture.

When Dark benched both Cepeda and Alou on the final Sunday, the Latinos were convinced it was a statement, that Spanish-speaking players could not handle the stress of big games.

That Saturday night, the players went home and listened to a telegraph wire re-creation by Giants announcers Lon Simmons and Russ Hodges. It was not unlike 1951, when they took a train from Boston to New York listening to Hodges, while traveling through Connecticut, giving them a play-by-play over the train's loudspeakers of Brooklyn's final game with Philadelphia. Hodges later announced the famed *"Giants win the pennant!"* when Bobby Thomson hit the "shot heard round the world."

The bachelor Willie McCovey, a man about town, was on a date and later recalled San Franciscans straining to pick up the Dodgers' broadcast from Los Angeles, which could be heard at night. The voice of Vin Scully was heard through static on the streets, in cabs, coming out of cars, and on transistor radios in The City. Here was Scully—the ultimate professional—trying to maintain calm despite his team's freefall, while Giants fans desperately rooted the other way. But Scully's voice told the tale—citywide; along the peninsula; across the bridge in Oakland, Berkeley, and the East Bay; in the hinterlands of Stockton, Sacramento, and Modesto; down toward Fresno, where Central California sympathies were evenly split between the Giants and the Dodgers; eight hours on the 101 where motorists rooting for both teams traversed the state, past Big Sur and Monterey.

Ernie Broglio, who hailed from the East Bay Area, outdueled Drysdale, 2-0, at Dodger Stadium. San Francisco's hopes were alive, and in all the aforementioned places and a thousand others, cars honked, people whooped and hollered. The Giants were not dead yet. In keeping with St. Louis's loosey-goosey style of partying and playing baseball that final weekend, the happy-go-lucky Broglio was throwing curves on 2-0 and 3-2 counts.

"That had to be the best game he ever pitched," said Perranoski. Frank Howard's misplay of a fly ball gave Broglio all his support. The next day the *L.A. Times* read, "Should O'Malley tempt fate by ordering champagne for the Dodger clubhouse today, he'd best order it on consignment."

They led by a game with one day to go. Amalfitano continued to be right: they *could not score*.

It all came down to September 30, 1962. On that day, James Meredith attempted to become the first black to enroll at the University of Mississippi. A riot ensued and much white and black blood was shed. Mississippi Governor Ross Barnett provided no assistance to his fellow Democrat, President John Kennedy, who called it the "worst thing" he had ever seen.

The "Mississippi burning" caught the attention of San Francisco's black and minority players, most of whom had experienced prejudice firsthand playing in the South, but when Cepeda and Alou did not see their names on the lineup card, they figured they were dealing with it on the West Coast, too. Dark's Southern heritage was an albatross he could not shake.

Dark started the Southern-born Billy O'Dell against Houston's Turk Farrell, who told the writers he did not intend to lose. In the fourth, Ed Bailey hit a long foul ball, then got the same pitch and hit it fair for a homer to give San Francisco a 1-0 lead. The score was 1-1 when Mays came to the plate in the eighth. He had not had a hit in 10 at-bats, and the Candlestick crowd booed him. He was considered a poor clutch hitter, "pop-up Mays."

Organist Lloyd Fox tried to simmer things down by playing, "Bye, Bye Baby." It was a phrase Hodges used to describe home runs, and a song was made out of it:

Oh when the Giants come to town
It's bye, bye baby
Always when the chips are down
It's bye, bye baby

Then Mays deposited a Farrell fastball deep into the left field seats for a 2-1 lead. "It became a blur of white, smashed through the noise of roaring throats, sailing high into the blue," wrote Bob Stevens, "and it gave San Francisco the best shot it has ever had at the long-awaited pennant." Mays had homered on the first pitch he saw in 1962, and now on the last pitch he saw—of the regular season, at least.

It was number 48 of the year for Mays, the most in the league. Stu Miller retired Houston in the ninth, striking out Billy Goodman for the last out as the crowd of 41,327 roared to its feet. The Giants mobbed Miller and celebrated on the green plains until the special police escorted them off the field.

The fans stayed in the stands. It was Fan Appreciation Day, and five cars were to be awarded to winners of the promotion, but just as important, the score from

Los Angeles was not a final. The Dodger game had started an hour later than the San Francisco game.

L.A. entered the final day having won twice in eight days, both times behind the clutch hurling of Johnny Podres. On the final Sunday, Podres faced Curt Simmons. It was Podres's 30th birthday.

The game was scoreless for seven innings. Los Angeles, supposedly the best base-running team in baseball, blew several opportunities. Lee Walls was thrown out trying to stretch a single into a double. Willie Davis was caught on a decoy play. The crafty Simmons picked off Tommy Davis. The Dodgers were reduced to a Little League team, their sense of fundamentals completely gone. They were desperate, befuddled, and bamboozled. *They could not score!*

The Dodgers' strong radio station was again heard—at Candlestick during the Fan Appreciation Day event and of course at all the places it had been listened to the previous evening. In addition, Russ Hodges maintained updates on KSFO. Cars pulled up to curbs. The 49ers fans at Kezar Stadium, where the team was playing Minnesota, listened in. The Giants gathered around the radio in their clubhouse. A Western Union ticker revealed the play a minute after it happened. The Dodgers' broadcast could not be heard in the Giants' clubhouse.

Podres dominated. He called it one of the best games of his career, better even than his 1955 game seven triumph over the New York Yankees in the World Series. But with one out in the eighth, Gene Oliver, whose three-run homer had decided an earlier win at Candlestick, deposited a Podres curveball barely over the left field fence.

Fans were being awarded cars when news of Oliver's homer was announced, and a "Giant roar" came up. When an attractive blonde ambled onto the field to claim her prize, the crowd roared even louder.

At that moment, John Brodie of the 49ers was calling signals at Kezar. It was fourth-and-one at the Vikings' 18, and he suddenly was drowned out by a crescendo of cheers. Thinking it was for him, he waved for quiet so his signals could be heard. The 49ers won, but fans stayed at Kezar to hear the Giants-Dodgers reports.

In the bottom of the ninth, Ken McMullen and Maury Wills flied out. It truly did look as if they simply lacked any capability of scoring, so woeful were the

Dodgers offensively. The long season, the dispute between Alston and Durocher, Wills's histrionics, the Koufax injury, Don Drysdale's loud complaints about everything; they were sapped of all strength, like the General Ripper character in *Dr. Strangelove* who fears being drained of his "precious bodily fluids."

The players listened to Hodges. Chub Feeney's footsteps could be heard in the background. Finally, Hodges told them that Jim Gilliam had popped to Julian Javier. There would be a playoff. Bedlam ensued everywhere. Dark proclaimed it a comeback for the ages, and he had been there in '51.

The contrast between the Giants and Dodgers clubhouses was extraordinary. It was also a little different from 1951. On the last day 11 years earlier, the Giants beat Boston and, with the Dodgers losing big against Philadelphia, seemed to have the pennant locked up. Then Brooklyn rallied. Jackie Robinson saved the day with a remarkable catch, and Brooklyn jumped for joy. By evening time, when the Dodgers won, it was the Giants who had the heart taken out of them. This time it was all Giants.

Dodgers players swore and threw things. Podres was beside himself, one of his greatest efforts having gone for naught. He drove to the Mayflower Hotel, his L.A. residence, where friends were waiting to throw a surprise birthday party, but he was in no mood to celebrate. Alston was full of recriminations, self and otherwise. In 21 innings the Dodgers had not scored a single run, and this was no light-hitting squad. They were stars, winners of over 100 games, World Champions three years earlier, the fabled Dodgers' franchise. There were no excuses.

In the last 13 games, San Francisco was only 7-6, but Los Angeles had gone 3-10. "It was like two drunks having a fight in a saloon and trying to stagger to the safety of the swinging doors," wrote Arthur Daley in the *New York Times*. "Both kept falling down. The Giants, however, could crawl better than the Dodgers."

The Dodgers had led for 111 days, compared to 54 for the Giants, and entered the final two weeks up by four. The two teams were 9-9 against each other in the regular season, most of their victories coming at home. The L.A. media began an anatomy of their collapse. Aside from internal dissension, defense in particular had failed the club down the stretch. They had finished last in the league in double plays. Koufax's injury, Drysdale's late-season failing after winning 25 games, bullpen collapses, power hitters reduced to an endless stream of grounders to shortstop, bad base running by the so-called Swift Set, and, above all, terrible fundamentals were cited. Others said they had "gone Hollywood," tempted by beautiful starlets, too much nightlife, the glitz, their press clippings. It went on and on.

San Francisco pitching was seen as the primary reason for the club's success, and in this regard it had benefited from three starters—Sanford, Pierce, and O'Dell—who had come over from other teams, in some cases as reclamation projects. "Sometimes a change of atmosphere helps," says Dark. "It certainly didn't hurt our pitchers."

"Wanted, one nearly new 1962 National League pennant, slightly soiled with tear stain in center," wrote the great Jim Murray. "Last seen blowing toward San Francisco. . . . Warning: if you return pennant to Dodgers direct, be sure to tape it to their hands."

After everything, there was still more baseball to be played before the National League could send a representative against the rested, waiting, all-conquering New York Yankees. A coin toss determined that the playoffs would open at Candlestick, then switch for the second and, if needed, third game at Dodger Stadium.

The Yankees had to cancel their flight to Los Angeles. Ralph Houk was concerned that they had been scouting the Dodgers and now they might be facing the Giants, but at least he did not have to deal with Mickey, Whitey, and company spending three or four days in Hollywood with nothing but "Johnny Grant parties" to keep them busy. They headed to San Francisco's Towne House Hotel to wait it out. Eleven years to the day after the "shot heard round the world" the teams started again. It was the fourth best-of-three playoff in Dodgers history.

Matty Schwab went to work on the basepaths. He had already warned the drivers of cars on Fan Appreciation Day not to park on the infield dirt because they would "sink to their hubcaps." Schwab kept it up all night on Sunday. When Wills and company arrived Monday they were again beside themselves, totally psyched by it.

Dodgers public relations director Red Patterson tried to lodge a protest with Warren Giles, who made himself scarce. He then appealed to umpire Jocko

Conlan, who approached Dark. The manager assumed an uncooperative, hardline stance. Conlan found Schwab and ordered him to dry up and solidify the basepaths. Conlan ordered it rolled, as was the custom at Dodger Stadium, and Dark exploded, saying it was because O'Malley ran the league.

"His word is law," said Dark, as if his knowledge of his own team's cheating should not have been allowed.

The Dodgers were mollified and encouraged by the October weather, which tends to be the best the Bay Area has to offer; warmer than the summer, mid-70s, no wind, perfect for sailing (a popular pastime in San Francisco).

Koufax started but struggled, allowing a two-out double to Felipe Alou. Mays hit a "Candlestick shot" over the right-center field fence. He had learned to adjust his swing for opposite field power so as to avoid hitting straight into the wind blowing from left field, instead "going with the flow" toward right. An inning later, when Jim Davenport homered and Ed Bailey whistled a single past Koufax, the pitcher was sent to the showers, his season over.

"I can't be the same after two months off," said Koufax. "My finger is okay, but I felt like the third week of Spring Training."

The Dodgers "displayed the muscle, the frightfulness, and the total immobility of a woolly mammoth frozen in a glacier; the Giants, finding the beast inert, fell upon it with savage cries and chopped steaks and rump roasts at will," wrote the fabulous Roger Angell, who had in the spring detailed the extraordinary popularity of the expansion Mets when the Dodgers and Giants made their initial visits to the Polo Grounds.

Billy Pierce breezed past L.A., tossing a three-hit shutout with six strikeouts. "It was the most satisfying game I ever pitched," said Pierce, who upped his record to 12-0 at Candlestick Park and 16-6 on the year. Pierce thanked Conlan afterward, possibly a peace offering after the pregame consternation over the infield rolling. "I congratulated him on calling an excellent game and he congratulated me—sort of a mutual admiration society." L.A.'s scoreless streak was now 30 innings, and they had not threatened in any way to break it.

In the opening playoff contest, Mays walked, singled, and hit two homers in four at-bats. The Dodgers played dirty, knocking him down a couple of times, but it only steeled his resolve. His second home run came after Sherry brushed him back. The crowd seemed to adopt him at that very moment. It was the line of demarcation in his relationship with the fans.

"I think it was the moment where the San Francisco fans finally took him to heart," said Pierce.

"I think the fans are starting to warm to me," said Mays, grinning.

"No team can be as bad as we've been," said Alston. "We've got to snap out of it sometime. I still don't know who I'm going to pitch in the second."

Alston then announced he was going with Stan Williams, who had been relegated to virtual obscurity since allowing a grand slam in a key game. It was an odd move, hotly debated by the Dodgers players, brass, and media on *Electra II*'s flight back to Los Angeles.

"What's he saving me for?" complained Drysdale to anybody who would listen. "The first spring exhibition game?"

The Giants flew to the City of Angels and checked into the Ambassador Hotel (the sight of Robert Kennedy's assassination in 1968). Some watched young comedian Johnny Carson debut as host of *The Tonight Show*. Singer Tony Bennett performed "I Left My Heart in San Francisco."

October 2 was hot and smoggy. A town of notorious front-runners had given up on their team. Cars drove straight into the parking lot. Only 25,231 showed up. The Dodgers had set the all-time attendance mark of 2,755,184 in 1962, eclipsing previous records by the Cleveland Indians and Milwaukee Braves.

Snider was in left field, Tommy Davis at third, and Moon at first. At the last second, Alston went with Big D on two days' rest. He had nothing and tried to rely on his famed spitball, drawing warnings from umpire Al Barlick. In the sixth Drysdale ran out of gas completely. With one out, Haller walked, followed by Jose Pagan's double, a successful sacrifice bunt by Sanford moving them along, and singles off the bats of Chuck Hiller and Davenport. The score was 4-0, Drysdale was headed for the shower, and the sparse crowd began to thin out. All that was left, it seemed, were Giants rooters wearing orange-and-black hats and gear, transplanted San Franciscans living in L.A. or those who had driven eight hours on the 101 to be there.

McCovey's RBI single seemed to seal it, and the remaining Dodger fans grumbled, booed, and then left. Alston's team was as done as a Thanksgiving turkey. The Dodgers had gone 36 straight scoreless innings without a peep.

They had gone down "not with a bang but a whimper," as the poet T. S. Eliot so famously wrote. There were none of the dramatics of 1951, of heroism in defeat. They were the French army circa 1940.

"Down in the dugout, manager Walt Alston was poring over the stagecoach schedules to Darrtown," wrote Jim Murray.

Gilliam's walk to lead off the sixth scarcely caused a ruffle, but Sanford's reputation was that of a six-inning pitcher. Additionally, the hard-throwing right-hander, already tired from the long season, was nursing a head cold and had to run the bases in the previous inning. Sanford looked "like five miles of bad road," according to Bob Stevens. Dark overreacted and called on Miller, instead of saving him for the closer's role.

Miller had nothing. Neither did O'Dell. Dark was now into his starters, panicking. O'Dell "threw some gas" on the fire that Miller admitted having started. Larsen came in and the Dodgers suddenly were scoring at will. The 36-inning shutout streak fell like the Siegfried line when George Patton's army knocked it down. After Los Angeles poured seven runs across, the Giants could see the Promised Land evaporating before their eyes.

"By the end of that inning, they were ahead and I could feel the goat horns sprouting," said Miller.

The sixth inning took an hour and 11 minutes to play. The seventh lasted 10 minutes. Fans started coming back. In the eighth, San Francisco scored twice to tie it, and Dodger frustration was again at an all-time high. Davenport and Mays got hits, Bailey contributed a pinch-hit RBI single, but Tommy Davis threw Mays out at third on a bad call. Stan Williams, now in the game, walked to load the bases but pitched out of it. He settled down, gaining some redemption, and in the bottom of the ninth Wills walked. Bob Bolin was lifted for Dick LeMay. Gilliam walked, Spencer hit for Snider, and Gaylord Perry came in. Dark gave him instructions to get the lead man. On the ensuing bunt he had Wills at third but panicked and went to first. Dark ripped the dugout phone off the wall and threw it to the end of the bench, stormed to the mound, wordlessly ripped the ball from Perry's hand, and called for McCormick.

Tommy Davis was intentionally walked to load the bases. Ron Fairly, who was 1-for-31, hit a short pop to center. Wills took a chance. A good throw by

Mays would have nailed him, but Mays's effort was up the line and Los Angeles won, 8-7.

The Dodgers picked up Wills and carried him off field. It got so out of hand he had to hide in the training room from teammates, in order to avoid injury. "I didn't want to get killed," he said. "Those guys were acting crazy."

"The feast continued here for a time yesterday," wrote Angell. Trailing 5-0, "At this point, the Dodgers scored their first run in 36 innings, and the Giants, aghast at this tiny evidence of life, stood transfixed, their stone axes dropping from their paws, while the monster heaved itself to its feet, scattering chunks of ice, and set about trampling its tormentors."

It was a total resurrection for Los Angeles. Williams was the happiest of them all, having redeemed himself after a month of purgatory. The Giants were filled with remorse at having blown a sure win. Alston called it "the biggest scrambler I've ever seen. I've never been in a wilder, woolier one, personally." There were recriminations about Sanford's effort. "One fella said to his face that he'd quit on us," O'Dell said.

The game "is best described in metaphor and hyperbole," wrote Angell, the master of the genre, "for there is no economy in it." The Mets (40-120) "could have beaten both teams."

Suddenly it was the Giants who were arguing and shouting. It looked like all the momentum had swung back to the Dodgers—shades of 1951, after Brooklyn's Clem Labine tossed a 10-0 shutout to force a deciding game. Game two required 42 players and took four hours, 18 minutes to play, the longest nine-inning game ever. NBC lost $300,000 when *The Huntley-Brinkley Report* and *Phil Silvers Show* were both preempted. Six years later this game resonated in the minds of NBC executives, who chose to cut away just as the Oakland Raiders were staging a last-minute comeback over the New York Jets in the infamous *"Heidi* game."

Actor Rock Hudson watched game two at a bar in Universal City. He announced, "We've got it made. Those Dodgers will kill them. The Giants won't have a chance tomorrow. They won't come close. You wait and see."

Director Alfred Hitchcock, dining at Chasen's, sounded like Winston Churchill predicting victory over Adolf Hitler. He said he had "the utmost confidence in the ultimate defeat of the Giants. The good guys always win in our fair city."

On Wednesday afternoon the "what have you done for me lately?" city transformed itself back into a Dodgertown of loyalists. More than 45,000 front-runners, including Doris Day, Rosalind Russell, and Frank Sinatra, arrived at Dodger Stadium.

The crowd contrasted with the "embarrassing acres of empty seats yesterday, when the park was barely half full," observed Angell. "Los Angeles calls itself the Sports Capitol of the World, but its confidence is easily shaken. Its loyalists are made uneasy by a team that appears likely to lose. Today, with a final chance at the pennant restored, the Dodger rooters were back, and there was hopeful violence in their cries. Fans here seem to require electronic reassurance. One out of every three or four of them carries a transistor radio, in order to be told what he is seeing, and the din from these is so loud in the stands that every spectator can hear the voice of Vin Scully, the Dodger announcer, hovering about his ears throughout the game."

The modern electronic Dodger Stadium scoreboard invited the fans to sing "Baby Face" and ordered the battle cry, "CHARGE!" during rallies. The scoreboard struck Angell—an observer of baseball for years in the venerable Polo Grounds and Ebbets Field—as a "giant billboard . . . like a grocer's placard," and that the "new and impressive Dodger Stadium . . . was designed by an admirer of suburban supermarkets. It has the same bright, uneasy colors (turquoise exterior walls, pale green outfield fences, odd yellows and ochres on the grandstand seats); the same superfluous decorative touches, such as the narrow rickraff roofs over the top row of the bleachers; the same preoccupation with easy access and with total use of interior space; and the same heaps of raw dirt around its vast parking lots. There is a special shelf for high-priced goods—a dugout behind home plate for movie and television stars, ballplayers' wives, and transient millionaires. Outside, a complex system of concentric automobile ramps and colored signs—yellow for field boxes, green for reserved seats, and so forth—is intended to deliver the carborne fan to the proper gate, but on my two visits to O'Malley's Safeway it was evident that the locals had not yet mastered their instructions, for a good many baseball shoppers wound up in the detergent aisle instead of the cracker department, with a resultant loss of good feeling, and had to be ordered to go away and try again."

These descriptions represent some of the most vivid of a time, a place, an era, and a stadium ever written.

Ron Fairly told Willie "Three Dog" Davis before the penultimate game that "this one is ours." Durocher wore the same T-shirt, shorts, and socks he wore the day of 1951, when Thomson hit his famed homer. "I wore them yesterday when we won, and they have magic powers," said Durocher, somehow overlooking the possibility that those items might have a mojo that would favor the Giants, not his new team.

The writers asked Dark if he brought along anything from 1951. "Yeah," he said. "Willie Mays."

The starters were the ailing Marichal versus the bone-tired winner of the 1955 game seven, Podres, on two days of rest. In the third inning San Francisco took a 2-0 lead on three Dodgers errors, including one by Podres. A Snider double and an RBI grounder by Howard cut it to 2-1. Roebuck replaced Podres with the bases full in the sixth.

"Even so, I pitched pretty good," said Podres of his exhausted effort. "I got us into the sixth inning before Eddie Roebuck bailed me out."

Roebuck, making his sixth appearance in seven days, pitched out of the jam with a force at home and double play. In the bottom of the inning Snider singled and the "Giant killer" Tommy Davis hit a 400-foot homer to give the Dodgers a 3-2 lead. Hope sprang eternal in the breasts of large-busted starlets!

Then the scoreboard flashed news that astronaut Walter Schirra, a USC graduate, had orbited the Earth six times. American Exceptionalism seemed to give the crowd a burst of adrenaline, exacerbated by the home team's increasing its lead to 4-2 in the seventh. Wills's fourth hit and 104th stolen base, his third of the day, led to the fourth run. A famed photograph shows the throw skipping past Davenport, with Wills totally disrupting him. Durocher ran all the way down the line with Wills as if he were Bobby Thomson, and it was over. Durocher *slid* as Maury scored, and the Giants seethed. Felipe Alou said right then and there that it steeled the Giants' resolve.

"For a time today, it seemed that all the recent doubts and discomforts suffered by Dodger fans were finally to be rewarded," wrote Angell, who in his *New Yorker* piece described how the club forged ahead "in the happiest fashion imaginable," behind the "old demi-god" Snider and the "young demi-god"

Tommy Davis, "who studies each pitch with the eye of a jewelry appraiser." Wills was "the ranking deity in Los Angeles this year." The Giants "forgot their newly discovered stratagem for getting Wills out," describing how the previous day Wills had stolen second, only to be cut down at third by "the best arm on the club," the sturdy right wing of Mays.

San Francisco went down quietly against Roebuck's sinker in the eighth. Los Angeles had a chance to increase its lead in the bottom half of the inning. Dark walked two batters intentionally, loading the bases. Roebuck came to the plate. He had thrown three innings and was dead tired. Alston allowed him to hit. The Dodgers groaned. Koufax and Podres begged Durocher to talk sense into Alston, to pinch-hit for the reliever and use Koufax or Drysdale in the ninth. Drysdale shouted and screamed for the chance. One of the best-hitting pitchers of all time, with some managerial foresight he could easily have been used as both the pinch hitter and the closer. Instead, Roebuck made the last out and trudged out for the ninth.

"I'd rather have Roebuck pitching for us with a two-run lead than anybody I've got," Alston later said.

"You're damn right I would have liked to pitch," Drysdale later told Bud Furillo. "Only they didn't ask me. I didn't think Roebuck should have started the ninth. He did enough."

Roebuck said Alston's theory was that his sinker would be more effective since he was exhausted, but the pitcher said he was "the most uncomfortable I've ever felt in a game." The smog was debilitating, and he just wanted to get it over with.

In the Giants' dugout, the silence was broken up by Dark. "Matty, grab a bat," he said.

Felipe Alou's little brother Matty, a contact hitter, was the worst guy a sinkerballer like Roebuck could face in that situation. Matty drilled Roebuck's second pitch to right field for a single.

"You can't imagine the pressure I was feeling by now," Roebuck admitted. He made $14,000 that year, and the Series share was $10,000. Wills tried to calm him down. Roebuck got Kuenn to hit a perfect one-hop double-play grounder to Maury, but *somebody* had moved Larry Burright two steps away from second base. He was a split-second late in the force at the bag, just enough to allow Kuenn to beat his throw to first base. No double play.

The question would swirl around Dodger circles like the famed "Who lost China?" accusation that dominated politics in 1949. "Who moved Burright?" According to Roseboro, Lee Walls yelled for Burright to play Kuenn as an opposite-field hitter.

Roebuck walked McCovey. Felipe Alou came to the plate. Alston visited the mound. But there was still no Drysdale. Big D seethed. Roebuck told the manager he just wanted to "finish this thing one way or another." It would turn out to be "or another."

"The clatter of typewriters died away in the press box," wrote Angell. Many writers were already in the elevator headed toward the Dodger victory celebration. Now, silence befell the cramped Dodger Stadium press box. None of the L.A. writers wanted to have to rewrite their stories. Half wanted more drama. Half just wanted it to end.

Roebuck had enjoyed success with Mays in the past, but Willie inside-outed a jam sinker up the middle.

"This white blur was coming right at me," Roebuck recalled. He had a large glove he called "The Claw." He stabbed, barely missed catching it for the second out and possibly setting up a double play. Instead it squirted off the webbing for an infield hit and a run scored. Bye Ed.

Drysdale?

"Stan Williams!" roared Durocher, not caring who heard him. "He'll walk the park."

Drysdale was beside himself as Williams entered.

The Giants were stunned. Alston had *Koufax and Drysdale* in the bullpen, but went with *Stan Williams*.

"He must have been saving them to pitch in the Series," deadpanned O'Dell.

Dark said that if he had Drysdale, "I'm thinking pretty seriously about seeing if he can't finish the ballgame," that in a game of this magnitude "there is no tomorrow."

Williams thought he was brought in because he had pitched well the day before—even though that increased the fatigue factor—and that he had won two playoff games against Milwaukee in 1959.

Alston figured the right-handed Williams would get the right-handed Cepeda, then the southpaw Perranoski could be brought in against the left-handed Bailey. Williams jammed Cepeda, who hit a short fly to right. Fairly had a decent arm but was a first baseman, not an outfielder. His throw was late. The Giants tied it at 4-4. Cepeda said it was one of the biggest RBIs of his great career. Consternation bordering on hatred was palpable in the Dodgers' dugout and bullpen, with open, verbal questioning of Alston. A pall fell over the Dodger Stadium crowd, broken up only by the wild shouts of scattered Giants rooters and the San Francisco players themselves.

Alston and Durocher "stalked slowly back and forth in their dugout, staring at their shoe tops and exuding an almost invisible purple cloud of yearning; they wanted the National League season extended by a few more innings or a few more games," wrote Roger Angell. "This wish, like so many other attitudes to be seen in this city, must be regarded as excessive. . . . The twitchy, exhausted athletes on both squads was reminiscent of action in the winter softball games played by septuagenarians in St. Petersburg, Florida." The Dodgers had permitted their "gasping pursuers" to catch them, and now they were about to pass them.

Alston did not go to Perranoski against the left-handed Bailey, who later admitted he had little chance against Perranoski. Williams threw a wild pitch. Mays moved to third, Felipe to second. Alston ordered Bailey walked intentionally. Roseboro came to the mound. He did not want the wild Williams loading the bases; he could easily walk in the go-ahead run, just as Durocher predicted. They looked toward the dugout to get Alston's attention, to come out and get Williams, or at least talk it over, but *"we couldn't find him,"* said Roseboro. Alston was in the runway smoking a cigarette.

Bailey was walked intentionally.

Davenport, a .320 lifetime hitter versus Williams, came to bat. The first two pitches to him were balls, then a strike. Williams, aiming now, walked him. Alou trotted home and San Francisco led, 5-4. The pall in the dugout and the stands barely concealed indignation.

Finally, too late, Perranoski was brought in. Naturally, Burright booted Pagan's grounder, and it was 6-4. Bob Nieman flied out.

The press box loudspeaker announced that United Airlines would have a special flight leaving at seven o'clock for San Francisco and the World Series.

Pierce was called on for the last three outs. He was as calm as a commuter waiting for the 5:15 to Greenwich. Wills grounded out, Gilliam hit a "can o' corn," and "I knew we were in pretty good shape," said Pierce.

The .205-hitting Walls stepped in for Burright and lifted an easy, soft fly to Mays, who did not make his usual "basket catch." Asked about it later, he yelled, "Are you crazy? That was $15,000 a man." In a year in which he owed money to everybody, he was not about to take any chances. There is a photo of the shirtless Mays, displaying the muscles of a steroid user long before such enhancements were thought of, in the post-game clubhouse. Mays wore a "million dollar" smile.

The game was over, and the stunned crowd spilled onto the freeways, the streets, the bars.

The Giants "went into the ritual Autumnal dance of victory in front of their dugout, leaping into the air like [they were dancing the] Watusi," wrote Angell.

"One of the most dramatic and nerve-racking pennant races in years came to an astounding end today," wrote John Drebinger in the *New York Times*, calling the crowd of 45,693 "incredulous" at the sight of their beloved home nine blowing a two-run lead in the ninth inning of a deciding playoff game for the second time in 11 years.

Park maintenance moved cases of champagne three different times in anti-cipation of the celebratory locale. The NBC crew had barely moved their equipment out of the Dodger clubhouse before the angry home team stomped in. The cramped Giants' clubhouse was a madhouse.

"This is the greatest moment of my life!" shouted McCovey, who posed for a wide-smiled photo with his rival Cepeda and pitching hero Pierce. Then they broke into a conga line. Dark smilingly begged off the champagne.

"If we drink all this stuff, we'd be sick for a week," exclaimed Bailey. "And if we had blown that game today, we'd have been sick for a year."

Former Vice President Richard Nixon, trolling for votes in his neck-and-neck gubernatorial campaign against incumbent Governor Pat Brown, the election only a month away, told Dark, "Your players have heart. You'll beat the Yankees."

The first game of the World Series was less than 24 hours away. The Yankees had been idling away the whole time; they had clinched the pennant early and were waiting out the playoffs. The Giants were loosey-goosey, carefree.

"This was it—this was the pressure," said Mays. "We've got no time to worry about the Yankees now. We'll deal with them as they come."

"Winning those playoffs was better than the Series," Felipe Alou later said. "Because of the rivalry, the animosity between the Dodgers and Giants, the way we came from behind. This was the biggest thing that ever happened to me in baseball—even more than the day I played in the same outfield with my two brothers."

The team started to party in the clubhouse, managed to deal with the press, showered, and was still partying as it headed to the Los Angeles Airport for the flight to San Francisco.

Dark reminded his players that they had a game to play the next day. They managed to cool it, but as the plane approached San Francisco International Airport, pilot Orv Schmidt announced, "There's a little disturbance down below."

People showed up en masse at SFO. When the parking lot filled up, many just parked on the side of Highway 101 and walked to the airport. The crowd, estimated at between 25,000 and 75,000 strong, overran the runway. The plane circled for an hour, and there was talk of landing in Oakland, across the bay. Many feared a crash. Felipe Alou in particular hated to fly.

Eventually, the DC-7 was allowed to land at a United maintenance base. A small gathering of mechanics and the Giants' bus driver politely applauded. The bus would drive the players north to Candlestick Park, where their cars were, but those who lived on the peninsula, to the south, decided to find their own way home. Cepeda, the Alou brothers, Pierce, and Marichal waded their way through the crowd. They eventually were given rides by fans they had never met before. They all made it.

The rest boarded the bus. At the main concourse, wives and family awaited but beyond that was a semi-dangerous throng. The day had been long and alcohol fueled. People broke through police barricades, French Revolution–style, converging on the bus.

"Those folks meant well, but they really shook us up," recalled Dark. They started to shake and rock the bus. Several recalled being terrified that the bus would be rolled over and they would be crushed. Writer David Plaut said it was a "miracle" the team escaped without serious incident or injury, to players or fans.

A chant began: *"We want Mays! We want Mays!"* But Mays had found a cab to take him to his peninsula home. Somebody suggested to "throw 'em Boles," his look-alike, but Boles wanted none of it. He literally feared for his safety.

Chub Feeney said that he had never seen anything like it in New York. "It certainly wasn't this way when we won in 1951," he exclaimed.

"But that was all in hysterical New York, not sedate San Francisco," said Art Rosenbaum sarcastically.

The event certainly suggested something about The City that nobody ever quite realized before; exactly what is still not clear, but its image did change somewhat from its sophisticated reputation.

The bus made its way out of the parking lot, but Feeney ordered it to stop at a nearby motel. Because of the late hour, rental cars were hard to come by, and owing to the strange events normal plans were askew. Feeney figured that the motel rather than Candlestick, which is off the beaten path, was a good place for players to arrange for rentals.

It was after midnight, the team had to play the Yankees in less than 12 hours, and "We're walking along the highway, across this empty field, in total darkness," recalled Feeney. "I thought to myself: Here we are. Here come the champions of the National League."

In 1962 the Giants and Dodgers played each other 21 times, with San Francisco winning 11 and Los Angeles 10. One million fans watched those games (including the playoffs) in person, while TV viewership reached 70 percent, and the radio listening audience reached 75 percent. A Bay Area phone service provided a paid service, providing play-by-play to 25,000 callers per day.

The Giants finished 103-62, followed by the Dodgers at 102-63, one game back. Cincinnati was 98-64, three and a half games behind. Pittsburgh (93-68) trailed by eight. The Braves (86-76) were 15.5 back, the Cardinals at 84-78 trailed by 17.5, followed by Philadelphia (81-80), Houston (64-96), Chicago (59-103), and at 60.5 games back, the lowly New York Mets (40-120).

Orlando Cepeda finished with 35 home runs, 114 RBIs, a .306 average, and 191 hits. Chuck Hiller batted .276 and Jose Pagan .259. Jim Davenport won a Gold Glove while batting .297 with 14 homers. Felipe Alou hit .316 with 25 homers and 98 runs batted in. Willie Mays had one of the best seasons of his career, finishing with a .304 batting average, a league-leading 49 home runs, 141 RBIs, and a .615 slugging percentage (third in the NL). Harvey Kuenn batted his customary .300 (.304). Rookie Tom Haller batted .261 with 18 homers, while Ed Bailey contributed 17 home runs. Playing part-time, Willie McCovey hit .293 with 20 homers and 54 RBIs in 229 at-bats.

San Francisco's ability to match the Dodgers' arms was ultimately what kept the team in the race. Billy O'Dell was 19-14 with a 3.53 earned run average. Jack Sanford was nothing less than spectacular, finishing 24-7 with a 3.43 ERA. Juan Marichal's injury prevented him from winning 20, but he finished with 18 victories and a 3.36 ERA. Billy Pierce, thought to be an American League retread after his bad spring, was unbeaten at home and 16-6 with a 3.49 ERA on the season. Stu "the Killer Moth" Miller finished with 19 saves and avoided the goat horns that he would have been forced to wear after his second playoff game performance. Mike McCormick, who took years to reach his potential, finished 5-5. Hard-throwing Bob Bolin was 7-3, and hard-partying Don Larsen was 5-4. Gaylord Perry was 3-1 but in Dark's dog house, considered timid on the mound after failing to throw out the lead runner at third base on a bunt in a key playoff situation.

Dodgers statistics for 1962 are some of the most pleasing to the eye in the club's history. Many, many Dodgers teams that went all the way could not match the overall numbers of the 1962 squad.

Ron Fairly batted .278 with 14 homers and 71 RBIs. Larry Burright hit .205. Maury Wills batted .299 with 208 hits in 695 at-bats and set an all-time base-stealing record of 104. He won a Gold Glove and was voted the National League's Most Valuable Player in a year in which some of the greatest names in baseball history competed against him in their primes. Jim Gilliam batted .270. Frank "Hondo" Howard's hot summer helped spur his overall .296 average with 31 homers and 119 runs batted in. Willie "Three Dog" Davis established himself as one of the best defensive center fielders in baseball while hitting .285 with 21 homers, 85 RBIs, and 34 stolen bases. Tommy Davis's numbers were simply astonishing: a league-leading .346, 230 hits, and 153 RBIs, along with 25 homers, 356 total bases, nine triples, and 18 stolen bases. It was one of the finest non-MVP seasons in history. John Roseboro hit .249 and earned kudos for stellar work behind the plate. Wally Moon batted .244. Duke Snider, on his "last hurrah," batted .278 with no power. Doug Camilli batted .284.

Don Drysdale's season is looked back upon with melancholy. It was the best of his career, or close to it, with a league-high 25 wins and 232 strikeouts against nine losses and a 2.83 earned run average, good for his only Cy Young award (which in those days was awarded to only one pitcher in both leagues), but still, 1962 is remembered as the year he lost control emotionally, failing to win when his team needed him most. Big D would have gladly traded his gaudy statistics and honorary hardware for a World Series ring. Johnny Podres was a solid 15-13 with a 3.81 ERA. Stan Williams was 14-12 with a 4.46 ERA. Sandy Koufax was so close, yet so far. His 14-7 record included no victories (and two losses) after the finger injury that shelved him at midseason. His 2.54 earned run average still led the National League. Like Drysdale, Koufax failed in the clutch and had not completely thrown the stigma of his early years—that of a pitcher lacking inner fire. Ed Roebuck's 10-2 record and 3.09 ERA were overshadowed by his ninth inning failings in the third playoff, as was Ron Perranoski's 20 saves and 2.85 ERA. Larry Sherry was 7-3 with 11 saves and a 3.20 earned run average but had not come through when he was given the chance to be the hero as he had been in 1959. Young Joe Moeller, returning in lonely solitude to Manhattan Beach after each home game, or to a single hotel room after each road contest, finished 6-5.

A look at the National League in 1962 reveals that it was indeed a golden age of Hall of Famers, veterans and youth, perhaps unequalled. Cincinnati's Frank Robinson, who at .342 was better than his MVP-lead-the-Reds-to-the-pennant year of 1961, followed Davis's .346. The great Stan Musial of St. Louis did not slow down, hitting .330. Ex-Giant Bill White of the Cardinals batted .324. Milwaukee's Hank Aaron batted .323.

Frank Robinson led the league with a .624 slugging percentage. Aaron's 45 homers trailed Mays, followed by Robinson with 39, Chicago's Ernie Banks (in his initial year as a first baseman after breaking in as a shortstop) with 37, and Cepeda with 35.

Davis's 153 RBIs led Mays (141), Robinson (136), Aaron (128), and Howard (119).

Jack Sanford's .774 winning percentage was second to Bob Purkey of Cincinnati (.821), followed by Drysdale (.735) and Pierce (.727). Koufax's 2.54 ERA led Bob Shaw of Milwaukee (2.80), Purkey (2.81), Drysdale (2.83), and Bob Gibson of St. Louis (2.85).

Drysdale's 25 wins led Sanford (24), Purkey (23), another Red (Joey Jay with 21), Art Mahaffey of the Phillies and Billy O'Dell (both with 19).

Elroy Face, the veteran reliever of the Pittsburgh Pirates, led the National League with 28 saves, followed by Perranoski with 20 and Miller's 19.

Drysdale's 232 strikeouts were followed by Koufax's 216, Gibson's 206, Turk Farrell of Houston (203), and O'Dell at 195.

Milwaukee ace Warren Spahn, still going strong at age 42, managed a league-leading 22 complete games. O'Dell had 20, Drysdale 19, and despite his late-season injury, Marichal had 18.

Ken Hubbs of Chicago won the Rookie of Year award, but later would meet a tragic fate when he drowned.

Roger Angell returned from the third and final playoff game to his hotel in Los Angeles on October 3. An art exhibit of life-sized pastel portraits of Dodger heroes was arranged in a semicircle, each elegantly framed and bearing a gold identifying plate. A velvet rope surrounded it, "like the new Rembrandt in the Metropolitan Museum," he wrote, guarded by a uniformed Pinkerton.

It was not unlike a portrait given to Brooklyn manager Charley Dressen midway through September 1951 bearing the inscription, "To the manager of the 1951 National League champions."

"No one was looking at the pictures," wrote Angell of the 1962 art exhibit. Angell then made his way to the airport and departed on that special United Airlines flight reserved for the media, transporting them from Los Angeles to San Francisco. The citywide party was still going strong when the *New Yorker* scribe arrived in The City. The faces of fans "all had the shiny-eyed, stunned, exhausted expression of a bride at her wedding reception," wrote Angell.

Bars and restaurants in San Francisco had been filled to capacity during game three of the playoff. When it ended, Market Street resembled V-J Day, with cars honking, orange-and-black confetti hung out windows, strangers shaking hands, hugging, and in the case of some men and women, doing a little more than that.

Transistor-tilting theatergoers shouting with glee broke up a matinee playing of *Oliver*. A restaurant owner poured champagne on the sidewalk, clubhouse-style. Handel's "Hallelujah Chorus" broke out at Grace Cathedral.

As the night wore on, the sense of religious deliverance turned into something ugly, with the cops called out to deal with drunk driving, fighting, and vandalism that caused tremendous property damage. Cable cars were tilted and rolled over, roads were closed, and numerous arrests were made.

The San Francisco bar scene was in full swing well past midnight. All of Northern California celebrated the Giants' monumental victory. It was more than just a great win for the Giants over the Dodgers. For the strange, schizophrenic *superior*-San Franciscans-with-an-*inferiority*-complex, it meant much more than that.

Los Angeles, Southern California, the Southland, La La Land, Tinseltown, Hollywood—the city that wasn't, they called it, but it was. They had everything—better weather, movie glamour, gorgeous girls, famed nightclubs, the endless strand, a bigger population, political and economic clout, better stadiums filled with more fans, and better teams at every level—high school, college, and professional. The Trojans and Bruins had little regard for the Golden Bears and the Indians, reserving their emotions for a national rival like Notre Dame. Cal's reaction was to *sue* USC, which made them look even more pathetic.

But now, finally, they had *beat L.A.!* In so doing, they had validated, confirmed their superior, narcissistic view of themselves as gents, not rubes, as sophisticates, not yokels. The great dragon of Los Angeles, not just the Dodgers but the very *idea* of L.A., had been slayed. It was a cultural and sociopolitical victory; a victory for clean air and water over smog; of cable cars over traffic jams; of literature and poetry over celluloid trickery; of Allen Ginsberg over John Wayne, Rudolf Nureyev over Shirley Temple, and liberalism over conservatism.

This all seemed to carry forward when, one month later, San Francisco's liberal Democrat, Edmund "Pat" Brown, defeated Los Angeles's conservative Republican, Richard M. Nixon, for governor. At the time, it seemed to be Nixon's political obituary, which could not come too soon for San Francisco Lefties. The north had its revenge over the south. They had validation.

Hannibal had crossed the Alps. Laying in wait was the Roman Empire of sports, the Yankees, who represented a city—the Big Apple, New York—that posed a whole new challenge. San Franciscans thought they lived in The City. New Yorkers knew they lived in *the* city.

NINE

Meltdown

"Let's wait a few minutes before you come in. It's pretty grim in there.
The guys are kind of in a daze."
—*Duke Snider advising the writers not to come into the locked
Dodger clubhouse after the game three playoff loss*

While the City of Angels contemplated what might have been, a drama, a
war, a meltdown for all times was still occurring and would continue for
hours in the Dodger Stadium home clubhouse. It would last all night and expand
to the Sunset Strip, to the San Fernando Valley, and to other locales.

The Dodgers' team policy was to allow immediate press access to their
clubhouse. They played mostly night games and writers needed to fill their stories
under late deadlines. This had been a day game, but they were still clambering
outside the locked doors. Twenty minutes passed before Duke Snider emerged.
He had lost in 1951, and he had lost again 11 years later.

"Let's wait a few minutes before you come in," he told the press. "It's pretty
grim in there. The guys are kind of in a daze."

The writers strained to hear accusatory shouts, whimpered cries, and
shattered beer bottles from inside. Snider went back in, and Wally Moon replaced
him. "How the hell would you feel if you'd just lost $12,000?" he asked.

The press was not let in until an hour had passed. Many Dodgers were gone
by then. Those still there were drunk or in shock. The stadium crews had not
moved all the champagne. Bavasi heard about it and called down an order that
if anybody drank any of it they could not expect a contract offer over the winter.

The response to this riposte was too foul to repeat, and the players consumed what was left without any care as to what Bavasi told them. Then equipment manager John "Senator" Griffin delved into his private stock of whiskey. The Dodgers were not in a beer drunk; they were in a vicious whiskey-mixed-with-champagne drunk, consumed on empty stomachs after playing a day game, on top of a day, a week, and a season of intolerable tension.

John Roseboro was not much of a drinker, so he dressed and left. "It was the worst scene I ever saw with the Dodgers," he said. "It was the one time we did not conduct ourselves with class."

They guzzled liked pirates or old-time Western saloon cowboys, getting nastier and louder. The scene was unprecedented in sports history and has probably never been equaled—not by the fightin', hairy "swingin' A's," *The Bronx Zoo* Yankees, or the mid-'80s Mets. Alston locked himself inside his office. Listening to the clawing, screaming players trying to get at him from outside, it was like George Romero's *Night of the Living Dead*; the poor manager huddled inside, waiting out the darkness.

"Come on out here, you gutless sonofabitch!" screamed one veteran. "Tell us about your strategy, skipper. How we gonna play the World Series, you bastard?"

"Walt, you stole my money," screamed Tommy Davis, apparently oblivious to the fact that Alston also was out his Series share. "$12,000. You stole it."

"Smokey lost it, boys," cried Podres, who had seen the agony and the ecstasy in seven years. "Old Smokey lost the pennant for us."

"We should have won," another screamed. "We could have won, too, if Durocher was managing this club."

Bottles crashed about and players walked among the broken glass. Uniforms were ripped to shreds or tossed in fury. Some players were blind drunk. Daryl Spencer and two others passed out in the shower. Spencer, who did not drink, had consumed a fifth of Seagrams VO in 30 minutes and later said he did not know how he got home. The club apparently made no provisions for drunk driving. No cabs were called. The players were left to their own devices. Dodger Stadium is not near where most players lived, which meant a perilous traversing of the L.A. freeways.

Griffin was annihilated, fell down wedged into a cubicle, and needed three men to pry him loose. Roebuck, one of the day's goats, dressed quickly and drove home in silence with his wife. "It was like a death in the family," he stated.

Williams stayed in the clubhouse, filled with remorse and self-recrimination. He eventually played putt-putt golf on the clubhouse carpet, but despite his poor performance, the wrath was deflected off of him and directed at Alston.

Of all the players, Drysdale spilled the worst bile. He was known to be loud and opinionated, but he was always a man of class, friendly, helpful, and not ostentatious. But that day was not his finest. Oddly, his tantrum could have been directed at himself. The 25-game winner and Cy Young award recipient had not pitched well in key games. Exhausted without Koufax in the rotation, taking it all on himself, he had not been reliable when most needed.

Bavasi lost his composure entirely, locking himself in his office, where he grabbed a blanket, turned off the light, and lay on the couch in the dark. He was literally ill from the stomach-churning game. He spoke to nobody because he knew he would say something terrible. His ringing phone went unanswered. Knocks on the door were repeated, shouts also unanswered. His wife could not get through, and she became concerned. He replayed the season over and over in the dark, hating everything, filled with doubt and guilt in a self-imposed hell on Earth. He stayed in his office for seven hours and left, stunned, at 12:30 in the morning. Drunk Dodgers were still pounding away in the clubhouse.

In Bavasi's mind, Alston had blown it, no question about it. Years later, despite his affection for Alston and subsequent glory attained by the Dodgers, he still blamed the manager for not bringing in Koufax or Drysdale.

"You've gotta go with your best," he said.

The Giants won the game on "spotty pitching, and spottier managing," according to the *1963 Official Baseball Almanac*. That was one of the kinder assessments. When the press was finally allowed into the clubhouse, Alston proved to be the one honest guy of the lot of 'em. He led the writers out of the clubhouse so as to avoid confrontations and was calm, candid, and honest, answering every question regardless of how baited or cutting. He defended all his moves; perhaps he had made mistakes, but he gave reasons for all of them instead of threatening to punch people in the face, as Gilliam had done when asked why he personally denied his teammate (Wills) the stolen base record in St. Louis.

According to Alston, he would have done everything the same if given a second chance. This did not endear him to anybody, and perhaps it was wrong-headed, but it was a stand-up performance. His voice never wavered while he patiently smoked cigarettes and took the questions. The writers, who had clambered that they had deadlines to meet, took their time questioning him, as if this were an inquisition after a shipwreck. It was in truth a day game, and they indeed had the time to dissect all of it, bit by bit, before filing their stories.

"I'm going to work their tails off on fundamentals next spring," said Alston, expressing no concern over the possibility that he might not be the manager by then. Finally, he thanked the writers and returned to the clubhouse, shutting the door behind him.

Andy Carey went home and burned all his World Series tickets, not realizing that they had already been deducted from his paycheck and he could not get his money back.

A lot of the Dodgers lived in the San Fernando Valley. They drove drunk to Drysdale's restaurant and got even more plastered, filled with hate for Alston, fueled by Big D's alcoholic venom. They went through the liquor stock and then went to TV personality Johnny Grant's house for more. The bars were closed and that was where the booze could still be found. They drank all night, "and it was pretty rough," said Perranoski. It was a miracle nobody crashed a car or was jailed for DUI.

The most classless of all was Leo Durocher, who stoked emotions like Javert in *Les Miserables*, performing the act of *j'accuse* against Alston. In the clubhouse he was approached by everybody and never made any effort to dispute the idea that had he been in charge they would have won, they would have their World Series shares, they would be getting ready for the Yankees the next day.

A victory celebration had been planned at the Grenadier Restaurant on the Sunset Strip. Stadium club caterer Tom Arthur owned it. There were no players in attendance, but Durocher was there. Liquor flowed and emotions were hot. One Dodger official allowed that if Durocher had been the manager, "we'd have won." Reports as to what happened next vary. According to some, Durocher told the club official he would have won the pennant.

According to other reports, he simply stated, "Maybe."

Others stoked him on, and Durocher allowed it all to build to a head. Later Durocher said that all he said that night was, "Who wouldn't like to go into the ninth inning with a two-run lead?" adding, "I was asked a question and I answered it." The Grenadier party was "not exactly a call to mutiny," he recalled.

But regardless of the particulars at the Grenadier, Durocher had worked and would continue to work behind the scenes trying for Alston's job. He looked down on the "country bumpkin," considering Alston unworthy of something he believed was his birth right of sorts. He had the opportunity to show class and did not.

Somewhere during his seven hours in the darkness, Buzzie Bavasi decided that he would not fire Alston. Loyalty, respect, and also the fact the team had just made oodles of money by breaking the big league attendance mark must have factored in the decision. Whatever motivated him, Bavasi stuck with the manager.

O'Malley had told Alston that if his plans backfired—principally, the decision to go against O'Malley's St. Louis admonitions to "get tough"—then "heads will roll." O'Malley respected Alston but was inclined to fire the manager until Bavasi told him, "If you fire Alston, then I go out the door with him."

O'Malley had a good front office in place and didn't want to tinker with it. A win here, a hit there; glory had been so close. It was not a bad season. It was, in fact, one of the best years in Dodger history, if one could separate the final result from what came before it. O'Malley told Bavasi it was his call.

The next day, Bavasi met Alston. "I wouldn't blame you if you fired me right now," said Alston, the stand-up guy.

"Everyone's entitled to a bad game, a bad year," Bavasi told him. They shook hands and that was that. Then, after Alston left, the phone rang. Hank Greenberg, a Hall of Fame slugger who was then the president of the Chicago White Sox, had been at the Grenadier. He told Bavasi about Durocher popping off, saying that Leo second-guessed and humiliated Alston in full view of everybody, including the varied Dodgers officials. The story got out and was printed in the papers.

Bavasi was very angry. Soon afterward a Friar's Club roast was held for Maury Wills. Bavasi was coming down the stairs with Vin Scully when Durocher appeared. Bavasi confronted him, calling him "an ungrateful sonofabitch." Durocher tried to lie his way out of it, but Bavasi knew what he had said. He fired him on the spot.

"Don't come around here anymore, you're through," Bavasi screamed. "I gave you a job when you needed one, and this is what you do to me?" Scully, thinking there would be a fight, "turned white."

Durocher later claimed that Bavasi "conducted an investigation," and when he found out Durocher had been the telling the "truth," he rescinded the firing. That was a lie. Durocher had said it, and the "investigation" confirmed it. What did happen is utterly remarkable; perhaps the most benevolent act in baseball history.

Alston told Bavasi not to fire Durocher. Alston knew that many Dodgers were "Durocher guys," and he would need them in 1963. If Durocher were made a martyr, they would gather against him. He wanted to win it on his own, with nobody feeling sorry for Durocher. It was a move not unlike the one Reggie Jackson made in 1977. Feuding with manager Billy Martin in New York, Jackson told owner George Steinbrenner not to fire Martin after a publicized shouting match between the two in Boston. Jackson felt that he would be blamed for the popular Martin's firing and all would suffer for it.

The 1963 Official *Baseball Almanac* provided a thorough encapsulation of the memorable campaign, written in the light of full disclosure. "It is a high-strung team of talented malcontents and aging veterans who blame each other a little and their manager a lot for 1962," it reported. "When Los Angeles lost the playoff, several of the veterans, passing around several bottles, began to abuse manager Alston, whose greatest ability seems to be winning pennants (three in nine seasons) and retaining his job title doing little and saying less than any other manager in the game."

"You never know what's going on," said Drysdale. "General manager Buzzie Bavasi makes all the decisions anyway."

"It took a combined effort of 25 players to lose the pennant," Bavasi said. "It's not easy to win a game when you don't get a run in three straight games. I don't place the blame on Alston or any one player. I blame 25 of them."

"The more you think about it, the more impossible it seems," said Alston. "We should never have let it happen and we don't plan to let it happen again."

TEN

The East-West Fall Classic

"Total triumph is unsettling."
—San Francisco Chronicle *columnist Charles McCabe*
contemplating a Giants World Championship

On the evening of the day the Giants won the pennant, the circulation manager of the *San Francisco Chronicle*, which uniquely printed its sports section on green and pink paper, asked the editor what the headline was for the next day's editions.

"It's 'WE WIN!'—white on black," the editor replied.

"How big?"

"Same size as 'FIDEL DEAD!'"

The papers cared only about the Giants. Richard Nixon's campaign was noteworthy because he had appeared in the Giants' clubhouse, a move meant to usurp San Francisco votes normally ticketed to the Democratic Party.

There were human interest stories about little kids using their piggy bank savings, running away from home to buy Series tickets. A constant refrain from the provincial writers harkened back to the "gay '90s," when owner Jim Mutrie called them "my giants." Now, in San Francisco, they were "our Giants." The social set was aghast.

"Good God!" one member of the landed gentry exclaimed. "People will think we're like *Milwaukee*, or something!"

Chronicle columnist Charles McCabe, who was not a sportswriter, normally wrote of the comings and goings at Trader Vic's, city hall, the Sausalito avant garde scene, and other unique aspects of San Francisco life. He now directed his attention to the Giants, whom he saw as a metaphor for his vision of what America should be. McCabe did not like greatness, as embodied by American Exceptionalism because for America to be exceptional, other countries had to be unexceptional. That was . . . unfair.

Therefore, he determined that despite having won 103 games, with perhaps the greatest superstar of all time in his prime playing center field, the Giants displayed "lovable incompetence." McCabe warned San Franciscans that victory would bring on a smugness that would be less comfortable than defeat. It was *not* what George Patton told his troops before they embarked on the rescue of Bastogne.

For the better part of two decades, whenever classic baseball was played (and often when very mediocre baseball was played), the great Roger Angell was there to chronicle it for the *New Yorker*. Angell's political and social sensibilities, which had not cottoned to the Los Angeles scene, were much more attuned to the San Francisco he found in October 1962.

The City has changed *drastically* as a result of the free speech movement, the antiwar movement, the gay liberation movement, the women's liberation movement, and in particular, the Summer of Love (1967). The San Francisco that emerged in the years after that event, after Vietnam and Watergate, bears little resemblance to The City that Angell found in 1962. There are still vestiges of it that will always be there, if one chooses to search them out, but in '62 it was a way of life.

San Francisco was indeed sophisticated, cultured, and foggy. It was The City of Dashiell Hammett's *Maltese Falcon*, with Humphrey Bogart leading moviegoers while "Spade turns up Powell Street." This was a far, far cry from Clint Eastwood's *Dirty Harry*, a mere decade in the future. It was a city of men in suits, elegant women, coifed hair, and evening manners; of the theater and the opera; of letters and iconoclasm.

"We've had a lot of trouble in the past few years," a woman told Angell, who by virtue of his *New Yorker* pedigree tended to run in effete literary circles. Thinking she was talking about a scandal in her family or some such thing, Angell was surprised to discover she was talking about the Giants' tendency to lose in September since their arrival in 1958. Instead of pointing out the long history of

September pratfalls that afflicted the New York Giants, Angell said nothing to the matron, "for I realized that her affair with the Giants was a true love match and that she had adopted her mate's flaws as her own. The Giants and San Francisco are a marriage made in Heaven."

How they were, and why they were, is not easy to describe. McCabe had a point, truth be told; they were *almost good enough*, just as San Francisco was. Almost good enough was good enough in these parts. Somehow, these people could turn their noses up at the team, the city, and the political figure that finished ahead of them. It was snobbery. Beating Los Angeles was like winning a competition with Howard Hughes to build rocket boosters for NASA (did they really want to do *that?*), but now—almost to their relief—another obstacle, even more daunting, had been set before them.

"You win the pennant, then you have to go out the very next day and play the Yankees," said Orlando Cepeda. "That didn't give us much time to savor our win against the Dodgers."

"The way the season ended, and the way the playoffs went, it took away a lot of the excitement of the World Series," said O'Dell. "We never really got the thrill of the Series that I believe everybody else gets."

This may well have been what made them so effective. For decades, National League teams that clinched the pennant early would spend an inordinate amount of time staring at the mounting Yankee forces, and soon they were defeated Gauls slain at the feet of the Roman Legion. Better to know death up close and quick, than to see it marching toward you over the horizon, across the valley, into your homes and villages.

Angell was shocked when he got a gander at Candlestick Park, especially after spending two days in Taj O'Malley and a pleasant evening in the salons of San Francisco cafe society. Candlestick was *nooooo* Dodger Stadium, Angell noted, "with its raw concrete ramps and walkways and its high, curving grandstand barrier, it looks from the outside like an outbuilding of"—yes, Angell got it the very first time he saw the place—"Alcatraz. But it was a festive prison yard during the first two Series games here."

The Giants used 12 pitchers in the playoffs, and the Yankees were well rested. The only advantages the Giants had was that it opened at Candlestick and they were tired, which *was* a strange advantage.

"Man, I'm tired," said Mays. "Man. We're all tired." Yes, they were exhausted, but they had *adrenaline*.

They also had the advantage of surprise.

"It's funny, we spend a week going over the Dodger hitters and here I am pitching against the Giants," said 33-year-old Whitey Ford.

When San Franciscans got a glimpse of the New York Yankees they felt like Belgians watching the victorious Americans arriving, but these larger-than-life icons were not there to liberate them. It was like somebody had hauled the statues from center field at Yankee Stadium and now they were come to life, walking about Candlestick Park. There is a truth about the Yankees; it existed then and it exists now. They *do* still have Babe Ruth and Lou Gehrig in their lineup. Those guys are *not dead*.

As if Ford, Mickey Mantle, Yogi Berra, and Roger Maris needed Ruth and Gehrig; these guys broke those guys' records. In 1962 there were a very small handful of people walking the Earth who were a bigger deal than Mickey Mantle and company—Dwight Eisenhower, John Glenn, and Douglas MacArthur, maybe. The only guys bigger than the Yankees, it seemed, were *former Yankees*, and in this a conundrum was posed. "Joltin' Joe" DiMaggio, San Francisco's own, the pride of North Beach, was unquestionably rooting for the Bronx Bombers.

This being 1962, it was before the Super Bowl, before Larry and Magic and Michael, and baseball still reigned supreme. The *World Series* was a near-religious event, and its day-games-played-during-school-days gave off a slight Holy Ghost quality, to be seen by kids whose fourth period teacher had a TV and let them watch, whose fifth period teacher did not. Snippets from the radio, 12-year-olds who were fans feeling superior to clueless classmates who were not.

The West Coast games started at noon to avoid late afternoon winds, which for the Giants—whose trip from L.A. to San Francisco and subsequent scramble for cabs, rental cars, and hitchhiked rides home—meant little sleep. They would need to rely on that adrenaline, which can often propel one to greater heights than standard preparation, at least in the short term.

The crowd arrived early, bearing picnic hampers for much gin-and-tonic tailgating. It was a polite, cheerful, well-dressed gathering, as if they were attending an outdoor opera concert, or "a country horse show," wrote Angell.

The fans watched the great Yankees take batting practice. A sense of creeping doubt began to replace the cheerful optimism engendered from the Dodger Stadium heroics. Mickey Mantle slammed four straight balls over the fence, causing one man to turn to his wife and say, "Well, at least we won the pennant." Berra, Maris, and Ellie Howard put on a pregame show. The sight of Whitey Ford confidently heading to the bullpen for warm-ups caused further shudders. At that point in his career, not only was Ford unbeatable in October play, he seemingly could not be *scored on!*

When the game started fans were in a perpetual state of worry, as in "uh oh, here comes Berra," or "don't relax, Mickey's comin' up this inning." New York jumped out to a 2-0 first inning lead, and the crowd feared a blowout. When Mays faced Ford in the second inning, they sensed that a great Hall of Fame treat had been offered them, that all the ups and downs of the crazy season were now well worth it. Mays singled and came around to score, breaking up Ford's World Series record of 33⅔ consecutive scoreless innings. Ford, who dispatched teams like an executioner, could not get Mays out and knew it.

"It doesn't matter what you throw him," Ford said. "Willie can hit it."

When Mays later drove in the tying run, the crowd seemed more relieved than happy, as if they had half-expected their heroes to fall flat on the national stage. The Giants had nine hits against Ford through six innings but could not put him away.

"Ford stands on the mound like a Fifth Avenue bank president," wrote Angell. "Tight-lipped, absolutely still between pitches, all business and concentration, he personifies the big city, emotionless perfection of his team."

Nevertheless, Mays's success against him and the flurry of hits by the home team did have the effect of demonstrating the possibility, at least, that the Giants could compete. O'Dell had better stuff and racked up strikeouts, but his control suffered. In the seventh Clete Boyer homered. New York added two more runs in the eighth and another in the ninth. The Giants also made mental and physical errors, "clustering under pop flies like firemen bracing to catch a baby dropped from a burning building," and making base running blunders.

"Ford retired the Giants on a handful of pitches and left the mound as if on his way to board the 4:30 to Larchmont," wrote Angell of Ford's six scoreless innings after the Giants scored in the third, posting a 6-2 victory.

"I'll never forget that homer," Clete Boyer said of his leadoff blast in the seventh, which broke up the 2-2 tie and was the game-winner. "I never got a hit against that guy when he was with the Orioles."

"The big play of the game was Ford," said Dark.

The night before the second game, Jack Sanford nursed a heavy cold while going over the Yankee hitters with O'Dell and Billy Pierce, two former American Leaguers.

"I need all the help you can get," said Sanford. "The Yankees scare the hell out of you." The game featured 23-game winner Ralph Terry versus the 24-game winner Sanford. Nursing his cold and with antihistamines, using a handkerchief constantly, Sanford was brilliant blending a sneaky fastball, a deceptive slider, a sharp curve, and pinpoint control to hurl a three-hit shutout, evening the Series at one in a classic October pitchers' duel, 2-0.

McCovey's monster homer off of Terry in the eighth made the score 2-0, and in this game at least, it seemed like 10 runs. Scoring almost appeared to be against the law. In the seventh and eighth, McCovey's homer, three singles, a walk, two sacrifice bunts, and a Yankee error produced just the one run. Terry pitched three-hit shutout ball until Bud Daley relieved him in the seventh.

"Our staff was in terrible shape but Jack fixed it today," said pitching coach Larry Jansen. "The name of the game is pitching. That's why we're still in it."

"When you pitch a Series victory against the Yankees, you can't complain about anything," said Sanford. "I just kept blowing my nose and pitching strikes. I guess I did pretty good for a dumb Irishman."

"Jack's always had good stuff, but today he had perfect control," said Jansen. "He kept the ball low and he wasn't afraid to go with his slider when he fell behind."

"We know we're in the Series," said Dark. "We played good ball in both games. We're every bit the pros the Yankees are supposed to be."

Giants fans filled with hope filed joyously out of Candlestick Park.

When the Series shifted to New York City, it took an entirely different tone. There was none of the hopeful joy of San Francisco. The Big Apple more resembled

General MacArthur's forces, having been dealt a blow, regrouping for the final surge, confident of victory and entirely aware precisely how to attain it—the methodology and the cost. They were in the *business* of winning. It was not a contemplated possibility; rather, Series victories were accomplished past acts.

The Yankees were like a veteran writer of books, the Giants a first-time novelist. The veteran scribe knows precisely how and when he will finish his book because he has so much experience and has done it many times. He is confident of his ability because there is no mystery in how he achieves his goals.

The first-time novelist, meanwhile, is armed with a great idea and inspiration, but is beset by writer's block and procrastination, doubts about his ability, alarmed by the looming deadline. Nevertheless, the Giants were filled with talent, and it could not be denied.

The Yankee crowds were a total 180 from Candlestick. Photographs reveal fans who either resembled bankers or were Sam Giancana look-alikes, gangsters and their molls in sunglasses, suits, and mink stoles. There was little cheering or pleading. They almost looked like foreigners dispassionately watching a game they did not comprehend.

The San Francisco women had been elegant, and in this regard the New York women looked similar in their expensive coats and coifed hair, but there was none of the noise, no excitement despite the fact that the crowd was a standing room only 71,431. The only emotion seemed reserved for Maris, who was booed lustily.

"C'mon, bum!"

Radios were tuned to a New York Giants football game. Conversation seemed more concerned with the latest Wall Street events or advertising trends. This was the New Rome at the height of hubris. The athletes below were merely paid gladiators brought forth for their amusement. In the sixth inning, large clusters of businessman-fans started to leave, "preserving their ticket stubs to the persevering verticals," Angell wrote, so they could "tell their friends they had been to a Series game." The *New Yorker* columnist suspected that many of the fans were not even New Yorkers, but rather out of town business execs whose tickets were perks.

Despite the lack of enthusiasm, however, those athletes on the green plains below engaged in an astonishing brand of great baseball; the building October tension that marks it as the very best of all sports. For six scoreless innings, Billy Pierce and Bill Stafford matched each other in dominating form.

In the sixth, Maris came to the plate, a tragic hero, unloved despite incredible accomplishments. Had he led Cleveland, or Kansas City, or St. Louis into a similar situation, he would have been elevated to the worshipful status of Rocky Colavito or Stan "The Man" Musial, but in New York all he was, was not the Mick. Ignoring the flack, like a bomber intent on hitting the target regardless, Maris delivered a clutch single to drive in two runs, breaking up the deadlock.

"We didn't want to give him anything good to hit, but I missed with a fastball and put it down the middle and Maris had his hit," said Pierce. The Yankees added a third run. Pierce was gone, replaced by Larsen, another oddly unheroic Yankee returning to his scene of triumph.

Stafford had a shutout until Ed Bailey's two-run homer closed the gap to 3-2 in the ninth. What was left of the crowd looked on, sure that "the Major," manager Ralph Houk, would quell the rebel uprising in time for the cocktail hour. Houk visited Stafford.

"I didn't see any blood on the mound, so I decided to leave Bill in," the grinning skipper said. "He was pitching a great game and I didn't want to deprive him of a chance to go all the way."

Houk left, the fans and his team supremely confident that any battlefield decisions he made were infallible. When Stafford got the last out with little trouble their confidence was now full arrogance. There seemed no stopping the Bronx Bombers from wrapping up the Series at home, winning in five as they had done in dispatching overmatched Cincinnati the previous year.

The fourth game was sink or swim for the Giants. To lose and fall behind, three games to one, giving New York the chance to close it out at home, would be an impossible hole to crawl out of. The crowd also transformed itself from the tourists of game three, replaced by real fans, a fair number of whom were rooting for the Giants. These were the same people who had been witnessing the Giants getting slaughtered at the foot of pinstriped hegemony since their last triumph, when manager John McGraw, pitcher Art Nehf, and infielder Frankie "the Fordham Flash" Frisch led the club to victory over Babe Ruth's Yankees in 1922. At that time, the Giants were the kings of baseball, the Yankees mere upstarts who rented the Polo Grounds and had never won a World Series.

Beginning in 1923, when the Yankees moved into Yankee Stadium, "the House That Ruth Built," they had won 19 World Championships, the Giants just two. Angell described the Giants rooters as "filled with the same pride, foreboding, and strong desire to avert one's eyes that was felt by the late General Pickett." For the first time, the full resonance of what this World Series really was hit home.

It was an East-West Fall Classic. For most of the season, the New York fans and media mentally prepared for the Dodgers and the first rematch of "Subway Series" opponents from the 1940s and 1950s. It was the Dodgers, more than the Giants, who dominated the last decade of three-team baseball in the Apple, and it was the Dodgers whose exodus brought on the most tears, the greatest angst, and now the most yearning. It was the Dodgers, above all others, who seemed to inspire the new Mets, whose lineup was chock full of the former *Boys of Summer.*

The first greatly anticipated Yankees-Dodgers World Series had not happened. In the odd 1959 season, Los Angeles never looked to be a real contender until they won at the end, while the Yankees stumbled for their only loss of the pennant in what would be the span of a decade. Throughout all of 1962, the battle of titans, Broadway versus Hollywood, had been built up to fevered anticipation.

Drysdale and Snider would return, along with the hated O'Malley, and the prodigal son, Koufax. The Yankees' trips to Los Angeles to play the Angels, and their princely reception at Johnny Grant parties, had served as buildup for the eventual arrival of the Bronx Bombers at Dodger Stadium for actual World Series games.

Dodger visits to the Polo Grounds for series with the Mets had served a similar purpose, whetting the appetite of their legion of Brooklyn fans, now spread throughout the tri state area in the aftermath of "white flight."

The surprise ending to the season, resulting in San Francisco's victory, had shocked many. It had taken much of the country, including most New Yorkers, a few days to get used to it. The first game of the World Series had been played less than 24 hours after game three of the playoffs, and there had been no time for the press to build up the battle of an inexorable object versus an impenetrable force.

But game four at the Stadium changed all that. It was a classic with classic moments that live on in Series memory. The fact that a great October duel was occurring played itself before the eyes of New York on October 8. Suddenly, the realization that the Giants versus the Yankees had every bit as much panache as the Dodgers versus the Yankees eased into the conscience of the sports world. It was, in fact, the New York Giants, not Brooklyn, who first opposed the great Yankees in the 1920s and 1930s, and in the beginning they gave as well as they got.

Suddenly, memories of Giant glory flooded across: Joe DiMaggio's last hurrah in 1951, the same year rookies Mickey Mantle and Willie Mays debuted on the world stage and the shadow of Leo Durocher loomed larger than life; and 1954, when the Giants beat Cleveland for the World Championship, with Mays making The Catch—as memorable a moment as any before or since.

After all, Yankees fans suddenly asked themselves, what was so great about *Milwaukee, Pittsburgh and Cincinnati* anyway? Boring Middle American villages. Sure, L.A. had those Johnny Grant parties, but San Francisco was built in the image of New York City. It had been that way since the transcontinental railroad was completed. Its citizenry, its skyline, and now its baseball team were paeans to Manhattan. What was not to like about a place that practiced imitation, the sincerest form of flattery?

Plus, they had *Willie Mays!* It was occurring to these New Yorkers that for all the love they exuded for Mantle, and all the traditions of Ruth, Gehrig, and DiMaggio, it was possible, just possible, that the very best of them all was the San Francisco center fielder.

The game four starters had the ring of a true classic: Marichal versus Ford. How many times in baseball history have two Hall of Fame pitchers faced each other in the World Series? It has happened, but not often.

Up until game four, the Giants tended to respond to enemy scores, but this time they staked the "Dominican Dandy" to a 2-0 lead in the second inning. Marichal seemed completely recovered from his September injuries and dominated New York bats with a two-hit shutout through four innings. Watching Juan's high kick and unhittable deliverance of spheres, the Yankees realized that they were in for the fight of their lives; in this game and in the Series, which suddenly seemed inevitably headed back to the West Coast, where anything could happen because in 1962 it already had!

Then in the fifth Marichal tried to bunt and took an inside pitch from Ford on his hand, clutching the bat. The Giants did not score. Dark looked askance at Marichal, who somehow was still suspect in his eyes. He blamed the pitcher for getting hurt, too much it seemed. Sal Maglie, in Dark's view, would have pitched through it, but it was the end of the line for Juan and Bob Bolin, a flamethrower but no Marichal, took over in the fifth.

The 23-year-old was inexperienced, and the Yankees circled him like hungry wolves, the tension getting thicker by the minute. Bolin pitched in and out of a tough jam, but in the sixth he got wild, walking Mantle and Maris, and the Yanks tied the game. At that point, hope was hard to keep afloat for the San Franciscans, who, minus the great Marichal, were trying to stem the legion in unfriendly territory. The fans, who had slowly built up momentum, now were into it, realizing for the first time that their team needed them.

For the Giants, some act of surprise, of great consequence, needed to occur in order to stop the bleeding, reverse the momentum, and keep them in the World Series. They looked to their most likely heroes—Mays, Cepeda, and McCovey, who were all curiously slumping—but the hero would be the most unlikely of all.

In the top of the seventh, with Ford out of the game, the Giants loaded the bases on a pinch-hit double by Matty Alou sandwiched in between two walks. Chuck Hiller and his three 1962 home runs stepped to the plate against Marshall Bridges. Hiller, who had struck out with men on in the fifth, got something he could sink his teeth into and lifted a fly ball toward the right field fence.

A famed photograph taken from beyond right field tells the story. The look on Hiller's face, as he drops his bat and heads out of the box, is one of hope and astonishment at what he may have just done. Catcher Elston Howard looks *worried*. The fans seated in the expensive box seats behind the screen have weary I've-seen-it-all expressions that capture the time and place. But these modern Roman senators are also just realizing that the gladiator, slated to die before thine eyes, has instead won the day against their chosen favorite.

Hiller, with 21 total homers in eight years, hit a grand slam and suddenly the Giants led, 7-3. Larsen was the winning pitcher six years to the day after his 1956 perfecto, and now, whether the Yanks had left their hearts in San Francisco or not, they were returning there, looking for another ring.

With momentum on their side, the key fifth game was San Francisco's golden opportunity to swing things around some more, giving them the all-important 3-2 lead heading back to Candlestick. But it was the ability to quell just such threats that had always marked the Yankees, and it was to be so again on October 10.

The 1962 Series produced a series of classic October photos, and in game five it was Willie McCovey stretching the full length of his 6'4" frame while Bobby Richardson slides safely into first base. Richardson later scored. The Giants made the mistake of handing the unsentimental Yankees a chance to get back in the fifth game. Bailey just missed a tying two-run homer by 15 feet.

Sanford struck out 10, but a wild pitch in the fourth and a passed ball in the sixth led to two New York runs in a 5-3 Yankee win. Tresh, establishing himself as a hero in a Series that increasingly saw little out of Mantle, Maris, Howard, Berra, or Richardson, hit a three-run homer, and Terry earned the win, his first in five postseason tries.

"I'm not particularly happy about it," said Dark. "I would have been happier if we won three in a row here."

Unlike the playoffs, each Series game had been taut and filled with professional tension. Each club showed not merely a desire to win, but the right to victory, which had not marked the final pangs of the NL pennant race and playoffs. Each game had been decided by a key, game-of-inches play—important strikes delivered, a double play just missed—and it appeared obvious that these were indeed the two best teams in baseball. A classic finish was in the offing.

A freak Pacific storm laid siege to San Francisco just as the two teams were getting ready for the sixth game. There were no games between Wednesday, October 10 and Monday, October 15. The massive storm hit Northern California with hurricane force winds, caused five deaths, knocked out power lines, ravaged property all the way to the Oregon border, and dropped nearly two inches of rain on The City. Commissioner Ford Frick postponed the games until the weather abated. Both teams trekked to the hinterlands to practice and wait it out. Dodger executive Fresco Thompson quipped, "Why call the game? When we play it's wetter than this."

Local and national pundits had ample time to extrapolate on the fate of the Giants, and the increasing awareness that the '62 Fall Classic may indeed be one for the ages. It was the media's opportunity to say all the things they were originally unable to say because of the short timeframe between the playoffs and the Series. Many posited the notion that Yankee victory would add to their smugness, but ultimate victory would result in a horn-blowing Market Street celebration, drawing rubes from the outlying provinces of Marin County, San Mateo, and Oakland, all to the consternation of the sophisticates.

"Total triumph is unsettling," wrote Charles McCabe, the resident "oracle of Mission Street."

Future defeat was seen as a fatal virus, and "Giant fans, like all neurotics, are unappeasable," wrote Angell. "I can see it now—the Dodgers should have won the pennant." L.A., after all, was the "city that could," where champions resided— the 1952 Rams, 1954 Bruins, 1959 Dodgers, and 1962 Trojans. Their victories had been attained on the backs of opponents from Berkeley, Stanford, and San Francisco who ranged from losers to worthy challengers.

When the rain finally stopped, bad drainage on the Candlestick playing surface postponed game six an additional 24 hours. Three helicopters were brought in to buzz the field, but the grass remained soggy. Frick called it "miserable conditions," but play resumed October 15. One man who could not wait for the rain to stop was Horace Stoneham, dismayed to see his booze supply depleted in the hospitality room of the Sheraton-Palace Hotel, where hundreds of writers had nothing to do but get drunk.

The Yankees, in typically smug fashion, made return plane reservations for the night of the sixth game. Instead, Billy Pierce tossed a sweet three-hitter. He was perfect until Maris homered in the fifth, but coasted to a 5-2 win over Ford, now human for the first time, it seemed.

The rain had allowed the Giants to rest, and to get their arms lined up. First and foremost, that meant ace right-hander Jack Sanford, the game seven starter. He allowed only a single by Tony Kubek in the first four innings. His opponent was up to the task. Ralph Terry retired the first 17 batters he faced.

In the fifth, the Yanks opened with two singles and a walk. Kubek then hit a 6-4-3 double-play grounder, but Moose Skowron scored and it was 1-0, Yankees. Tresh made a marvelous catch of a long drive to left field by Mays. Another classic photo shows Tresh fully extended, the ball "snow coned" on the tip of his glove.

Billy O'Dell relieved Sanford with the bases loaded in the eighth but pitched out of the jam. It all came down to the excruciating bottom of the ninth inning, with San Francisco trailing 1-0, hoping to get to Mays and McCovey, scheduled fourth and fifth up in the inning.

It looked promising when pinch hitter Matty Alou's bunt single led off the inning. It was Matty whose hit of Ed Roebuck started the fateful ninth inning rally in the game three playoff with the Dodgers. Alou's drag bunt was only the third hit of the afternoon against Terry.

Terry was working hard and had much on his mind. He had given up Bill Mazeroski's walk-off homer to lose the 1960 World Series to Pittsburgh and certainly did not want to be the "goat" again. The crowd was pleading, hope against hope, a wall of sound and violent, anguished cries. Bearing down, Terry struck out Felipe Alou and Hiller while Matty stood forlornly at first base.

Now, the moment all had been waiting for, the Giants raison d'être, what San Franciscans had expected since the Giants came west: Willie Mays with everything on the line. Baseball does not get better than this!

Terry worked Mays low and away, maybe because of an old scouting report. Mays, reacting to the Candlestick winds, had adjusted his power toward right field. Terry said he thought that he put "real good stuff on it, but Willie opened up and just hit it with his hands." He wristed the ball, powering a shot into the right field corner.

Matty Alou had speed and at first it seemed that he could score the tying run from first base, but Mays's double got stuck in the soggy grass. Roger Maris got to it, whirled, and made a good throw. Coach Whitey Lockman held Alou at third base. To this day, the decision is disputed, but replays seem to indicate that Lockman made the right call.

"I'd make the same decision 1,000 times out of 1,000," Lockman insisted. Dark agreed. Both Maris and the cut-off man, Bobby Richardson, had strong, accurate arms.

"Matty would have been out by a mile," said Ralph Houk.

"Roger Maris was playing me to pull, and he cut the ball off before it could get to the fence," recalled Mays. "If that field was dry, the ball rolls to the fence, Matty scores, and I'm on third."

Instead, Mays was on second, Alou was on third, and McCovey was coming to the plate. Leading 1-0 with two outs, Houk came to the mound to confer with Terry and Howard. McCovey had scorched a triple in a prior at-bat and had hit a homer in an earlier Series game. First base was open, but Terry said, "I could get McCovey out. I felt I had a pretty good line on him. . . . Maybe I was overconfident."

The decisions that were made doubtfully would be made today: leave Terry in, don't intentionally walk McCovey, and pitch to him. McCovey stepped in, a left-handed threat against the right-handed Terry. The odds seemed to favor Willie Mac, but then again these *were the Yankees!*

Terry threw a slow curve, down and away, hoping to fool the slugger. McCovey hit what at first looked like the last out, a fly ball to Maris in right. Then the wind got ahold of it for a three-run game-winning home run—except that at the last second the wind pushed it foul.

The crowed was shocked. Standing, imploring, they watched McCovey pick up his bat and get back into the box. Next was a fastball, Terry challenging him. McCovey leaned into it and hit one on the screws, a searing line drive. Richardson moved just a step to his left, stuck his glove up as much to protect himself as anything, and caught it. The impact knocked him to his knees, where the devout Christian bowed before jumping up to join his teammates in celebration of the Yankees' 20th World Championship in 39 years.

"I hit that ball as hard as I could," said McCovey. "I wasn't thinking about anything when I connected, but when you hit it good, you assume it's going to be a hit."

Photos of the post game scene show kids with "flood" pants, varsity jackets, and various officials wearing visors, a popular item of the day, surrounding the celebrating Yankees, who carried Terry off the field on their shoulders

"I said it would go seven, because you don't beat the Yanks in less than seven," said Dark.

"I was afraid I was going to faint when McCovey hit that ball," said Terry. "I probably would have fainted if it had gone through. . . . A man rarely gets the kind of second chance I did. . . . I was real thankful I had a chance to redeem myself in the seventh game of the World Series, because I'd been the loser in the seventh game at Pittsburgh in 1960."

"This was the best pitched Series game I've ever seen," said Joe DiMaggio. "In fact, the pitching was great all Series."

"It may be noted that the Yankees are the least popular of all baseball clubs, because they win, which leaves nothing to 'if' about," wrote boxing writer A. J. Liebling, in San Francisco during the last two games for a prize fight.

There was plenty to "if" about for the Giants. What-ifs? cropped up about the length and sogginess of the outfield grass; *if* not "a foot either way" Mc-Covey's liner would have won it, although replays showed Richardson could have gone much further than that to spear it.

Dark was asked if Mays would have scored from second had McCovey's liner gone to the outfield. He replied that Mays would have been dressed by the time the Yankees got the ball home, an ode to his instincts as a base runner and speed.

"I'm just as proud of my players as if they had won the Series," said Dark. "They played just great. When you go down to the last out and the Series is decided by maybe one foot on a line drive, you've battled all the way."

It was the most time-consuming Series since the 1911 Fall Classic lasted 13 days.

"It was a crazy Series, but it was a crazy season," said Dark. "You never forget a year like '62."

Horace Stoneham threw a party in the stadium club, which included 400 people and all the players. In those days, rings only went to the winners. He bought the players solid gold money clips reading "San Francisco Giants—1962 National League Champions," with crossed bats and balls. Each player's name was carved on the bat, personalized. McCormick said he carried his for years, but stopped because "I think its value is probably too great" to risk theft or loss.

In the end, all the star power on both sides failed to live up to its ultimate billing in a Series dominated by great pitching. Terry was the Series MVP and Outstanding Pitcher, but with a few lucky bounces those honors could just as easily have gone to Jack Sanford, whose hard-luck 1-2 record was accompanied by a 1.93 earned run average in 23⅓ innings pitched.

"We were told he was a six or seven inning pitcher," Mantle said of Sanford. "We figured if we kept it close, Sanford would lose his stuff by the eighth."

"We learned a lot of things about the Giants in the Series, but we were wrong about Sanford," said Houk. "He's a heck of a pitcher."

The Yankees hit .199, the third lowest for a winning team ever. The Giants outhit them by 27 points and outscored them, 21-20, but it was a reversal of fortune from 1960. The batting averages were Tresh (.321), Clete Boyer (.318), Mantle (.120 on 3-for-25), Maris (.174), Howard (.143), Pagan (.368), Mays (.250), Cepeda (.158), and Kuenn (.083). Much of the post-Series anguish was directed at Orlando Cepeda, who disappeared against the Yankees.

"I know better than anybody else how terrible I was," said Cepeda. "I do nothing right. I try everything but nothing helps. I feel bad because I let the others down. It's terrible when you're not doing your share. I'm very tired. Between here and Puerto Rico, I play 300 games this year. That is too much."

The Giants thought about trading him. "He just couldn't get his bat around," said Stoneham. "Sometimes he was missing pitches by six inches. That's not what he's being paid $47,000 a year for."

In the Series, Felipe Alou hit third, second, first, sixth, third, and first. His .269 average included a hit in every game but the third and the seventh. San Francisco lost both by a run.

"Davenport surprised me more than any other Giants," said Ralph Terry. "We didn't think he was that good and even though he didn't hit too high, he hit the ball real well."

Charles Schulz, a Bay Area resident, Giants fan, and creator of the *Peanuts* cartoon strip, may have captured San Francisco's sense of longing as well as anybody. In three panels, Charlie Brown sits quietly in a near-catatonic trance, then burst into tears, cursing to the Heavens: "Why couldn't McCovey have hit the ball just three feet higher?"

On Sunday, October 21, President John F. Kennedy asked if the U.S. Air Force could take out all the missiles that had been discovered by reconnaissance flights on the island of Cuba. Cuban dictator Fidel Castro, a major thorn in JFK's side, had invited the Soviets to park nukes there. The reply was, "Only the ones we know about." President Kennedy then asked about casualties, both civilian and military. The answer was 10,000 to 20,000. This influenced Kennedy's decision to forgo an air strike and set up a blockade around Cuba.

Another U-2 flight discovered bombers being rapidly assembled and cruise missile sites being built on Cuba's northern shore.

The press learned there were offensive weapons in Cuba and questioned President Kennedy. He asked the reporters not to break the news until he informed the American people on network television the next evening. If they denied him the element of surprise, he warned, "I don't know what the Soviets will do."

On Wednesday, October 24, Soviet ships approached the quarantine line. EX-COMM wondered if Nikita Khrushchev had had enough time to instruct the ship captains. Later that day, they got their answer. Soviet ships stopped dead in the water after receiving a radio message from Moscow.

"We were eyeball to eyeball and the other guy just blinked," said Secretary of State Dean Rusk.

On Sunday, October 28, Nikita Khrushchev announced over Radio Moscow that the Soviets would dismantle their nuclear missiles in Cuba. Khrushchev could have insisted that the United States respond to the greater demands in the second letter, but he did not. By backing down, Khrushchev ruined his career but prevented nuclear disaster.

ELEVEN

The October of Their Years

"You have to have a lot of little boy in you to play baseball."
—*Roy Campanella*

Walter Alston was rehired shortly after the 1962 World Series. Buzzie Bavasi called him in Darrtown, Ohio.

"Smokey, if you haven't got anything better to do next spring, meet me in Vero Beach," he said to him. There were no more hard feelings. The fact that Los Angeles had just set the all-time attendance record certainly played a part in the decision.

Alston dealt with Durocher until 1964. In 1963 he led the Dodgers to ultimate glory—a pennant and four-game sweep of the New York Yankees—won in front of a Dodger Stadium throng.

With Durocher out of his hair, he repeated the act in 1965. His managing of that team is considered one of the most masterful of all time. The Dodgers had zero offense, leaving it up to Alston to manufacture runs, and then make maximum use of the Koufax-Drysdale duo to win numerous 1-0 and 2-1 games en route to a pennant and World Series triumph over Minnesota.

Alston did the exact same thing in 1966, when Los Angeles captured another pennant before their hitting woes caught up to them in a four-game sweep at the hands of Baltimore.

Alston oversaw another "youth movement" between 1969 (when the club was known as "The Mod Squad" after a popular TV show) and 1973. In 1974 he steered the club to 102 victories and a Championship Series triumph over

Pittsburgh, but the vaunted Oakland A's beat them for their third straight World Championship.

Alston retired at the end of the 1976 season with 2,040 career victories. Aside from his five pennants and three World Championships, he managed five teams to second place finishes. Alston was elected to the Hall of Fame in 1983.

"Out of my whole managerial career, I'd like to have back the last week of the '62 season, and the playoffs," he said. It was his only known regret.

Alston passed away in 1984.

Leo Durocher eventually got what he deserved.

Before that, his rehiring surprised everybody. When it was announced at a press conference, Walt Alston's voice was heard on a squawk box. "I am not convinced he said those things [at the Grenadier]," Alston stated. "And I've always gotten along well with him."

Durocher stayed on through the successful 1963 campaign and the 1964 season, when Sandy Koufax's injury derailed the club's chances in August. He took over the Chicago Cubs in 1966, ending the club's policy of "revolving managers." His first observation of the Cubs was that they were not a ninth place team. In his first year they were a 10th place team, but Durocher steered Chicago to respectability for the first time since 1945.

In 1969 he had the Cubs flying high, in first place all season, but was blamed for overmanaging, playing tired players, insisting on a four-man rotation with little bullpen relief, and placing undue pressure on his team, when they blew the lead against the Amazin' Mets. The man who claimed he would have steered the Dodgers to the 1962 pennant had failed to produce when placed in similar circumstances seven years later. Alston, by then as respected a manager as there was in the game, refrained from gloating.

Durocher managed a few more years in Chicago, then briefly in Houston, before retiring. Only five managers had more wins. All were in the Hall of Fame, but "the Lip" never got in while he was alive. Embittered, he told friends to reject his induction after his death, which occurred in 1991 at the age of 86. In 1994 the Veteran's Committee voted him in.

In 1963 baseball's rules committee expanded the strike zone, restoring it to the pre-1950s standard: the top of the shoulders to the base of the knees. This propelled Sandy Koufax and Don Drysdale to great heights in what may be the greatest pitching decade ever. Drysdale matured, resurrected his relationship with Alston, and apologized to the manager and anybody else he offended. He was a temperamental man who got in trouble with his mouth during his career and later as a broadcaster with the Angels, but he was also a gentleman who knew when he was wrong and was not afraid to admit it. All who knew him said he was a class act who never put on airs. He just wanted to win.

In 1963 Drysdale beat Jim Bouton of the Yankees, 1-0, in a classic Dodger Stadium matchup en route to a Los Angeles four-game sweep. While he won his only Cy Young award and a career-high 25 games in 1962, 1965 must go down as his best season. He was 23-12 with a 2.77 ERA, but pitched with broken ribs (unknown by the manager) down the stretch; all clutch victories that led Los Angeles to the pennant. He pitched brilliantly in the World Series, a seven-game thriller over Minnesota.

However, Drysdale was hit hard in the first game of the 1965 Series. Koufax was slated to start, but the game fell on Yom Kippur. Koufax sat it out, and Big D took his place. After losing, he approached Alston and wryly told him, "I bet you wish I was Jewish, don't you?"

Pitching at Dodger Stadium, he atoned for his poor performance in Minnesota and the club won the title. In 1966 Drysdale and Koufax held out in contentious contract negotiations with Bavasi. Drysdale threatened to join the Screen Actor's Guild, to leave baseball for the movies. He and Koufax made a movie with David Janssen, *Warning Shot*, and told the press they were individually wealthy and did not need baseball. Bavasi told the writers, "good luck with their acting careers." The Dodgers' general manager was so consumed by the negotiation that he forgot to submit L.A.'s bid for USC pitcher Tom Seaver in a special draft, thus denying the club a chance at a homegrown Hall of Famer in the 1970s.

When they returned, Koufax was brilliant, Drysdale was not (13-16), but they still combined to pitch the Dodgers into the 1966 World Series. Drysdale again pitched below par in the Series opener with Baltimore, but was excellent in an outing at Memorial Stadium. Lack of offensive support—which marked his career in L.A.—made him a 1-0 loser.

When Koufax retired after the season ended, Drysdale resumed his role as staff ace, which he had held from 1957 to 1962. In 1968, the "Year of the Pitcher," the 31-year-old pitched six straight shutouts, completing a Major League record of 58⅔ straight scoreless innings. The record was attained at Dodger Stadium on June 8, a few days after Robert Kennedy was shot at the Ambassador Hotel, only a few miles away. Drysdale was a Kennedy admirer and was shaken by the experience.

After attaining the record, Drysdale's season fell flat, and he finished 14-12 with a 2.15 ERA on an average club. He retired in 1969; the sturdy right-hander suddenly experienced arm troubles after a durable career. His record was 209-166 with a 2.95 ERA and 2,486 strikeouts.

Drysdale announced for the California Angels during Nolan Ryan's prime years. He later joined Vin Scully in the Dodgers' broadcast booth. He was elected to the Hall of Fame in 1984. Drysdale had a strange incident occur in Montreal when he was apparently drugged, possibly by a woman at the hotel bar, who may have wanted to lure him to her room to steal from him or worse. His marriage to the beauty queen Ginger did not last, but he did remarry, to the great UCLA women's basketball star Ann Meyer. He died tragically young in 1993 at the age of 56.

Sandy Koufax also benefited from expansion of the strike zone in 1963. All previous assumptions or questions—about his toughness, his competitiveness, his relationship with Walt Alston—were dispelled that season when he exploded above and beyond all expectations.

He was 25-5 with a 1.88 earned run average, 11 shutouts, and 306 strikeouts. He earned the Cy Young as well as National League MVP awards, then was named the MVP of the World Series when he beat the New York Yankees twice, 5-2 and 2-1. It was one of, if not the most, dominating seasons ever recorded by a pitcher.

In the opener at Yankee Stadium, a ballyhooed Koufax-Ford matchup was all Sandy when he set the big league record for strikeouts in a World Series game, with 15. Koufax shocked the mighty Yankees. Their commentary was laced with defeatist phraseology, with Ralph Houk stating they had "27 outs left" before facing him in game four. Mickey Mantle, Yogi Berra, and others expressed amazement that Koufax had managed to lose five games that season.

Koufax was just as good in 1964, carrying a 19-5 record with a 1.74 ERA and 223 strikeouts in 223 innings pitched until he was injured in August. With

Koufax out for the year, Los Angeles dropped out of the pennant race. In 1965 he may have been better than ever, going 26-8 with a 2.04 ERA. His perfect game against the Chicago Cubs was the fourth no-hitter of his career, and his 382 strikeouts set the new Major League record. He won his second Cy Young award and added two wins over the Twins as the Dodgers won the World Series.

Could Koufax be better? Yes, he could, and he was in 1966 when he was 27-9 with a 1.73 ERA and 317 strikeouts, leading the anemic-hitting Dodgers to the National League title. Squaring off against rookie Jim Palmer of Baltimore in the World Series, Koufax was betrayed by Willie "Three Dog" Davis, who despite being a superb defensive center fielder somehow could not handle catching or throwing that day in a 6-0 loss at Chavez Ravine.

Duke Snider felt that Koufax from 1963 to 1966 was the greatest pitcher ever. "He comes closer to being unhittable than any other pitcher I ever saw," said Frank Shaughnessy, the late president of the International League, who had seen Christy Mathewson, Grover Cleveland Alexander, and Walter Johnson.

"Against that guy we should get four strikes," one batter said. Koufax announced his retirement after the 1966 season. He was 30 years old with a 165-87 record, 2.76 ERA, and 2,396 strikeouts. He said that the pain of injuries was too great, that he wanted to enjoy his life without enduring a debilitating ailment that would prevent him from living like a normal man. Koufax said the pain of hot salves applied to his arm before games was even greater than the pain of pitching. He hated the freezing ice applied to his arm after games and claimed he was on so many medications to dull his senses that he was constantly "high," worried about operating a car or thinking straight.

Koufax's acting career never amounted to anything. He tried broadcasting and was on the national *Game of the Week* crew for a few years, but his personality was so dull that he was not very good at it. He wrote an uninspiring autobiography and had biographies written about him, the best of which was written by Jane Leavy in 2002. He remained, for the most part, mysterious. Of all the myths he was most eager to and worked hardest to dispel was the idea that he was an intellectual, uninterested in baseball greatness, the idea that it had all been an accident. He had worked too hard, he stated, for that to have been the case.

Koufax married the daughter of movie star Richard Widmark and tried to live a quiet life in Santa Barbara, but the marriage was not successful. In 1970 the *Associated Press* named him Player of the Decade.

"I'm not being modest, but I never had 10 good years in the decade," said Koufax. "I had about five. A lot of people had 10 good ones. . . . This award was a very big one. But there were so many great players in the decade, it had to be hard to single out one.

"I might have chosen Mays or maybe Mantle or Aaron. I'm still surprised I got it, because I haven't pitched since 1966. . . . It's hard to single out the highlights, because big years are more important than single big moments. Consistency is the main thing."

Koufax made a point in his autobiography that he approached games in May the same as September pennant-clinchers. The moments that did stand out for him included "the perfect game against the Cubs," which "might be the biggest, but I'll never forget my victory in the seventh game of the 1965 World Series and that win over the Yankees in New York to start the 1963 Series. . . . You know, I never won 30 games in a year, but that doesn't gnaw at me at all. To do it, you have to be terribly good and terribly lucky.

"But you have to get the decisions, too, and if you don't get a lot of runs, you won't. 30 is a heck of a number. Heck, I would have liked to win 40, or all of them for that matter. . . . As the years go by, I miss baseball less, but I still get the urge to pitch when Spring Training comes around. Or when the pennant race goes into the last week.

"But you have to face the fact that everything ends."

He was named to the Hall of Fame in 1972 at the age of 36, the youngest inductee ever. For years, Koufax's public appearances, which always generated enormous excitement, have mostly been when he worked with Dodger pitchers in Spring Training. In an episode of HBO's *Entourage*, an untrue rumor of Koufax's demise was the premise for the Kevin Dillon character's purchase of a vintage 1966 Koufax number 32 jersey.

Tommy Davis won the batting title again in 1963 and seemed headed straight to Cooperstown until, early in 1965, he suffered a terrible leg injury on the basepaths. Without Davis, the Dodgers—known as the "Hitless Wonders"—had little offense, but won the World Championship behind the extraordinary pitching of Koufax and Drysdale. After the 1966 pennant-winning campaign,

Davis was traded to his hometown New York Mets. His injury healed but he never approached the explosive athletic prowess of 1962–63 again. Still, he was a consistent .300 hitter who played for the White Sox, Pilots, Astros, A's, Cubs, Orioles, Angels, and Royals in a well-traveled career. He was a strong contributor to the A's championships and a member of the Orioles when they were contenders. Davis retired at the end of the 1976 season with a .294 career average. He was Seattle's hitting coach in 1981.

Maury Wills had a starstruck Dodger career. He batted .302 in 1963 and stole 94 bases in 1965 and 38 in 1966, leading the National League in that category for six straight seasons. After the 1966 season, he made outspoken contract demands of Bavasi. Walter O'Malley developed an open dislike of him and ordered him dealt to Pittsburgh. He went to the expansion Montreal Expos in 1969 but returned a prodigal son after playing 47 games for the Expos.

In that 1969 season, the first year of divisional play, the veteran Wills helped lead "The Mod Squad" into contention in "The Wild, Wild West" (the name of another popular TV series). Wills played through the 1972 campaign, until Bill Russell was able to assume the mantel. He finished with 586 stolen bases and a .281 lifetime average, and later managed the Seattle Mariners (1980–81). His son, Bump, played at Arizona State University and made it to the big leagues. In the 1970s Wills lived in the swingin' singles community of Marina Del Rey, where he fell into the cocaine habit that marked the disco era. He managed to overcome his demons and, like many Dodger icons, had a long career as a special instructor, naturally focusing on the art of base running.

Ron Fairly felt that the 1962 loss spurred the Dodgers to future successes.

"The disappointment in '62 was definitely a springboard for the success we had in '63," he said. "We were just about the same ballclub, but we had greater resolve during the course of the '63 season. We swore we wouldn't let 1962 happen again."

Fairly was a reliable Dodger, at first base or in the outfield, until 1969. With Wes Parker fixed at first base, he was traded to the Expos in 1969 and was a mainstay under manager Gene Mauch at Montreal. He then went to the St. Louis

Cardinals in 1975, followed by stints with the Oakland A's and Toronto Blue Jays. He retired in 1978 with 215 career homers and a .266 average. Fairly became a broadcaster for the Angels and, of all teams, the Giants, then the Mariners in 1993.

Willie "Three Dog" Davis played with the Dodgers until the end of the 1973 season. He made two of the worst defensive plays ever in the same inning—in a 1966 World Series game at Dodger Stadium—and then followed that up with one of the best. In 1969 Davis went on a 31-game hitting streak. Overall, he was considered one of the finest defensive center fielders of his era, but was generally an underrated player. He played at the same time as Willie Mays and Mickey Mantle. Davis retired in 1979 with 182 career homers, 398 stolen bases, and a .279 batting average.

Jim "Junior" Gilliam played through the 1964 season and became one of Walt Alston's most trusted colleagues. He was reactivated in 1965 and again in 1966, helping the club win pennants down the stretch both years. His lifetime batting average was .265 with 203 stolen bases. He mastered the art of the sacrifice bunt, the sacrifice fly, and moved countless runners along with ground balls to the right side. When Jackie Robinson publicly asked for a black coach in 1972, it was Gilliam who first fulfilled that wish. In 1978, at age 49, Gilliam died tragically of a brain hemorrhage. Alston cried while giving his eulogy.

Frank "Hondo" Howard was traded to the Washington Senators after the 1964 season. Over the next seven years he was considered one of the most dangerous sluggers in the game, winning two American League home run crowns. He was constantly considered a threat to break Roger Maris's record. Howard slammed 10 home runs in one week in 1968 and 48 in 1969 under new manager Ted Williams. He went to Texas when the Senators moved there in 1972 and finished with Detroit in 1973. He had 382 lifetime home runs and a .273 batting average. He played briefly in Japan and managed the Padres in 1981 and the Mets in 1983. Hondo also coached for several teams.

In 1965 Juan Marichal clubbed John Roseboro over the head with a bat at Candlestick Park. Marichal claimed that Roseboro "buzzed" his ear with his throws back to the mound while he was at the plate, a highly possible event that was part of the intense rivalry between the two teams. Willie Mays came to his rescue, murmuring, "John, oh John!" while holding his bloody head in his hands, and preventing a riot from breaking out. Sandy Koufax, nursing a shutout until that point, was so shaken up he delivered a home run pitch to Mays, who helped San Francisco win the game on the strength of that clout.

Roseboro recovered from his injuries and helped the Dodgers win the pennant and World Series. Roseboro was the Dodgers' catcher through 1967 before a trade to the Twins along with Ron Perranoski. He starred under manager Billy Martin on their 1969 division champions, and then went to the Senators, where he played for Ted Williams in 1970. "Gabby" finished with 104 career home runs and a .249 average. He coached for the Senators and for the Angels from 1972 to 1974. Roseboro founded a public relations firm, Fouch-Roseboro in Beverly Hills, which dedicated itself to black-owned businesses and causes.

Marichal was deeply sorrowful over what he had done. Eventually, he asked Roseboro for forgiveness, and it was granted. They became close friends, regularly seen at old-timers games and charity events. Roseboro was gracious with Marichal's family, and Marichal became emotional when the former catcher passed away in 2002.

Duke Snider went to the Mets in 1963, then the Giants in 1964. He retired with 407 career homers, a .295 career average, and was elected to the Hall of Fame in 1980. Snider was a broadcaster for the Dodgers and wrote a book called *Few and Chosen: Defining Dodgers Greatness Across the Eras* (2006).

Doug Camilli was a Dodger catcher through the 1964 campaign and was traded to Washington, where he played until 1969. His career average was .199. He coached for the Red Sox in the early 1970s.

Wally Moon stayed on the L.A. bench though 1965. He retired with 142 homers and a .289 batting average. Moon coached for two decades at the college, minor league, and big league levels.

A headline in the *Sporting News* after the 1962 season ended read, "Dodger Yelpers to Face Bavasi's Pruning Shears." It referred to outspoken players, particularly those who had ranted and raved in the postgame meltdown in the Dodger Stadium clubhouse after the last playoff game. Norm Sherry, exposed as one of the "yelpers," was sold by his hometown team to the New York Mets. He retired at the end of the 1963 season and managed the California Angels from 1976 to 1977. Later he became the pitching coach for the Expos, Padres, and Giants.

Larry Burright was traded with Tim Harkness to the Mets. His big league career ended in 1964 with a .204 average.

Andy Carey was released and retired. Daryl Spencer was released in May 1963, finishing with Cincinnati, then eight years in the Far East. He hit 152 home runs in Japan. Lee Walls was a bench player for two more seasons, then went to Japan. He coached for several teams through 1983 but died at the age of 60 in 1993.

Stan Williams was traded to the New York Yankees in 1963.

"I felt very badly about that trade," he said. "I thought I was being used as a whipping boy for the '62 season, for the playoff loss. I resented their making an example of me. Sure, I was part of it, but I'd have liked the chance to redeem myself."

Williams was a member of the 1963 American League pennant-winning Yankees who lost to Los Angeles in the World Series. He went to the Cleveland Indians in 1965, staying in that organization until 1970. He was 10-1 pitching for manager Bill Rigney's 1970 American League West champion Minnesota Twins. Williams pitched for St. Louis and Cincinnati before retirement in 1972 with a 109-94 mark, and a 3.48 earned run average. He moved back to the Long Beach area, where he had lived on the same block with several teammates from 1962. His son Stan was a star under legendary coach John Herbold at Lakewood High School, which in the 1970s was one of the all-time great prep baseball dynasties in history. He earned a scholarship to the University of Southern California, where he pitched for another legend, Rod Dedeaux, then played in the minor leagues.

Ron Perranoski was named Fireman of the Year in 1963 and was a Dodger bullpen ace through 1967, when he left as part of the club's "youth movement" in the post-Koufax era. Perranoski was a star at Minnesota, the team that lost to L.A. in the 1965 Series and, after a downturn, revived themselves in large measure with players obtained from Los Angeles. He was the best closer in the American League on Minnesota's 1969–70 division champions and returned to Los Angeles in 1972. He was with the California Angels in 1973 and then retired with a 79-74 record, 179 saves, and a 2.79 ERA. Perranoski was the Dodgers' pitching coach under Alston and Tom Lasorda until 1981 and later worked for the hated Giants.

Johnny Podres pitched for Los Angeles until 1966, then went to the Tigers, and eventually joined the expansion San Diego Padres in 1969 before retirement with a 148-116 record and a 3.67 earned run average. He later became a highly respected pitching coach for San Diego, Boston, and Minnesota, perhaps getting his best recognition for the work he did with the Phillies' staff.

Ed Roebuck was sent to Washington in the middle of the 1963 season, then was part of the infamous Phillies squad that blew the 1964 pennant. He finished his career in 1966 with a 52-31 record, 62 saves, and a 3.35 ERA.

Joe Moeller pitched parts of seven years in Los Angeles, living in his idyllic south bay during the Beach Boys era of the 1960s. He left the club after the 1971 season.

Pete Richert was traded to Washington after the 1964 season, then went to the Baltimore Orioles in 1967. He became one of the top relievers in the league, but in the 1969 World Series his throw up the first base line hit Mets' pinch hitter J. C. Martin, who was running inside the base line, on the arm, skirting into foul territory and allowing New York to win game four, 2-1, in extra innings. Richert came back to Los Angeles in 1972 and retired in 1974 with an 80-73 mark to go with a 3.19 ERA.

Larry Sherry went to Detroit in 1963, Houston in 1967, then the Angels before retiring with a 53-44 record and a 3.67 earned run average. He was a coach with the Pirates and was on his brother Norm's staff at Anaheim in late 1970s.

Batboy Rene Lachemann graduated from Dorsey High in Los Angeles. His last year as the Dodgers' batboy was 1962. He joined his brother Marcel at the University of Southern California and later signed as a catcher with the A's organization, reaching the big leagues in Kansas City and Oakland. He managed at Seattle in the early 1980s and was a coach under Tony LaRussa during the "Bash Brothers" era at Oakland in the late 1980s. He managed with the Florida Marlins in the 1990s and returned as a coach in Oakland. His brother, Marcel, played in the big leagues with Oakland, was Rod Dedeaux's pitching coach at USC, and managed the California Angels (1994–95).

Vin Scully was already a legend. He was the finest baseball broadcaster and likely the best all-around sportscaster in the business by 1962. His description of Koufax's perfect game against the Chicago Cubs in 1965 is considered less announcing and more poetry, but it is not a singular moment in his career. He is simply the very best who has ever done what he does, and long, long ago he was recognized as the "most valuable Dodger," responsible for the team's image, its great attendance, and its joyous relationship with the fans of Los Angeles. Scully may be the greatest ambassador baseball has ever known. He was as respected a sports figure as can be conceived and an icon in Los Angeles matched by none (*possibly* John Wooden).

"1962 was a crucible year for a lot of the players," Scully recalled. "They added a healthy Sandy Koufax and that '63 team was off and running. To win the pennant and then sweep the lordly Yankees in four straight—that's probably the greatest moment in the history of the Dodger organization."

Walter O'Malley, the most powerful man in baseball by 1962, continued to be one of *The Lords of Baseball*, the title of a book describing the impact he and a handful of visionaries had on the sport. Despite his hated status in Brooklyn, he goes down as a hero in Los Angeles and one of the most remarkable executives in baseball history. By the end of the 1960s, O'Malley was ceding authority to his son, Peter, who was cut out of a different mold. A graduate of Penn's Wharton School of Business, Peter O'Malley successfully husbanded the Dodgers into the succeeding decades with no bumps in the road. Walter O'Malley passed away in 1979, and Peter sold the family interest to Rupert Murdoch and the News Corporation, the parent company of Fox News, in the late 1990s. In 2008 Walter O'Malley was inducted into the Hall of Fame.

Buzzie Bavasi left the Dodgers to run the fledgling San Diego Padres in 1969 and later was involved with Gene Autry and the California Angels. His son, Peter Bavasi, became a respected baseball executive .

Fresco Thompson ran the Dodgers' farm system through 1968, and in 1969 was slated to take over from Bavasi when he died of a heart attack.

Al Campanis ascended to the position instead and was extremely successful running the Dodgers when they captured five pennants and a World Championship in the 1970s until the mid-1980s. In 1987 he was a guest of Ted Koppel on the ABC national news show, *Nightline*. The subject of Jackie Robinson, and the question as to why there were so few black managers was posed. Campanis may have been intoxicated, having been imbibing in his Astrodome suite. He told Koppel blacks lacked the "necessities" to manage. The hue and cry was far-reaching and resulted in his immediate dismissal. His grandson was an All-American catcher at USC.

TWELVE

Legends of the Fall

"You can't compare Joe to me."
—*Willie Mays, putting down Joe DiMaggio in 2001*

The Giants slipped to third place under manager Alvin Dark in 1963. In 1964 they contended in a tight five-team race. The Dodgers dropped out when Koufax was hurt in August. The Giants fell by the wayside in September, leaving it up to St. Louis, Cincinnati, and Philadelphia to slug it out in the last week.

Dark's remark that minorities players were "a different kin'" of ballplayer combined with additional personal and professional troubles in 1963–64. His problems with Orlando Cepeda never went away, and Dark's marriage also was "on the rocks." Horace Stoneham questioned his ethics. In 1964 Stan Isaacs of *Newsday* wrote about Dark's troubles with black and Latino players.

"We have trouble because we have so many Negro and Spanish-speaking players on this team," Dark was quoted saying. "They are just not able to perform up to the white ballplayer when it comes to mental alertness. You can't make most Negro and Spanish players have the pride in their team that you can get from white players."

Dark denied it, stating that nobody would be so stupid as to say such things to a writer, which actually made sense, but Isaacs said he had taken notes and, regardless of whether they were direct quotes, many felt it reflected Dark's attitude at some level. It was speculated that Dark might not have said it to Isaacs, but that it was an accumulation of remarks by Dark overheard over time. New York writer Leonard Schecter, who later edited Jim Bouton's *Ball Four* and was not popular—some called him "a pariah"—confirmed he had heard similar comments from Dark in the past.

This was 1964, a seminal year in the civil rights struggle. A major characteristic of those heated times was animosity not just between Southern whites and blacks, but also between Southern whites and Jews, who were seen by some opponents to integration as making up a disproportionate amount of the white "Freedom Riders" descending upon Dixie to "stir up trouble." Some speculated that Dark's Southern Baptist background was seen as anathema to Jewish writers from New York (Isaacs, Schecter). Many questioned the veracity of the writers.

Jackie Robinson rushed to his former opponent's defense. "I have known Dark for many years, and my relationship with him has always been exceptional," he said. "I have found him to be a gentleman and, above all, unbiased."

Sports Illustrated, *Newsweek*, and *Time* all printed follow-ups favorable to him. Dark kept his job but was later fired when the team floundered. If he could manage the Giants to 103 wins and the seventh game of the 1962 World Series, it was speculated, then why could he not repeat the act in succeeding years? The answer was obvious: the Giants' veteran pitching staff of Jack Sanford, Billy Pierce, and Billy O'Dell would not ever be as effective again. Juan Marichal was a genuine star, but Gaylord Perry, Bob Bolin, Ron Herbel, and Bob Garibaldi— the hope for the future—had not yet come to fruition and in some cases never would. In cosmopolitan San Francisco, Dark's way of doing things was seen as part of the past.

"You never forget a year like '62," Dark said. "Even with all the Giant-Dodger battles I've been a part of, I still have to rank that season right at the top."

Charlie O. Finley, who was always part of the past, the present, and the future, had been born in Alabama before moving to the Midwest, and then of course associating himself with the West Coast. He was an innovator who embraced New Age concepts like flashy colors, long hair, and the sexualization of culture. While nobody ever could say he was a man of prejudice, he was a man of his surroundings and past. Finley befriended Bear Bryant, 'Bama's legendary football coach, who entered the Birmingham locker room and supposedly said Reggie Jackson was "just the kind of n----r boy" he could use to integrate his program, five years before he did just that in confluence with a loss to Southern California.

In 1966 Finley gave Dark another chance when he hired him to manage the Kansas City A's. Under Dark, the team improved. By 1967 much of the team's future foundation was in the system, either breaking into the Majors or enjoying success in the minors. But Dark ran into trouble with Finley in the aftermath of a "plane incident " involving pitcher Lew Krausse. Finley accused Dark of colluding with the players in the drafting of an open letter to, and critical of, Finley.

Between 1:30 and 5:30 AM on a late August night in 1967, Dark and his coaching staff were fired, rehired, and fired again by Finley. Finley at first fired Dark because the players had supported him. Dark then "saved" his job by providing an optimistic, and ultimately prophetic, prediction of future championships with the young players under contract.

Dark, who had informed his coaches they had lost their job, called to say he had saved them after all. Then Finley called pitcher Jack Aker, a major instigator of the "letter campaign." As fate would have it, Aker was not in his room, having broken curfew, a big no-no for Finley. Finley apparently put announcer Monte Moore on the hunt, looking for Aker in nearby watering holes, or with a local "Baseball Annie."

Aker was finally produced, and like a prisoner hauled before the King, was taken to Finley's room. Moore provided the details of his escapades, detailing them as if he were a private dick assigned to the case. Aker was in no moral position to argue his side, if indeed at 5:30 in the morning he had the wherewithal to make any cogent points.

Then Aker, trying to save himself, said that Dark had been in on the letter, contradicting Dark's assertions that he had nothing to do with it. Apparently, Dark did possess knowledge of it before it was released, even though he did not help draft it and did not urge its release. Dark was fired and Aker stayed with the team for several years.

Dark managed in Cleveland with no success before getting rehired by Finley in 1974. Dick Williams, winner of consecutive World Championships, had enough of Finley's all-night phone interruptions and thought (incorrectly, as it turned out) that the Yankees, his dream job, would hire him.

The world had changed drastically between 1967 and 1974. Al Dark looked like a dinosaur by this time. His Christian upbringing and Southern demeanor seemed more out of place than ever. In the Bay Area, the only "cool" Southerners were "wild eyed" party animals like Ken Stabler, or rockers like Lynyrd Skynrd, who packed the Coliseum's "day on the green" concerts.

But it was precisely Dark's Christianity that allowed him to own up to his own flaws as a man. He pointed to Biblical teachings, freely quoting New Testament verse in describing the transformation he had gone through in response to questions about his handling of minority players.

The A's were a free-wheelin' bunch, more like the "Hell's Angels" who were headquartered in Oakland than the "better angels of our nature." They were not a bad group. They pretty much stayed out of trouble, avoided police blotters and the like. Perhaps if they had played in New York their off-field habits would have been more exposed, but like the party-hearty Raiders, they benefited from the low key Bay Area press corps. But they were no tent revival. Dark was.

Sal Bando said Dark "couldn't manage a meat market." Early in 1974, I sat behind home plate at the Oakland-Alameda County Coliseum with my dad. Dark made a move my father disagreed with, and he made no bones about it. A well-dressed lady sitting with several of the most well-heeled children on the planet tapped him on the back. She told my dad that she would appreciate more "kindness of heart." An inning or so later I was looking through the A's program and saw a photo of Al Dark and his family—the well-coifed woman and the well-heeled children sitting behind us.

How much Al Dark contributed to the A's 1974 World Championship is debatable. Their regular season record of 90-72 was in decline from those of the previous three seasons, but their postseason run was the best of any of those teams—with Baltimore and the Dodgers falling easily. Dark benefited from a healthy roster of All-Stars and future Hall of Famers in their prime, which never hurts. This included one of the most airtight pitching staffs, top to bottom, in the history of the game. But like Pat Riley in Los Angeles and Phil Jackson in Chicago, credit must be given to coaches who did not screw it all up, because many others with talent-laden clubs have done just that. It was certainly viewed as redemption for Dark—for his baseball sins and otherwise. The fact that Oakland defeated Walter Alston's Dodgers was almost too perfect.

Like all of Finley's managers, Dark was eventually fired when all his talent began to go the free agent route. He managed the San Diego Padres in 1977.

"I would certainly do a lot things differently today," Dark said years later of the 1962 campaign. "I tried to treat all the players the same. I would treat them all differently now."

Willie Howard Mays, exhausted or not exhausted, near-bankrupt or not, was at the very height of his game in 1962. He maintained that high level for four more seasons. In 1964 he led the league with 47 home runs while driving in 111. In 1965 he slugged a league-leading 52 home runs with a .645 slugging percentage, drove in 112, and batted .317. He earned the Most Valuable Player award, but the Giants finished second.

In 1966 he hit 37 homers and drove in 103, but again San Francisco finished behind the Koufax-Drysdale Dodgers. Baseball was slightly frustrating for Mays, what with the bridesmaid finishes behind L.A. and battling the constant winds that blew his home runs in from beyond the left field fence.

Sluggers like Hank Aaron, Eddie Mathews, Roger Maris, and even teammate Willie McCovey benefited from short porches or prevailing winds, but not Mays. In 1967, the year he turned 37, Mays started to slow down. Today, 37 is not considered old, but Mays lost a considerable step or two and never got it back. McCovey replaced him as the club's bona fide home run slugger, star, and even marquee name. Every year, the second place syndrome continued to haunt Mays and the Giants. After the Dodgers it was the St. Louis Cardinals. In 1969 they placed second behind Henry Aaron and Atlanta in the National League West. In each of three seasons, *Orlando Cepeda* played on the team that beat them (St. Louis, 1967–68; Atlanta, 1969).

Mays's record between 1967 and 1971 fell substantially from that of his 1951–66 levels, but he continued to play at or near an All-Star performance. Whether he deserved to make the All-Star Game every year or not was immaterial; he was an icon, and he was on the team each season, setting records and even earning game MVP honors in 1968 at the Astrodome.

In 1970 Mays got his 3,000th career hit. Long considered the most likely to break Babe Ruth's career home run record, his late-career tailoff and the Candlestick winds combined to prevent the attainment of that goal, leaving it up to Hank Aaron (who got there in 1974). Mays turned 40 in 1971, but his career was revitalized by an exciting Giants club that raced out to the lead, overcame the "June swoon," and held on to beat the Dodgers in another thrilling divisional pennant race. He batted .271 with 18 homers but seemed to run with a little extra bounce in his step. San Francisco lost to Pittsburgh in the playoffs, however, and it was Mays's last hurrah.

He was shockingly traded to the New York Mets in 1972 for Charlie Williams. *Sports Illustrated* dutifully recorded some early Maysian heroics at Shea Stadium. The prospect that he could revive the Polo Grounds ghosts, and along with Tom Seaver make the Mets "amazin'" again, was quickly determined to not be in the cards. In 1973, under manager Yogi Berra, the Mets were improbable winners of the National League East, and even more improbable winners over Cincinnati's "Big Red Machine" in the NLCS.

The 43-year-old Mays, who hit .211 and had nothing to do with the Mets' success, found himself playing center field in front of the Bay Area fans, at the Oakland-Alameda County Coliseum, when the Mets battled the A's in the World Series. Mays had no business being out there, but Berra could not bring himself to sit the aging hero, hoping against hope there was one last miracle left. It was not to be.

Mays looked befuddled—on a routine ground ball single that snaked under his glove, on his knees arguing a call at home—and the Mets lost in seven. He retired, and people have lamented for decades that this was the very picture of how a great athlete should *not* go out.

He finished with 660 home runs and a .302 average. He entered Cooperstown in 1979. Somewhere along the line, Mays became *bitter*. His remarks to writers, fans, and banquet rooms full of people paying to hear what he was paid to say were stories of racism and unfairness. He had avoided bankruptcy in the 1960s but never made the big dough. Watching Tom Seaver, Reggie Jackson, and Dave Winfield cash in filled him with bile.

Fans asking for autographs, sitting next to him in planes, or other situations, were likely to hear foul epithets instead of grace. He respected baseball, worked with Giants youngsters and helped many, but when asked to compare himself with all-time greats he showed zero humility.

He taught Bobby Bonds to be wary of the media and see racial prejudice and dark clouds behind all interaction. He later taught his godson, Barry Bonds, the same thing. Bonds, one of the least impressive personalities in baseball history, is a mirror reflection of Mays. Mays never reproached Bonds for juicing, even though the younger man likely passed Mays's records because of it.

The Giants kept him around. Provincial San Franciscans found a way to love him, just as they love Bonds. He offered some helpful hints in Spring Training and some public relations value, but scribes approaching him do so cautiously, knowing that his buttocks must be kissed in order to get cooperation.

The difference between Willie Mays and his contemporary, Ernie Banks of the Cubs, is a vast chasm as wide as all space.

Orlando "Cha Cha" Cepeda never really ceded the first base job to Willie McCovey. The outspoken Puerto Rican slugger hated playing the outfield. He would talk to the fans and show little hustle. He was young and immature.

"When I was with the Giants, I didn't like playing for Alvin, but I feel much differently today," said Cepeda. "I was 24, 25 years old and he said certain things to me that got me very upset. Now, I wish I had paid more attention, because he'd been through it, he was a good ballplayer, he knew the game. Instead of fighting him, I should have listened to him and learned from him.

"Back then, he did some things that were hard to figure out. Sometimes, I believe he had it out for me personally. But I wasn't always easy to live with, either. It worked both ways—my fault, his fault."

Cepeda's best year was 1961, but he was consistent in 1962, 1963, and 1964, hitting more than 30 home runs each season and finishing with 97 RBIs in each of the 1963 and 1964 campaigns. His ability was unquestioned, and Cepeda appeared to be a Hall of Fame contender.

In 1965 he sustained an injury that limited him to 33 games. It probably cost San Francisco the pennant, although the loss of Tommy Davis around the same time was an "equalizer" for the Dodgers. After playing 19 games in 1966, Cepeda was traded to St. Louis for left-handed pitcher Ray Sadecki, a 20-game winner for the Cardinals who never panned out in San Francisco.

Cepeda hit .301 overall in 1966, but in 1967 he led *El Birdos* to the National League pennant—over the Giants. One of his teammates was Roger Maris. The two stars who had opposed each other in the 1962 World Series, both of whom had "worn out their welcomes," found comfort in what many consider the best baseball town in the Majors. Cepeda had better years—he batted .325 with 25 home runs and 111 runs batted in—but he assumed a leadership role that he never had before. Playing in the shadow of Mays, with McCovey battling for his position, at odds with Dark, and beset by his own youth, Cepeda had not been in this kind of position in San Francisco. He loved The City, but at the age of 30 in 1967, he reached a comfort level with St. Louis. The Cardinals defeated the Boston Red Sox in the World Series.

In 1968 the Cardinals came within one game of a repeat championship but were beaten by Detroit in a seven-game Series. Cepeda was traded to Atlanta and in 1969 helped the Braves win the National League West. From 1967 to 1969, Cepeda's teams finished in first place, always with San Francisco in second. It was a period of vindication for him. He batted .305 with 34 home runs and 111 RBIs in 1970, but Cepeda's painful legs and various injuries took their toll on him. Had he remained healthy he likely would have compiled lifetime statistics worthy of Cooperstown, but it was not to be. He made a brief return to the Bay Area, along with Matty Alou, when Charlie O. Finley acquired him for the Oakland A's in 1972, the year they won the first of three World Series. Injuries prevented him from making any contribution, but the designated hitter rule allowed him to make a comeback at Boston in 1973, when he batted .289 with 20 home runs and 86 runs batted in. After playing 33 games for Kansas City in 1974, Cepeda retired with 379 career homers and a .297 average.

In 1988 Cepeda and Dark reconciled at an old-timers game. Dark apologized and Cepeda said he felt it took a big man to do that. Cepeda, like Mays and McCovey, became a regular at Giants games. When the club moved to Pacific Bell Park in 2000, it did an excellent job of paying homage to its history. Rightfully, Cepeda was a big part of that. He maintained a home in Puerto Rico but also lived in the Bay Area. His identity, despite success in St. Louis and elsewhere, was with San Francisco.

Cepeda had on occasion brushed with the law, mainly drug-related offenses. Some speculated that being kept on the Giants' payroll with little responsibility tended to lead him astray. His drug problems were said to have kept him out of the Hall of Fame, but in truth it was his knees, which prevented him from achieving the 400 career homers that might have made the difference. Had he batted .300 lifetime instead of .297, that might have helped.

Willie McCovey played 135 games in the outfield, and 23 games at first base in 1963, when he materialized as a genuine superstar with 44 home runs and 102 runs batted in. In 1964 he played 83 games in the outfield, 18 games at first base, but slumped badly (.220). In 1965 he assumed the first base position from the injured Cepeda, hit 39 homers, and followed that up with 36 (1966) and 31 (1967).

Mays's productivity began to tail off markedly in 1967, and McCovey picked up the slack. He was the *Sporting News* National League Player of the Year in 1968, when the "Year of the Pitcher" apparently had no effect on him. Willie Mac slammed 36 homers, drove in 105 runs, and had a .545 slugging percentage.

His best season was 1969, when his two home runs earned him the MVP of the All-Star Game played in Washington, D.C., and he finished with 45 home runs, 126 RBIs, a .656 slugging percentage, and a .320 average. He was widely hailed as the most feared hitter in baseball, and many felt of all time.

The Giants were a close second in 1969, but were still second. Late in the season, Tom Seaver and the New York Mets beat them soundly. Seaver won 10 straight games to finish 25-7, personally leading the Amazin' Mets to the East Division title, the National League pennant, and a World Series victory. It was nothing less than spectacular. Seaver's season goes down as one of the greatest in baseball history, his contributions bordering on the otherworldly. It was considered a fait accompli that he would win the Most Valuable Player award as well as the Cy Young award, not to mention the Hickock Belt (Professional Athlete of the Year) and *Sports Illustrated*'s Sportsman of the Year honor.

However, two pitchers (Bob Gibson of the Cardinals, Denny McLain of the Tigers) had won the MVP awards in 1968's "Year of the Pitcher." Sandy Koufax had won the MVP award six years earlier and very easily could have repeated the trick in 1965 and 1966. In response to pitching dominance, the mound was lowered in 1969, although it did not stop Seaver.

Many members of the Baseball Writers' Association of America (BBWAA) had been complaining that since pitchers had the Cy Young award—which in 1967 became an award to the best pitcher in each league, not just all of baseball—they should be excluded from MVP consideration. They had "their own award" (the Cy Young) in the view of some. When the BBWAA voted for the National League MVP in 1969, several excluded Seaver from their ballots entirely. The system includes votes for one (the top pick) through 10. Ten points are awarded for the first, eight for the third, one for the 10th, and so forth. McCovey barely edged Seaver out. All the Mets' pitcher needed was a couple of seventh or sixth place votes, which he more than deserved by a long shot, but by being excluded entirely he lost vital points that he needed to beat out McCovey.

The vote, despite McCovey's great season, was considered a fraud, especially by the influential New York media base. Furthermore, the writers who excluded Seaver remained anonymous. The BBWAA voted thereafter to publicly reveal the voting of their members in future ballots, but Seaver was denied what was rightfully his. A class act, Seaver never complained and had only kind words for Willie Mac.

In 2001 McCovey and Mays were at Pac Bell Park. Both displayed zero humility, bragging and talking themselves up like there was no tomorrow. Mays, asked whether Barry Bonds's recent 500th home run and good reception from the home crowd reminded him of the moment in 1962 when the Candlestick fans "warmed up" to him after favoring Joe DiMaggio, veered from the essence of the question.

"You can't compare Joe to me," said Mays, as if Joe D's World Championships, three MVP awards, and general deity status meant nothing. Mays went on to repeat his memorized statistics, indicating he had been making this same argument to anybody who asked long before this moment.

Then McCovey was asked about the 1969 MVP vote. He, too, took umbrage at the concept that his obvious greatness should be questioned. "Of course I deserved that award," said McCovey. "Seaver had no business winning the MVP. I should have won it in '68 instead of Bob Gibson, too."

In 1968 McCovey's Giants finished second to Gibson's Cardinals. That was the year Gibson pitched 48 straight scoreless innings and compiled a Major League record 1.12 earned run average. Many consider it the greatest single season pitching performance ever recorded, and Gibson was so obviously deserving of the award over all challengers that he won it with 14 first place votes and 242 points. Cincinnati's Pete Rose, not McCovey, was second with the Giants' first baseman a distant third. Pitcher Denny McLain won unanimously in the American League.

McCovey was often given cover by the press, possibly out of a sense of political correctness that is especially practiced in San Francisco. He has always been described as a class act, and in truth is a decent enough fellow, but those who have dealt with him personally have found him to be a piece of work. When invited to functions such as golf club banquets and the like he insists on payment, ostensibly referring to his "stature" as a man. There is a racial twinge to his near-extortions, as if the prejudice he experienced in the South of the 1950s must be "paid for" by liberal whites in the Northern California of the 2000s.

McCovey hit 39 home runs and drove in 126 runs in 1970, but by 1971 his knees were aching. The pain had a considerable effect on his performance, reducing him to 18 home runs, but San Francisco still won in the West. He made a big comeback with a 29-home-run season in 1973, but was dealt to San Diego for the 1974 through 1976 seasons. Early in 1976 he was traded to Oakland, but in 1977 he came home to the Giants. He ascended to godlike status, above and beyond anything Mays ever experienced, and was probably even more popular than Barry Bonds became. In 1977 McCovey hit 28 home runs, and in 1978 contributed a series of remarkable clutch hits as San Francisco shocked baseball.

The Giants led the two best teams in the league, Cincinnati and Los Angeles, well into the summer before fading down the stretch (with the Dodgers winning). Attendance and excitement returned to Candlestick after a moribund period, helped by the fact that cross-bay Oakland was a shell of the earlier dynasty. McCovey struggled in his last two seasons, 1979–80, as did the team. Interest again waned, and he finally retired with 531 lifetime home runs, a .270 average, and his 1986 induction to the Hall of Fame.

The Giants, as with Mays, Cepeda, and Juan Marichal, did a good job of respecting their past, particularly when Pac Bell Park was built. McCovey became a regular, hobnobbing with fans, players, and writers. Beyond right field, past a walkway, a part of San Francisco Bay was named McCovey Cove. Barry Bonds has been virtually the only left-handed slugger able to reach it, but his "splash shots" amid kayakers and boaters have made for spectacular visuals. A statue outside the stadium was erected for McCovey, who for the most part has been a class act.

When Juan Marichal came out of game three of the 1962 World Series at Yankee Stadium, there was still some hope that he might be available to pitch in some capacity later in the Series. When it shifted to San Francisco and was delayed by rain, the writers speculated that the "Dominican Dandy" might start game six or seven.

"He won't pitch again in this Series even if it rains for a week," Alvin Dark said. While the manager had Billy Pierce and Jack Sanford ready, Marichal took it that Dark was mad at him, first for the bone fracture in his foot and second for the hand injury he suffered in game four. The media took Dark to mean this, too. It bothered Marichal all winter. In 1966 a new set of X-rays found the broken bone that the 1962 X-rays had not.

Marichal recovered after 1962 to win 20 games six times between 1963 and 1969, but in a league dominated by Sandy Koufax, Bob Gibson, and Tom Seaver, never won the Cy Young award. In 1968 he and Denny McLain threatened to win 30 games all summer. McLain got there but Marichal finished 26-9 with a 2.43 earned run average. With Gibson pitching St. Louis to the pennant and setting the ERA record of 1.12, Marichal's best shot at the Cy Young fell by the wayside.

Marichal was pleasant and intelligent. His marriage to Alma was a good one, and he was a fan favorite. He wrote a book called *A Pitcher's Story* that, despite being ghostwritten by Charles Einstein, reflected his unique voice and his Dominican heritage and gave insight into the Latino ballplayer's mind. Still, a dark cloud seemed to hover above him. The controversies with Dark started it, but when he clubbed John Roseboro over the head with his bat in 1965, he was demonized, especially in Los Angeles. He was sorrowful in the succeeding years, made up with the Dodger catcher, and by 1971, when his 18 wins and victory on the last day gave San Francisco the division, he was as popular as any Giant.

Marichal always seemed to have maladies and small injuries, and after 1971 they became debilitating. He pitched until 1975, finishing with Boston, and like Sal Maglie going to Brooklyn, he wore Dodger blue in 1975. He finished with a 243-142 record and a 2.89 earned run average and was elected to the Hall of Fame in 1983. However, his failure to win any Cy Young awards, falling well short of 300 career victories, the fact he was not a strikeout pitcher, and the lack of any lasting image—as with Koufax and Drysdale—of him victorious on the World Series stage, reduced Marichal in the minds of many when comparing him to the all-time greats, including contemporaries Koufax, Gibson, Seaver, and Steve Carlton. While he was undoubtedly the ace of a staff that included Gaylord Perry, Perry's longevity (and 300 wins) may have pushed him ahead of Marichal in the pantheon.

Marichal remains an iconic figure on the Dominican island and has successfully straddled his role there with his role as a baseball hero in America. In this respect, he is a cultural ambassador, and many continue to say that awards and lifetime numbers aside, none was better.

In the wake of the Cuban Missile Crisis of October 1962, Cuba and Fidel Castro were public enemy number one in America. Ford Frick banned big leaguers from playing in any games against Cubans. Felipe Alou appeared in an exhibition game against a Cuban team in Santo Domingo. He feared reprisals in his home country if he did not help them beat the Cubans. He was fined and said it proved Latinos "were, are, and will always be foreigners in America and we cannot hope that we will ever be totally accepted."

He played in San Francisco through the 1964 season, then with the Braves through 1969. Alou returned to the Bay Area with the Oakland A's in 1970, hitting .271 on a second place club. From there Alou played for the New York Yankees, Montreal Expos, and Milwaukee Brewers, retiring after the 1974 season with a .286 lifetime average and 206 homers. He became a coach, and then a well-respected manager of the Expos. When Dusty Baker left after the 2002 season, Alou was hired as manager of the Giants, where he handled Barry Bonds as well as his own son, an excellent outfielder, Moises Alou.

The respect he received from players, fans, and the media during his managerial career proved that his 1962–63 off-season statement that Latinos "were, are, and will always be foreigners in America and we cannot hope that we will ever be totally accepted," was not a truthful statement, although he honestly felt it to be at the time.

Alou remained deeply Christian, outspoken, and erudite. In Montreal he dealt with French-speaking reporters and mastered the repartee. He was a thinking man's manager, but despite achieving things he may have thought unavailable to him in the 1960s, kept his distance and was sensitive. A sportstalk host on the "Giant 68" radio station KNBR, complained that Giants hitters on Alou's team swung at everything instead of showing plate discipline. They were "brain dead Caribbean" hitters, said the radio host.

Alou went ballistic and called the radio host "Satan." It all might have blown over except that KNBR made fun of Alou's use of the term "Satan," replaying an old *Saturday Night Live* skit in which the "Church Lady" character blames all ills on *"Saaaatan!"* Alou took all of it poorly, and in a matter of major political correctness the radio host was fired while Alou acted as if the KKK had burned a cross on his lawn. When the Giants stumbled, Alou left managing altogether.

Tom Haller played for San Francisco through the 1967 season. His best year was 1966, when he hit 27 home runs. He played four years in Los Angeles, where he was a mainstay, then went to the Tigers in 1972. He hit 134 career homers and batted .257, coached for the Giants, then became their vice president of baseball operations from 1981 to 1986. He died at the age of 67.

Ed Bailey made the All-Star Game in 1963 and in 1964 was traded to the Braves, where he was involved in a big fight with the Mets. He returned to San Francisco in 1965 and retired in 1966 with 155 home runs and a .256 average.

Chuck Hiller was traded to the Mets in 1965 and later played for the Phillies and Pirates, retiring with a .243 average. He later was a coach with several teams, including the Giants.

Jim Davenport played his whole career with the San Francisco Giants and was a fan favorite. He retired after the 1970 campaign with 77 home runs and a .258 average, but his longball numbers were a big drop after the 14 he hit in 1962. He hit only four in 1963 and never reached double figures again. Davenport managed San Francisco in 1985 and was a coach at Philadelphia and Cleveland. His son played at the University of Santa Clara. In a game in which I was one out away from a complete game victory against the Broncos, young Davenport hit a home run to break up my shutout.

Jose Pagan was traded to Pittsburgh in 1965, stayed through 1972, playing for the 1970 and 1972 division champions, and the 1971 world champions. He finished with Philadelphia, a .250 hitter, and later was a coach with the Pirates.

Harvey Kuenn was with the Giants through the middle of the 1965 season, when he was traded to the Chicago Cubs. He was the last out of Sandy Koufax's '65 perfect game at Dodger Stadium. Vin Scully's famed description of that out, his sing-song delivery as he said, "two-and-two to Harvey Kuenn, Sandy one strike away," may have made Kuenn more famous than anything else he did in his outstanding career. He retired after the 1966 season with a .303 average, and from 1971 to 1982 was a coach with his home state Milwaukee Brewers. In the middle of the 1982 season he was named manager of the Brewers, a heavy-hitting crew led by Robin Yount known as "Harvey's Wallbangers," after the cocktail. The Brewers rallied to defeat Gene Mauch's California Angels in the playoffs but lost a thrilling World Series to St. Louis. He left Milwaukee after the 1983 season and died in 1988 at the age of 57.

Matty Alou played for the Giants until 1965 and was part of the famed "three brothers outfield," consisting of Felipe, brother Jesus, and himself, in 1963. He led the National League with a .342 average at Pittsburgh in 1966 and was a perennial batting title contender in the late 1960s. Matty played at St. Louis in 1971, but late that season Charlie O. Finley acquired him. He was instrumental down the stretch, helping the Oakland A's win the 1972 World Series title. He retired after the 1974 season with a .307 average. Brother Jesus, known for his neck contortions before taking his place in the batter's box, was a productive Giant hitter through 1968, and played in the big leagues until 1979, including with two A's world champions (1973 and 1974).

Carl Boles played in the minors for three years, then in Japan before retiring after the 1971 season, having hit 117 homers with a .265 average over there. Ernie Bowman played one more year in San Francisco. His career ended with a .190 average.

Manny Mota was sent to Houston at the end of 1962, then traded to the Pirates, where he played from 1963 until 1969. He joined the Dodgers, where he was a pinch hitter deluxe until 1982. His 1,560 pinch hits are the most in history. Mota batted .312 in his career and became the Los Angeles batting coach. His son played at Cal State Fullerton and became a sportscaster.

Jack Sanford stayed with San Francisco through the middle of the 1965 season, when he was dealt to the Angels, then the A's, finishing 137-101 with a 3.69 ERA. He was a coach with the Indians.

Billy O'Dell was a Giant through 1964, then went to the Braves prior to a mid-1966 trade to the Pirates, retiring at the end of the 1967 season with a 105-100 record and 3.29 ERA.

Billy Pierce pitched two more years in San Francisco. He retired after the 1964 season having won 211 games against 169 defeats with a 3.27 earned run average.

Mike McCormick was traded to Baltimore after his subpar year and dealt with strange arm problems. He went to the Senators in 1965 but returned to the Giants, where he blossomed for one season, 1967. With both Juan Marichal and Bob Gibson hurt that season, McCormick's 22 wins earned him the National League Cy Young award. He stayed in San Francisco until mid-1970, then concluded his career with the Yankees and Royals. His record was 134-128 with a 3.73 earned run average.

Stu Miller went to Baltimore. "I did not have a very good outing in a clutch situation during the playoffs, and I think that had a lot to do with it," he assessed. Miller lasted five more years with the Orioles and Braves, retiring at the end of 1968 with a 105-103 record, 154 saves, and a 3.24 ERA.

Bob Bolin pitched for San Francisco through the 1969 season, and later with Milwaukee and Boston, retiring after 1973 with an 88-75 record and 3.40 ERA. Don Larsen was traded to Houston in 1964, and then played for the Orioles and Cubs. He retired in 1967, 81-91, with a 3.78 ERA. He continued to maintain some heroic status in New York because of his perfect game in 1956, and he was cheered when he was on hand in 1998 the day fellow Point Loma High School graduate David Wells pitched *his* perfect game at Yankee Stadium. Bob Garibaldi never reached his potential. He became a basketball referee.

Gaylord Perry was in Alvin Dark's doghouse. Despite great tools, he continued to disappoint and was certainly not the pitcher his brother Jim was. In 1964 Perry entered a game at Shea Stadium in New York with men all over the bases and the outcome on the line. According to his autobiography, *Me and the Spitter*, out of desperation he went to his infamous spitball, pitched out of the jam, and, with the staff depleted, threw the equivalent of a complete game in a marathon extra inning win, completing a doubleheader sweep.

He finally reached his potential as a 20-game winner in 1966 and toiled for nine years with San Francisco. After the 1971 campaign, the two-time 20-game winner, one of the best pitchers in baseball, was traded to Cleveland for the drunken "Sudden Sam" McDowell. While McDowell was the butt of jokes in San Francisco, Perry won the 1972 Cy Young award in Cleveland.

In 1974 Perry won 15 straight games and was approaching the 16 consecutive wins of Jack Sanford in 1962, the American League record of 16, and the Major League record of 19 by Rube Marquard of the New York Giants. He was beaten in a ninth inning rally at Oakland.

Perry won another Cy Young award at San Diego in 1978 and also pitched for the Yankees, Braves, Mariners, and Royals. He retired after the 1983 season with a 314-265 record, a 3.10 ERA, and was inducted into the Hall of Fame in 1991. He and Jim hold all combined records for brother victories. Jim helped Minnesota win the 1965 American League pennant and the 1969–70 West Division titles. He was the 1970 AL Cy Young award winner and was a minor league pitching coach in the Oakland A's organization when I played for them in the 1980s. Despite the trade to Cleveland and his many travels with different clubs, Gaylord—like a number of Giants who played for different teams—always considered himself a Giant and has long been a favorite at old-timers games.

Horace Stoneham sold the Giants to Bob Lurie and Bob Short in 1976. He died in 1990 at the age of 86. Chub Feeney almost became Commissioner of Baseball in 1968, but the job went to Bowie Kuhn instead. Russ Hodges announced Giants games with Lon Simmons until he passed away in 1971. He was elected to the Hall of Fame.

Lon Simmons announced for the Giants and the Oakland A's, off and on, into the 2000s. When I pitched in a 1982 Major League Spring Training exhibition game for the Oakland A's against the San Francisco Giants at Phoenix Municipal Stadium, both Simmons and the great Bill King announced parts of my three scoreless innings, a thrill and highlight of my short pro career.

Simmons was the San Francisco 49ers' announcer. His call of Jim Marshall's "wrong way run" in 1964 for Minnesota at Kezar Stadium lives forever in NFL Films. He retired as the 49ers' play-by-play man prior to the 1981 season, the year the Niners won their first Super Bowl. Simmons was brought back and was in the booth when the club won their third World Championship in January 1989.

When baseball moved into the cable era, Simmons was able to freelance radio and TV work. He lived in Half Moon Bay and also in Alameda and was in the Pac Bell Park booth when Barry Bonds hit his 73rd home run in 2001, graciously handing the microphone to a younger colleague. Even after moving to Hawaii, Simmons was periodically brought back to announce, do guest appearances, or be the master of ceremonies at events honoring Giants of the past.

Lon Simmons is one of *the* all-time class acts, in sports history or any other history. When I was a columnist for the *San Francisco Examiner*, a newcomer with the Bay Area sports media in 2001, Simmons showed me around, introducing me to people. I was a nobody, but he treated me as if I was the deciding vote on his Hall of Fame induction. With no help needed from me, Simmons is a member in good standing of the broadcaster's wing of the Baseball Hall of Fame.

THIRTEEN

Yankees Forever

"If you don't know where you are going, you will wind up somewhere else."
—*Yogi Berra*

Ralph Houk managed the 1963 New York Yankees to a 105-57 record, but after losing the World Series to the Dodgers became the general manager. His tenure as GM (1964–65) was not considered a good one. Whatever made him a good manager did not seem to make him a good front office executive. The "new breed" player was on the scene, and Houk was unprepared for this type of character.

The Yogi Berra–Johnny Keane fiasco of 1964–65 was a black mark in Yankee history. According to reports, the team did not respect Berra when he managed in 1964. Houk gave up on the season by August, determined to fire Berra at season's end. An arrangement was made to replace him with Keane, who was then managing the St. Louis Cardinals. The Cardinals were floundering, seemingly out of the chase with Philadelphia in control. It was widely reported that the Cardinals would fire him.

Then both the Yankees and Cardinals rallied to win the pennant, meeting each other in the World Series. By then, the dye was cast. Berra and his team knew they were facing a manager who would be replacing him in 1965. Even though it was an open secret, many in the media argued that the decision should be reversed—that Berra was a competent manager and Keane should stay in St. Louis. But there were too many personalities involved, and feelings had been hurt. Houk did fire his longtime friend Berra; it marked a sad day that started a decade of estrangement between the Hall of Fame catcher and his team.

Keane was brought in. The Yankees were confused by the whole sequence of events. Within a short period of time it was obvious that the Keane hiring was a mistake. In 1966 Houk returned as field manager, but the club was old, a shell of their greatness and, at 66-73, in last place in the American League. Houk led a rebuilding project and the club was 83-79 in 1968, then 93-69 in 1970. But the 1969 Amazin' Mets, not to mention "Broadway Joe and the Super Jets" and the NBA champion Knickerbockers, owned the town. At 93-69 and in second place in the East was far from Yankee standards, especially since Baltimore dominated at that time.

After managing clubs that played around the .500 mark in the early 1970s, Houk went to Detroit from 1974 through 1978, then did a stint with the Boston Red Sox, of all teams. He finished with 1,619 career wins.

Mickey Mantle, who won his third Most Valuable Player award in 1962, could easily have had one or two more and said he wanted to add a couple more in future years. He never did. In 1963 Mantle had more injuries, reducing him to 65 games. It did not stop his club from blowing past all American League competition. Mantle was available for the Fall Classic, but against the incredible Dodger pitching staff in the World Series he was rendered useless (.133 in the four-game loss).

The Johnny Grant parties got wilder and wilder. It was rumored that Angels owner Gene Autry helped encourage them so as to tire out the opposition. Mantle and his mates probably stayed fairly safe and sound during two 1963 World Series games played in Los Angeles, but during regular season trips to the West Coast to face the Angels, they regularly got out of control. In 1964 Dean Chance of the Angels had a season for the ages. His dominance of the Yankees was the highlight of his 20-win, 1.65 ERA, Cy Young season.

In June Chance threw a 14-inning shutout against New York. He beat them every time he faced them, usually by shutout. Mantle told writers he was ready to vomit whenever he faced Chance. He had a France-surrenders-to-Germany attitude, telling Angels catcher Buck Rodgers, "This is a waste of time. I got no chance." His heavy partying at the Johnny Grant parties assuaged his despair the night before games and helped him drown his sorrows afterward.

But Mantle, sober or not, was so great he still managed to hit .303 with 35 homers and 111 runs batted in during the 1964 season. After three consecutive subpar World Series performances (1961, 1962, 1963), he had a big Series against St. Louis, slamming three homers and batting .333. It was his last World Series. He finished with 18 Series homers and 40 RBIs.

Hampered by injuries, his lifestyle, and the general malaise surrounding the Bronx Bombers after that star-crossed season, Mantle suffered a drastic drop in his performance from 1965 on. In 1968 Mantle was set to pass Jimmie Foxx. Struggling, and a shell of his old self, he appeared unable to hit one out. Detroit's Denny McLain, cruising on his way to a 30-win season and with victory in hand, tossed a batting practice fastball to Mantle, who jumped on it for his 536th career home run. It was his last.

Mantle thought about playing in 1969, but he had nothing left and retired in the spring, weeping at his announcement. His final desultory years, in which he tried to play first base before there was a DH, unfortunately dropped his lifetime batting average under .300, to .298. He had 1,509 RBIs.

Mantle was inducted into Cooperstown in 1974. His appearances at old-timers games brought thunderous cheering. His status as a true New York sports icon was over and above almost all others. His blond, All-American boy persona was the stuff of legend, his memory enhanced by nostalgia for the 1950s and early 1960s—the age of innocence.

Mantle retired to Dallas, where he tried to live a normal married life with his wife Merlyn. After years of dalliances with groupies, all of which she knew about, it was not easy. Billy Martin came out for "hunting" trips, which were little more than intense drinking sessions in which both were lucky they did not kill each other with an inadvertent shotgun blast. On one occasion, Martin claimed that Mantle killed a neighbor's cow.

Mantle and Whitey Ford would get together at Fort Lauderdale during Spring Trainings, which meant more drinking. His alcoholic "vacations" were a relief from the daily grind of domestic life in Dallas. Eventually, Mantle's sons came of age. He never had much in common with any of them; none were great players. Drinking became their common denominator, father and sons getting drunk together. The kids, naturally, struggled with sobriety for years as a result.

In the 1980s, the growing memorabilia market made anything touched, worn, hit by, or signed by Mickey Mantle worth huge sums. Mantle became the star of the memorabilia-and-signing-session industry. It helped make him wealthier than he ever was in his pre–free agency career, but with time on his hands he drank day and night, and was often embarrassingly inebriated in the presence of fans and kids.

Mantle had a foul mouth and a short temper. He was often asked to endorse products but hated the takes and retakes he had to endure in the making of commercials. Nobody really cared. He was Mickey Mantle, a bulletproof hero. Whether race played a part or not, whether his New York imprimatur made him extra special—for whatever reason, Mantle's faults were overlooked, whereby people were peeved at Willie Mays's bitter attitude. At least Mays maintained sobriety and good health.

It all caught up to Mantle, who died of liver disease in 1995. His most heroic act occurred in the final year of his life. Looking like death warmed over, knowing he was going to die, Mantle made numerous public appearances, begging people not to drink as he had. He was the ultimate cautionary tale, a tragic hero in the end.

Roger Maris was also hurt in 1963, reducing him to 90 games and 23 home runs, but the club won with ease anyway. Fans and critics said it proved that Maris never meant that much to the team. In 1964 he hit 26 home runs as the Yanks won their fifth straight pennant. Maris never did much in the postseason with New York. In 1960 he had two homers and a .267 average, but after that he hit .105 (1961), .174 (1962), .000 (1963), and .200 (1964). His work ethic, sobriety, and family man reputation meant little in the Big Apple; they loved the martini-swiggers of the Sinatra age. In 1965 he was hurt again. With the team struggling, suddenly his production was essential to the club's success, and he was "blamed" for being hurt.

Many athletes have complained about the New York "fish bowl." None were ever hurt more, or more unfairly, than Maris was. Mercifully, he was traded to St. Louis prior to the 1967 season. It was a wonderful jolt for his career. Even though he hit only nine home runs, the great Cardinal fans took to the midwesterner Maris, applauding his great defense in right field on a club that won with pitching and fundamentals. He was well paid and appreciated for his efforts helping St. Louis, where he was a teammate with Orlando Cepeda, to the

World Championship. He did the same thing in 1968 on a club that lost in seven games to Detroit in the Series. He then retired when Cardinals owner August Busch arranged a Budweiser distributorship for him.

His part ownership in a beer company seemed a little strange. He was never a teetotaler, nor was he a drunk. After all, that was Mantle's forte. Maris had a low-key retirement, occasionally receiving cheers at old-timers games. He eventually made appearances in New York, where time had healed wounds and he was given standing ovations. He, too, was a tragic figure who died far too soon, in 1985 of cancer.

In 1998 Mark McGwire and Sammy Sosa chased and both broke his 61 home run record. Both paid homage to Roger throughout the chase. His widow and kids were in the stands at St. Louis when Big Mac hit number 70. It was a gracious moment. In 2001 Billy Crystal directed an excellent movie, *61, for HBO. That same year, Barry Bonds hit 73 homers. It was the "steroid era." Bonds, McGwire, and Sosa all blasted past Maris's record of 61 over this time. Many others came close. It was a joke. In light of what we now know about performance-enhancing drugs, Maris's records—as well as his character and place in history—deserve all the respect denied him when he played. Those who broke his records deserve little respect and much scorn.

Lawrence Peter "Yogi" Berra was a 15-time All Star who played in 14 World Series and holds numerous World Series records, including most games by a catcher (63), hits (71), and times on a winning team (10). He is first in at-bats, first in doubles, second in RBIs, third in home runs and bases on balls. Berra was elected to the National Baseball Hall of Fame in 1972.

But he is *really* best known for his many Yogiisms, including:

"Surprise me." (On where his wife should have him buried.)

"You've got to be very careful if you don't know where you're going, because you might not get there."

"If you don't know where you are going, you will wind up somewhere else."

"If you can't imitate him, don't copy him."

"You better cut the pizza in four pieces because I'm not hungry enough to eat six."

"Baseball is 90% mental—the other half is physical."

"What's everyone blaming me for? Blame Felix. I wouldn't have hit into the double play."

"It ain't over till it's over."

"Nobody goes there anymore; it's too crowded."

Everything Yogi Berra ever touched turned to gold. If it was a military operation, that meant D-day, the greatest in all history (he actually said taking part in the beach landings at Normandy "was fun"). If it was playing baseball, that meant 11 World Championships and three MVP awards with the Yankees. If it was friendship, that meant Joe Garagiola, his boyhood pal from St. Louis, who became America's baseball buddy, bestselling author, and announcer. If it was coaching, that meant World titles with the Mets and Yankees. If it was managing, that meant taking the 1964 Yankees and 1973 Mets to the seventh game of the World Series. If it was marriage, that meant a long and happy one. Fatherhood? His son went to Harvard and played in the big leagues. Investments? Ivan Boesky called him for advice. Endorsements? Countless, his face known and loved by millions, thanks in small part to a long-running AFLAC commercial. His words carry more resonance, it seems, than Hemingway or Dickens. His sayings are legendary. It could fill a book and has—several of them.

If Berra had been at the World Trade Center on 9/11 nobody would have ever heard of Osama bin Laden. If he had been on the *Titanic*, the iceberg would have melted. You want this guy sitting next to you during turbulence. You want to share a hospital room with him before surgery.

In 1964 the Yankees all made fun of Berra and he was going to be fired. He told Phil Linz to stop playing his harmonica on the bus but Linz refused. Berra knocked it out of his hands. "On any other team, they would have folded," said Jim Bouton. "With the Yankees, we won 40 of 50 and the pennant."

In the 1973 playoffs and World Series, every move he made seemed to work out. He is the one guy associated as a hero with both the Mets and Yankees. Berra is as much a symbol of New York as the Statue of Liberty, and has an accent that is straight out of the Bronx even though he is from Missouri. He lived in New Jersey for years. Mob guys give him respect.

Whitey Ford was 24-7 with a 2.74 earned run average in 1963, but lost the Series opener to Koufax 5-2. He was beaten twice in the four-game sweep. He was 17-6 with a 2.13 ERA in 1964, when Berra made him player/pitching coach. He lost his one start to St. Louis in the World Series and retired in 1967 having won 236 games with a 2.75 earned run average. He was 10-8 with a 2.71 ERA in Series play, earning induction to the Hall of Fame in 1974, when he fittingly entered with Mantle.

Like Juan Marichal, Ford is slightly below the likes of Koufax, Bob Gibson, and Tom Seaver in the all-time pantheon, but as a big game pitcher his name ranks among an elite group that includes Christy Mathewson, Koufax, Gibson, Catfish Hunter, Curt Schilling, and Josh Beckett.

Bill "Moose" Skowron was traded in 1963 to Los Angeles, where he hit .203 for the World Champion Dodgers. He played until 1967 with Washington, the Chicago White Sox, and California, hitting .282 with 211 homers, and a .293 average in 39 World Series games, along with eight homers.

Joe Pepitone took over as the starting first baseman when Skowron left in 1963. He was immediately hailed as one of the next great Yankee stars when he hit 27 home runs. A review of Pepitone's career in the 1960s indicates that the term "star" may have applied to him, or close to it. He hit 28 home runs in 1964, 31 in 1966, and 27 in 1969 with 100 RBIs. He went to Houston in 1970, then to the Cubs until 1973 before retiring after a stint with Atlanta. His career numbers: .258 with 219 homers. Pepitone, however, is best known as symbolizing the "new breed." He was the first player to bring a blow dryer into the clubhouse. Jim Bouton and pitcher Fritz Peterson once secretly filled it with talcum powder during the seventh inning of an apparent easy Yankee win. After blowing the game the clubhouse was silent when Pepitone turned on the blow dryer. The powder made him look like "an Italian George Washington," wrote Bouton in *Ball Four*. On another occasion, Pepitone put a piece of popcorn on his genitals and brought it to the attention of the team's trainer, claiming some new form of venereal disease.

"Jesus, Joe, what the hell have you done to yourself?" the trainer exclaimed. Pepitone's prowess with women, his career coinciding with the sexual revolution in the funnest Fun City of them all, was legendary. He was proud of his *size* and happy to publicize it so the women of America would be enticed.

When he played in Chicago, he tooled to and from the ballpark, on the road and at home, in a limousine and wore a fur coat, Joe Namath–style. He grew his hair long, sported a Fu Manchu, and epitomized the style of his day. He drank and experimented with drugs.

The polar opposite of Joe Pepitone was Bobby Richardson. He never hit more than .267 after his near-MVP performance of 1962 and retired as a Yankee in 1966 with a .266 lifetime average. He became a Christian pastor and successful coach at the University of South Carolina. He helped make college baseball popular in the South. Long dominated by Southern California, over the next decades the Southeastern Conference came to achieve parity with the Pacific 10.

Clete Boyer played for the Yankees through 1966 and then went to the Braves, where he played between 1967 and 1971 (including their 1969 division championship). He retired with a .242 average but did not win the Gold Gloves he otherwise deserved because his career paralleled Baltimore's Brooks Robinson. His brother Ken was the Most Valuable Player of the National League when he starred for St. Louis in 1964, leading the Cardinals to a World Series win over Clete's Yanks.

Tony Kubek's production dropped each year after 1962. He hit only .188 versus Los Angeles in the 1963 Series and retired after 1965 with a .266 average. He became Joe Garagiola's popular broadcast partner on NBC's Saturday *Game of the Week*.

Elston Howard became the first black American League MVP in 1963, when he hit 28 home runs, drove in 85 runs, and batted .287 (no less than 11 blacks had won in the NL since 1949). He batted .313 in 1964 and finished his career with Boston, ironically the last club to bring a black player to the big leagues. He helped the Red Sox down the stretch of their "Impossible Dream" pennant, then retired in 1968 having batted .274 lifetime with 167 homers. He became a coach under Billy Martin and helped keep the peace during the volatile *Bronx Is Burning* summer of 1977, when Martin and Reggie Jackson feuded. He coached under other managers and remained a loyal Yankee.

Tom Tresh never realized his great potential. He hit .269 with 25 home runs in 1963 and slammed 26 home runs in 1965, but was traded to his home state Detroit Tigers in 1969, retiring shortly thereafter with a .245 average.

Hector Lopez played in New York through 1966 and hit .269 in his career. He batted .286 in 15 Series games. Johnny Blanchard was traded to Kansas City and retired in 1965 with a .239 average, but he was a .345 hitter in 15 Series games.

Ralph Terry was 17-15 in 1963 but did not start a game in either the World Series with the Dodgers (1963) or the Cardinals (1964). He was traded to Cleveland in 1965, where he was 11-6. After stints in Kansas City and with the Mets, he retired in 1967 with 107 wins.

Bill Stafford was never effective again, not winning more than five games for the Yanks and A's until 1967, finishing at 43-40 lifetime. Rollie Sheldon was 5-2 in 1964 and went to Kansas City in 1965 before retiring after playing for Boston in 1966. Jim Coates went to Washington in 1963 and later pitched for the Reds and Angels through 1967, finishing with 43 wins. Bud Daley retired after 1964 with the Yanks, a 60-64 pitcher. Marshall Bridges went to the Senators in 1964 and then retired after the 1965 season. Luis Arroyo pitched six games in 1963 and retired with 44 career saves.

Mel Allen hosted a popular national TV baseball program called *This Week in Baseball*, his "How about that?" line heard by millions for years. Phil Rizzuto stayed on as the Yankee announcer for many years. Eventually, former Cardinal Bill White became his partner (before White became president of the National League). Aside from exclaiming *"Holy cow!"* Allen was also famous for stating, "How about that Bill White?!" White was his "straight man." "Scooter" passed away in 2007.

Jim Bouton became a true star in 1963 and 1964. He was 21-7 with a 2.53 ERA in 1963. In the World Series, he lost a classic 1-0 pitchers' duel at Dodger Stadium to Don Drysdale. In 1964 Bouton was 18-13 with a 3.02 earned run average, then pitched New York to two wins over the Cardinals with a 1.56 ERA in the World Series. His unnatural straight-overhand pitching delivery, which caused him to knock his hat off his head on most pitches, put too much strain on his arm and he suffered a debilitating injury in 1965, when he had a 4-15 record.

Bouton had not built up any goodwill with the Yankees. He hung out with Pepitone and Phil Linz, "new breed" types who were not considered sufficiently respectful of the Yankee tradition. He did a "crazy Guggenheim" face that the club felt was a disgrace to the pinstripes. The writers loved him because he dealt them all the dirt they wanted, but teammates and club executives knew it was coming from Bouton. As the Vietnam War heated up, Bouton's outspoken opposition to the war made him popular with liberal writers, but unpopular with patriotic teammates and Yankee bigwigs.

Bouton noted that when the police came on the field to break up a fight, Ralph Houk wondered what in the hell they were doing there. "They should be over at the university where they belong," he said, in reference to antiwar protests at Columbia.

A more conventional player may have survived his injuries, but the club was just waiting for an excuse to unload him, even though he was popular with the fans—"my public," he called them.

Bouton struggled, did a turn in the minor leagues, and became a knuckle-ball pitcher. He was rescued by expansion when he made it with the first-year Seattle Pilots (later the Milwaukee Brewers) in 1969. He was traded to Houston late in the season, and was a member of the hard-throwing Astros' pitching staff that kept the surprising club in "The Wild, Wild West" into September.

Bouton could not get pitching out of his system. He played on an independent minor league club, where one of his teammates was Kurt Russell, later a marquee actor. In 1978 kindred spirit Ted Turner, who shared Bouton's left-wing political views, signed him to an Atlanta Braves contract. He made it back to the Major Leagues, more a sideshow than a legitimate big leaguer, but fans enjoyed seeing him.

What made Bouton's return to The Show even possible in 1978, however, was the publication of his book, *Ball Four* in 1970. *Ball Four* is to this day the highest-selling sports book, and one of the greatest bestsellers of all time. Controversial as it was, and in some cases still is, it may well be the best baseball book—and sports book—ever written. It made Bouton rich and famous; it changed his life and changed baseball the way Babe Ruth's home runs and introduction of the lively ball did in 1920.

It was the brainchild of New York sportswriter Len Schecter, who suggested that Bouton tape record his observations on baseball and life in diary form throughout the 1969 season, all to be edited by Schecter in time for a release date in the summer of 1970 by an obscure publishing house. Schecter was a hated figure among athletes, coaches, and front office executives. His style was to hang around like a parasite, overhearing snippets of conversation not meant for his ears, then print it as fact in his articles.

Bouton spent parts of 1969 with Seattle, in the minor leagues, and with Houston. While the book centered on events on those teams and in that year, he also spiced it up with ribald memories of the Yankee clubs he played on in the 1960s, his feelings about Vietnam, and the political attitudes of teammates. One of the key selling points of the book was Bouton's "oddball" reputation, which he never ran from, and how he differed from average baseball players.

What infuriated most about *Ball Four* was his unmasking of Mickey Mantle as a diva, albeit a good guy at heart. Other revelations that offended some readers included his total lack of respect for Ralph Houk (particularly his tenure as the general manager) and Yankee pitching coach Jim "the Chicken Colonel" Turner; the backward attitude of coaches and baseball people in general; the sexual antics of married players and the drug use of players, mainly the use of "greenies" (amphetamines that pepped players up before games); and his own politics, which caused several teammates to call him "a Communist."

Every young kid in America, including me, read *Ball Four*, or so it seemed. When young minor leaguers like myself got to professional ball, we knew what to expect—clubhouse rituals, groupies, partying, humor—because Bouton had described all of it perfectly.

It spawned many books, by Bouton and others, in particular *The Bronx Zoo* by Sparky Lyle. It created a genre: the "tell all." Bouton was the Jacqueline Susann of baseball, only his book was not a novel. Bouton did not get into any of the 1962 World Series games, but he was a member of the Yankee staff. He returned to San Francisco as a member of the Astros in 1969 and wrote that it brought back good memories, particularly the unique smell in the Candlestick visitor's clubhouse.

When the book came out, Mantle, his former Yankee teammates, and everybody else associated with the Yanks, was incensed at Bouton. He was persona non grata at Yankee Stadium. Mantle did not talk to him for a long time. He was called an "(expletive deleted) Shakespeare." He and Schecter were described as "pariahs." Commissioner Bowie Kuhn investigated the drug allegations. Numerous players faced angry wives suddenly apprised of previously hidden road trip dalliances, even though Bouton's descriptions were tame and did not name names. He was a "traitor" who broke the unwritten clubhouse "code of silence" for money—lots and lots of it.

Bouton also cashed in as a New York sportscaster, but he was not very good at it. A television version of *Ball Four* was laughable and short lived. Bouton was not a good actor, either. Many felt he got what was coming to him when his own extramarital affairs were exposed, causing his wife to leave him. Later, his beloved daughter passed away. By that time, there were exposés of *Ball Four*, and athletes' peccadilloes far above any of that were well-known. Time healed most of the wounds. Bouton never re-entered baseball in an official capacity, not because of the book, but because at heart he was not cut out for it. He had ability and was competitive, which led him to brief success, but baseball's customs and even the game itself bored him.

Nevertheless, he became a caretaker of baseball purity. He found the likes of Barry Bonds, with his steroids and an attitude that made Mantle look like Mother Theresa, to be a stain on the game.

FOURTEEN

The 2000s

In 2002, with interleague play now a regular event, the San Francisco Giants visited Yankee Stadium. With the reigning single-season record holder, Barry Bonds, the return of the Giants caused enormous excitement in the Big Apple. At the time, it was seen as a preview of the World Series (the Giants made it, but New York was upset by eventual World Champion Anaheim). The games were total sellouts, although by this time all Yankee games sold out, with attendance now topping four million per season. Average crowds at Yankee Stadium are now over 50,000, a virtually unheard-of concept in 1962, and a testament to the remarkable popularity of baseball since several teams approach this kind of support. In San Francisco, the "Giant 68," KNBR, replayed game seven of the 1962 World Series. A large audience tuned in.

In 2007 the Yankees visited AT&T Park in San Francisco for the 45th anniversary of the '62 World Series. A ceremony was held including the likes of Ralph Terry as well as numerous Giants luminaries. Many retrospectives of the Series were offered, with the *San Francisco Chronicle* (by now vastly improved over the 1962 version) running large-scale articles about the Series, its impact on the Giants and The City.

ESPN Classic and other sports stations have showed game seven of the 1962 World Series many times, along with numerous highlight reels. In 2008 the Los Angeles Dodgers honored their 50th year in Los Angeles by playing a special game at the Los Angeles Memorial Coliseum. In 2009 the Yankees will move into a brand new Yankee Stadium.

The 1962 season and World Series remain among the most exciting in the history of baseball. The year itself is seen as a touchstone of American culture. In that sense it rivals the Declaration of Independence (1776); Abraham Lincoln's assassination (1865); Babe Ruth's 60 homers, the Jack Dempsey–Gene Tunney fight, and Charles Lindbergh's Atlantic crossing (1927), symbolizing the "Roaring '20s"; the winning of World War II (1945); later winning the Cold War when the Berlin Wall fell (1989); and 9/11 (2001).

It was the last year of innocence before Jack Kennedy's assassination, Vietnam, the protest generation, and the 1968 assassinations of Martin Luther King Jr. and Robert Kennedy. It preceded Watergate, and the political corruption and divisiveness that appear unhealable.

It remains the ultimate in nostalgia—far off enough to be part of our past, for sure, but modern enough to be part of our times. It was the "Sunset Strip summer" of Bo Belinsky, and the end of sophistication and elegance that marked both San Francisco and New York.

For those who lived through it, 1962 was a year of memory like none other. This was particularly true for Californians and New Yorkers, for whom the recounting of tales of this magical season, from March to October, washes "like magic waters" over them as they, in the words of James Earl Jones in *Field of Dreams*, perpetually search for "something good."

Bibliography

Adell, Ross, and Ken Samelson. *Amazing Mets Trivia*. Lanham, MD: Taylor Trade Publishing, 2004.

Allen, Maury, with Bo Belinsky. *Bo: Pitching and Wooing*. New York: The Dial Press, 1973.

Allyn, Bruce J., James G. Blight, and David A. Welch, editors. "Back to the Brink: Proceedings of the Moscow Conference on the Cuban Missile Crisis January 1989." Occasional Paper 9, CSIA and University Press of America Lanham, MD: University Press of America, 1992.

Alston, Walter, with Jack Tobin. *One Year at a Time*. Waco, TX: Word, Inc., 1976.

Anderson, Dave, Murray Chass, Robert Creamer, and Harold Rosenthal. *The Yankees: The Four Fabulous Eras of Baseball's Most Famous Team*. New York: Random House, 1979.

Angell, Roger. *Five Seasons*. New York: Simon & Schuster, 1977.

———. *Game Time: A Baseball Companion*. Orlando, FL: Harcourt, Inc., 2003.

———. *Late Innings: A Baseball Companion*. New York: Simon & Schuster, 1972.

———. *The Summer Game*. New York: The Viking Press, 1972.

Appel, Marty. *Yogi Berra*. New York: Chelsea House Publishers, 1992.

Archibald, Joe. *Right Field Rookie*. Philadelphia: MacRae Smith Co., 1967.

The Baseball Encyclopedia. New York: Macmillan, 1996.

Berra, Yogi. *The Yogi Book: "I Really Didn't Say Everything I Said!"* New York: Workman Publishing, 1998.

———, with Dave Kaplan. *Ten Rings: My Championship Seasons*. New York: William Morrow, 2003.

———, with Tom Horton. *Yogi: It Ain't Over . . .* New York: McGraw-Hill Publishing Co., 1989.

Biskind, Peter. *Easy Riders, Raging Bulls: How the Sex-Drugs-and-Rock 'n' Roll Generation Saved Hollywood*. New York: Simon & Schuster, 1998.

Bitker, Steve. *The Original San Francisco Giants*. Champaign, IL: Sports Publishing L.L.C., 2001.

Bjarkman, Peter C. *The New York Mets Encyclopedia*. Champaign, IL: Sports Publishing L.L.C., 2003.

Blight, James G., and David A. Welch. *On the Brink: Americans and Soviets Reexamine the Cuban Missile Crisis*. New York: Hill and Wang, 1989.

Bouton, Jim. *Ball Four*. New York: The World Publishing Co., 1970.

————, with Neil Offen. *I Managed Good, but Boy Did They Play Bad*. New York: Dell Publishing Co., Inc., 1973.

Breslin, Jimmy. *Can't Anybody Here Play This Game?* New York: Viking, 1963.

Brodie, Fawn M. *Richard Nixon: The Shaping of His Character*. New York: W.W. Norton & Co., 1981.

Brosnan, Jim. *Great Rookies of the Major Leagues*. New York: Random House, 1966.

Brugioni, Dino A. *Eyeball to Eyeball: The Inside Story of the Cuban Missile Crisis*. New York: Random House, 1990.

Bundy, McGeorge. *Danger and Survival: Choices about the Bomb in the First Fifty Years*. New York: Random House, 1988.

Cantor, Norman F., with Mindy Cantor. *The American Century: Varieties of Culture in Modern Times*. New York: Harper Perennial, 1997.

Chadwick, Bruce, and David M. Spindel. *The Giants: Memories and Memorabilia from a Century of Baseball*. New York: Abbeville Press, 1993.

Coulter, Ann. *Treason*. New York: Crown Forum, 2003.

Cramer, Richard Ben. *Joe DiMaggio: The Hero's Life*. New York: Simon & Schuster, 2000.

Creamer, Robert. *Stengel: His Life and Times*. New York: Simon & Schuster, 1984.

Davis, John H. *The Kennedys: Dynasty and Disaster 1848–1983*. New York: McGraw-Hill Book Co., 1984.

Dean, John. *Blind Ambition: The White House Years*. New York: Simon & Schuster, 1976.

Dearborn, Mary V. *Mailer*. New York: Houghton Mifflin Co., 1999.

Devaney, John. *Tom Seaver*. New York: Popular Library, 1974.

DiMaggio, Joe. *Lucky to Be a Yankee*. New York: Grosset & Dunlap, 1947.

Drucker, Malka, with Tom Seaver. *Tom Seaver: Portrait of a Pitcher*. New York: Holiday House, 1978.

Durso, Joseph. *DiMaggio: The Last American Knight*. New York: Little, Brown and Co., 1995.

Eig, Jonathan. *Luckiest Man: The Life and Death of Lou Gehrig*. New York: Simon & Schuster, 2005.

Einstein, Charles. *Willie's Time*. New York: J.B. Lippincott Co., 1979.

————, with Willie Mays. *Willie Mays: My Life In and Out of Baseball*. New York: E.P. Dutton & Co., Inc., 1966.

Enders, Eric. *100 Years of the World Series*. New York: Barnes & Noble Publishing, Inc., 2003.

Eskenazi, Gerald. *The Lip: A Biography of Leo Durocher*. New York: William Morrow and Co., Inc., 1993.

Ford, Whitey, with Phil Pepe. *Few and Chosen: Defining Yankee Greatness Across the Eras*. Chicago: Triumph Books, 2001.

Fox, Bucky. *The Mets Fan's Little Book of Wisdom*. Lanham, MD: Taylor Trade Publishing, 2006.

Fox, Larry. *Broadway Joe and His Super Jets*. New York: Coward-McCann, Inc., 1969.

Fursenko, Aleksander, and Timothy Naftali. *One Hell of a Gamble*. New York: W.W. Norton & Co., 1997.

Garment, Leonard. *Crazy Rhythm: My Journey from Brooklyn, Jazz, and Wall Street to Nixon's White House, Watergate, and Beyond . . .* New York: Da Capo Press, 2001.

Giants 2001 Media Guide. San Francisco: Giants Media Relations Dept., 2001.

Golenbock, Peter. *Amazin': The Miraculous History of New York's Most Beloved Baseball Team*. New York: St. Martin's Press, 2002.

Grabowski, John. *Willie Mays*. New York: Chelsea House Publishers, 1990.

Graham Jr., Frank. *Great Pennant Races of the Major Leagues*. New York: Random House, 1967.

Gruver, Edward. *Koufax*. Dallas: Taylor Publishing Co., 2000.

Gutman, Bill. *Miracle Year, 1969: Amazing Mets and Super Jets*. Champaign, IL: Sports Publishing L.L.C., 2004.

In the Face of Evil: Reagan's War in Word and Deed. Capital Films I, LLC, 2004.

Hano, Arnold. *Willie Mays*. New York: Grosset & Dunlap, 1966.

Helyar, John. *Lords of the Realm*. New York: Villard Books, 1994.

Herskowitz, Mickey. *A Hero All His Life*. New York: HarperCollins Publishers, 1996.

Hodges, Gil, with Frank Slocum. *The Game of Baseball*. New York: Crown Publishers, Inc., 1969.

———, and Al Hirshberg. *My Giants*. Garden City, NY: Doubleday & Co., Inc., 1963.

Honig, Donald. *The National League*. New York: Crown Publishers, 1983.

Houk, Ralph. *Ballplayers Are Human, Too*. Transcribed and edited by Charles Dexter. New York: G.P. Putnam's Son, 1962.

Huchthausen, Peter A. *October Fury*. Hoboken, NJ: John Wiley & Sons, Inc., 2002.

Holy Bible. Philiadelphia: The National Publishing Co., 1970.

Kahn, Roger. *Joe & Marilyn: A Memory of Love*. New York: William Morrow and Co., Inc., 1986.

Karnow, Stanley. *Vietnam: A History*. New York: The Viking Press, 1983.

Kennedy, Robert F. *Thirteen Days: A Memoir of the Cuban Missile Crisis*. New York: New American Library, 1969.

Koufax, Sandy, with Ed Linn. *Koufax*. New York: The Viking Press, 1966.

Kuenster, John, ed. *From Cobb to Catfish*. Chicago: Rand McNally & Co., 1975.

Leavy, Jane. *Sandy Koufax*. New York: HarperCollins Publishers, 2002.

Lebow, Richard Ned, and Janice Gross Stein. *We All Lost the Cold War*. Princeton, NJ: Princeton University Press, 1994.

Lee, Bill,with Richard Lally. *The Wrong Stuff*. New York: The Viking Press, 1983.

————, with Jim Prince. *Baseball Eccentrics*. Chicago: Triumph Books, 2007.

Leventhal, Josh. *The World Series*. New York: Tess Press, 2004.

Lichtenstein, Michael. *Ya Gotta Believe!* New York: St. Martin's Griffin, 2002.

Los Angeles Dodgers 2001 Media Guide. Los Angeles: Los Angeles Dodgers, Inc., 2001.

Macht, Norman L. *Tom Seaver*. New York: Chelsea House Publishers, 1994.

Mantle, Mickey, and Phil Pepe. *Mickey Mantle: My Favorite Summer 1956*. New York: Doubleday, 1991.

————, with Mickey Herskowitz. *All My Octobers: My Memories of 12 World Series when the Yankees Ruled Baseball*. New York: HarperCollins Publishers, 1994.

Marichal, Juan, with Charles Einstein. *A Pitcher's Story*. New York: Doubleday & Co., Inc., 1967.

Markusen, Bruce. *Tales from the Mets Dugout*. Champaign, IL: Sports Publishing L.L.C., 2005.

Matthews, Christopher. *Kennedy & Nixon: The Rivalry That Shaped America*. New York: Simon & Schuster, 1996.

Morgan, Ted. *Reds: McCarthyism in Twentieth-Century America*. New York: Random House Trade Paperback, 2004.

Mosley, Leonard. *Dulles: A Biography of Eleanor, Allen and John Foster Dulles and Their Family Network*. New York: The Dial Press/James Wade, 1978.

Navasky, Victor S. *Kennedy Justice*. New York: Atheneum, 1971.

Newhan, Ross. "Vintage Seaver." *Los Angeles Times* (http://www.latimes.com/sports/la-sp-seaver5jul05,1,3895492,full.story), July 5, 2007.

New York Times. *The New York Times Book of Baseball History: Major League Highlights from the Pages of the New York Times*. New York: The New York Times Book Co., 1975.

Official 1969 Baseball Guide. St. Louis: *The Sporting News*, 1971.

Official 1970 Baseball Guide. St. Louis: *The Sporting News*, 1971.

Official 1971 Baseball Guide. St. Louis: *The Sporting News*, 1971.

O'Neal, Bill. *The Pacific Coast League*. Austin, TX: Eakin Publications, Inc., 1990.

Parmet, Herbert S. *JFK: The Presidency of John F. Kennedy*. New York: The Dial Press, 1983.

Parrott, Harold. *The Lords of Baseball*. New York: Praeger Publishers, 1976.

Pearlman, Jeff. *The Bad Guys Won!* New York: HarperCollins Publishers Inc., 2004.

Plaut, David. *Chasing October: The Dodgers–Giants Pennant Race of 1962*. South Bend, IN: Diamond Communications, 1994.

Reeves, Richard. *President Kennedy: Profile of Power*. New York: Simon & Schuster, 1993.

Reichler, Joseph. *30 Years of Baseball's Great Moments*. New York: Crown Publishers, 1974.

Ritter, Lawrence. *The Glory of Their Times*. New York: The Macmillan Co., 1966.

———, and Donald Honig. *The Image of Their Greatness*. New York: Crown Publishers, Inc., 1979.

Robinson, Ray, ed. *Baseball Stars of 1965*. New York: Pyramid Books, 1965.

———. *Baseball Stars of 1970*. New York: Pyramid Books, 1970.

Rusk, Dean, with Richard Rusk. *As I Saw It*. New York: Norton & Co., 1990.

Schlesinger, Arthur M., Jr. *Robert Kennedy and His Times*. Vol. 1. Boston: Houghton Mifflin Co., 1978.

Schott, Tom and Nick Peters. *The Giants Encyclopedia*. Champaign, IL: Sports Publishing Inc., 1999.

Seaver, Tom, with Marty Appel. *Great Moments in Baseball*. New York: Carol Publishing Group, 1992.

———, with Dick Schaap. *The Perfect Game*. New York: E.P. Dutton & Co., Inc., 1970.

Shamsky, Art, with Barry Zeman. *The Magnificent Seasons: How the Jets, Mets, and Knicks Made Sports History and Uplifted a City and the Country*. New York: Thomas Dunne Books, 2004.

Smith, Robert. *Baseball*. New York: Simon & Schuster, 1947.

Smith, Ron. *The Sporting News Selects Baseball's Greatest 100 Players*. St. Louis: The Sporting News Publishing Co., 1998.

Stein, Fred, and Nick Peters. *Giants Diary: A Century of Giants Baseball in New York and San Francisco*. Berkeley: North Atlantic Books, 1987.

Stout, Glenn. *The Dodgers: 120 Years of Dodgers Baseball*. New York: Houghton Mifflin Co., 2004.

———. *Yankees Century: 100 Years of New York Yankees Baseball*. New York: Houghton Mifflin Co., 2002.

Talbott, Strobe, ed. and trans. *Khruschev Remembers*. Introduction, commentary, and notes by Edward Crankshaw. Boston: Little, Brown, 1971.

Travers, Steven. *A's Essential: Everything You Need to Know to Be a Real Fan!* Chicago: Triumph Books, 2007.

———. *Barry Bonds: Baseball's Superman*. Champaign, IL: Sports Publishing L.L.C., 2002.

———. *Dodgers Essential: Everything You Need to Know to Be a Real Fan!* Chicago: Triumph Books, 2007.

———. *Dodgers Past & Present*. Minneapolis, MN: Voyageur Press, 2009.

———. *God's Country: A Conservative, Christian Worldview of How History Formed the United States Empire and America's Manifest Destiny for the 21st Century*. Unpublished.

———. *The Good, the Bad and the Ugly Los Angeles Lakers*. Chicago: Triumph Books, 2007.

———. "L.A./Orange County Prep All-Century Teams," *StreetZebra*, January 2000.

———. *The 1969 Amazing Mets*. Guilford, CT: The Globe Pequot Press, 2009.

———. "Once He Was an Angel." *StreetZebra*, 1999.

———. "Once He Was an Angel." Unproduced screenplay.

———. *One Night, Two Teams: Alabama vs. USC and the Game That Changed a Nation*. Lanham, MD: Taylor Trade Publishing, 2007.

———. *Summer of '62*. Unproduced screenplay.

———. "Time to Give Barry His Due," *San Francisco Examiner*, April 18, 2001.

2001 New York Mets Information Guide. New York: Mets Media Relations Dept., 2001.

Whittingham, Richard. *Illustrated History of the Dodgers*. Chicago: Triumph Books, 2005.

Will, George. *Bunts*. New York: Touchstone, 1999.

Wise, Bill, ed. *1963 Official Baseball Almanac*. Greenwich, CT: Fawcett Publications, Inc.

Yankees 2000 Information & Record Guide. Bronx, NY: New York Yankees Media Relations Dept., 2001.

Zimmerman, Paul D., and Dick Schaap. *The Year the Mets Lost Last Place*. New York: The World Publishing Co., 1969.

Index

About the Author

Steven Travers is a USC graduate and ex-professional baseball player in the Cardinals and Athletics organizations. He is the author of the bestselling *Barry Bonds: Baseball's Superman*, nominated for a Casey Award (best baseball book of 2002). He is also the author of *The USC Trojans: College Football's All-Time Greatest Dynasty* (a National Book Network "top 100 seller"); *One Night, Two Teams: Alabama vs. USC and the Game That Changed a Nation* (subject of a CSTV/CBS documentary and major motion picture, as well as a 2007 PNBA nominee); five books in the Triumph/Random House *Essential* series (*A's, Dodgers, Angels, D'backs, Trojans*); *The Good, the Bad & the Ugly Los Angeles Lakers*; *The Good, the Bad & the Ugly Oakland Raiders*; *The Good, the Bad & the Ugly San Francisco 49ers*; *The 1969 Miracle Mets*; *Dodgers Past & Present*; *Pigskin Warriors*; *What It Means to Be a Trojan*; and *The USC Mafia: From the Frat House to the White House to the Big House.*

Travers has written for the *Los Angeles Times*, and was a columnist for *StreetZebra* magazine in Los Angeles and the *San Francisco Examiner*. He also penned the screenplay, *The Lost Battalion*. He helped lead Redwood High School of Marin County, California, to the baseball national championship his senior year; attended college on an athletic scholarship; was an all-conference pitcher; and coached at USC, at Cal-Berkeley, and in Europe. He also attended law school, served in the army, was a sports agent, and is a guest lecturer at the University of Southern California. A fifth generation Californian, Travers has a daughter, Elizabeth, and still resides in the Golden State.

For readers who want to contact Travers, his contact information is:

Steven Travers

(415) 455-5971

USCSteve1@aol.com